THE INJUSTICE OF JUSTICE

Millennial Mind Publishing
2389 South, 300 East, Salt Lake City, Utah 84115
www.american-book.com
Printed in the United States of America on acid-free paper.

The Injustice of Justice

Designed by Silvia Bukovac, silvia@art-attack.hr

Publisher's Note: *This publication is designed to provide accurate and authoritative information in regard to the subject matter covered. It is sold or distributed with the understanding that the publisher and author is not engaged in rendering legal, accounting, or other professional service. If legal advice or other expert assistance is required, the services of a competent professional person in a consultation capacity should be sought.*

Library of Congress Cataloging-in-Publication Data is available upon request.

ISBN 1-930586-13-2

Eve Meyer, The Injustice of Justice

Special Sales

These books are available at special discounts for bulk purchases. Special editions, including personalized covers, excerpts of existing books, and corporate imprints, can be created in large quantities for special needs. For more information e-mail cln@american-book.com or call 1-800-296-1248.

THE INJUSTICE OF JUSTICE

Eve Meyer

The Injustice of Justice is the true story of a Boulder County murder case that was tried in 1992, during the re-election campaign of District Attorney Alex Hunter. The author's son was convicted of killing a man and his 10-year-old son and is serving consecutive life sentences for those crimes. Courtroom scenes are taken from the actual transcripts of that case. All comments separate from the transcripts are the opinion of the author and should not be taken for fact.

It is not the author's intent to plead her son's guilt or innocence, or to harm the family and friends of the victims in any way. Instead, the author hopes this record will help answer questions about the manner in which her son's trial was conducted; questions that may raise reasonable doubts about her son's guilt and earn her son a new trial.

Contents

Verily, verily, I say unto you,
That ye shall weep and lament,
But the world shall rejoice; and
Ye shall be sorrowful, but your
Sorrow shall be turned into joy.
John 16:20

Foreword

Until January 2000, I worked as a police officer for the last 24 years. I have seen the scrounge of the earth, the innocent victims and everyone in between. The children, brothers and sisters, moms and dads, rich and poor, there are no prejudices when it comes to victims. The lives taken either by way of an untimely death or on the other side, by being incarcerated forever. No one is in a better position to see the overall effects of a crime than a cop. The public, the lawyers, and the judges see the criminal. Friends and family of the victim and the perpetrator are forced to live with the aftermath and forevermore ask the universal question, "Why."

Police officers conduct a thorough, unbiased investigation to answer that very question. When there is a solution to the crime the question is answered and justice is served. But, justice can leave a long and weary trail of torn hearts and souls, not only of the victims' family and friends, but of the perpetrators as well.

Although it is hardly perfect, I have respect for the criminal justice system. Persons working within the system strive to do their job in a lawful, professional manner. Because we are human beings dealing with many unknowns and subject to mistakes, checks and balances have been built in the system.

These checks and balances are in place to protect and insure that the person accused is rightfully prosecuted and sentenced accordingly. The appeal process is a way of double-checking for the benefit of the defendant. This luxury is not given to the other people affected, the ones left behind. They must live with the loss of loved ones and finish out their lives as best as possible.

Yes, when convicted of a crime, the criminal is afforded avenues of appeal. However, no matter the results of the appeal, one side will accept it and the other will continue to ask, "Why."

Ron Black

You Be The Jury

You are about to go on a journey – a journey inside a courtroom where an 18-year-old boy has been accused of a double homicide. The mother of the accused will take you back to the day their world turned upside down, to the past and how it shaped the future. She will recount the numerous newspaper articles about the pre-trial publicity – the same newspaper articles that many on the jury admitted to reading and believed their contents.

You will be there with her as she reads over the actual trial transcripts trying to find resolve to the many unanswered questions. You will read some of the pre-trial motions, the opening statements, testimonies of expert witnesses and the closing arguments. This journey does not last long, as the trial itself lasts only three days, and the jury took only three hours. Three days and three hours to decide the fate of one young man and to change forever the lives of one family.

This journey is one that will stir every emotion in you. You will close the book and its story will linger.

You will experience *The Injustice of Justice.*

Part 1

The Journey Begins

Nine Years Later

I was excited about our trip to the Florida Coast. The ocean brought me so much strength and inner peace. I also treasured the time with my husband, Steve. So much had happened…so much tragedy. Our road trips were a way for us to find each other again and renew our love for one another.

As we drove down the highway, the music played softly on the radio. I glanced at the back seat where the large box held volume after volume of court transcripts, then leaned my head back against the headrest and closed my eyes. My thoughts drifted to a time when life had been simpler.

Being a single mother hadn't been easy. I had tried so hard to provide for the boys. I knew I'd been a very tough parent, no excuses. I had to work and support them and I expected them to do their part – do well in school and stay out of trouble.

Sometimes the boys would giggle at how I grilled them like a drill sergeant. I always knew when one of them was lying. Each of them had their own facial expressions and tones of voice that they couldn't hide from me. I always knew when something wasn't quite right. God had blessed me with a sixth sense of 'knowing' when something wasn't right that always took the boys by surprise.

My eldest, Scott, is a handsome young man with blonde hair and blue eyes. He was very outgoing. He had taken the role of protector for his brother David. Scott was more like a father figure than a brother to Dave. He had always brought so much pride and love to our family…except in school…oh, how he hated school. I couldn't understand how someone who was always the star athlete in football and track could hate school so much. He was a great athlete and had so much going for him with his natural talent in sports. His coaches always paved the way for him when his grades faltered. I never understood this. And the girls…they swarmed around him. Scott had a very bubbly personality. He was always smiling and always finding the good in every situation.

Dave is my youngest. He was the sweetest child anyone could ever have. Dave was very different from Scott; he was very shy, but an excellent student in school.

I let my thoughts drift back to the day we moved to Colorado. We were so excited about our new start in a pretty neighborhood in Louisville. The house was located on a quiet cul-de-sac. Scott never had trouble meeting new people, but Dave did. Scott took Dave by the hand and led him around the neighborhood to introduce him to the kids that lived there.

Scott also had a way with the younger kids wherever we lived. He became a big brother to all of them, especially the ones with single parents. It was amazing the way Scott made kids feel important about themselves, that there was nothing they couldn't achieve -- especially when it came to sports. Scott had so much self-confidence, and he tried to pass that on to the younger kids he was around.

I'll never forget one day after football practice with the high school team, Scott rushed over to the field where his brother was practicing with a town league squad. He stood on the sidelines watching the men coach his brother's team. All of a sudden, he walked over and got the kids in a huddle and started giving them pointers on what they needed to do. Of course, the men coaching the team didn't like it one bit, but Scott wanted the kids to be successful and do it right. The funny thing was, the kids wanted to listen to Scott, not their coaches.

My thoughts suddenly shifted from football to the night I received a call from my sister in New Jersey. Our mother was dying and probably wouldn't make it through the night. She had suffered for many years with emphysema. I knew this day was coming, but I still wasn't prepared. Scott was devastated by the news. His grandmother, the one person that Scott could tell everything, was his whole world. They had one of the strongest relationships I've ever seen.

Thinking back on all the discussions I'd had with Mom about this day wasn't helping. My mom knew that when she died, there would be turmoil among her children. She told me, "Don't come stand over my dead body. I know you love me and there will be no sense for you to be here. Stay away."

And I did stay away, but that would prove to be a mistake. Back then, I didn't realize how important it was for Scott to say goodbye to his grandmother. I didn't realize, until later, that he needed closure.

What had gone so wrong? How did things get so out of control? Soon after my mother's death, Scott started getting into trouble with the law. I'll never forget the first call from the police station. Scott and his best friend had been picked up for shoplifting at a local grocery store. I couldn't believe it! That was just the beginning of a tragic path my son would head down.

"Eve, we're just about there." Steve's voice brought me out of my dream-like state. I sat up in my seat and looked around. I hadn't realized that we'd traveled so far. I smiled and took a deep breath, inhaling the wonderful smell of the sea air.

It was very early in the morning. The sun was just barely coming up. We checked into our room and unpacked our suitcases.

"Want to go watch the sun rise, Eve?"

"I'd love that." I picked up my big beach bag and packed it full of the large volumes of transcripts. "OK, I'm ready." Steve took my hand as we walked out of our room onto the sandy beach.

We found an empty cabana and sat down. Steve took me in his arms and held me close. I laid my head on his shoulder and looked out at the ocean.

"Eve, I don't know how to help you anymore. You're filled with so much sadness."

"I know, but there's such a struggle going on in me. I've just got to find a way to bring the truth out and find a way to help Scott." I sat up and looked in my husband's eyes. "Steve, I don't know what happened that night, but I know Scott didn't get a fair trial. There's more to this story than we know."

"I agree with you, but what can we do?"

I put my head back on Steve's shoulder. "I don't know, but I have to find a way. I've just got to find a way."

I closed my eyes and let my mind drift back to when our nightmare began.

The past two years had been draining with Scott and the trouble he had been getting into.

I remembered back to the afternoon the police came to our door looking for Scott. He wasn't home and I didn't know where he was. Much later that night I would learn that he apparently walked into a local bar and offered a stranger $50 to go to a car dealership and pretend he was his father. The man agreed. After they had selected the car they wanted to "test drive" Scott took him back to the bar and headed for the East Coast…back home to where his grandmother had been. He didn't make it. The law caught up with him just a few states away.

I couldn't understand why Scott felt the need to steal from others, which was what landed him in jail this time. Each incident seemed to be getting worse. Each time he promised it would be the last.

The Release

Scott had spent the last two months in jail on theft charges. Steve and I felt it was doing no good to just keep bailing him out of trouble. He obviously needed to appreciate more what he had at home. We had hoped he had learned his lesson this time, and finally agreed to post his bail. He had convinced us that we would never go through anything like this again.

My heart was racing as I drove to Brighton, where Scott had asked me to meet him after his release from the Adams County Jail. He was waiting with that familiar smile on his face, the one that always made me feel like everything was going to be OK. It was so good to see him.

I parked the car and jumped out. Where have all the years gone? I wondered as we hugged. He wasn't my little boy anymore.

"Scott, it's so good to have you out of there." We got back into the car and started the trip home.

"Mom, I'm sorry for all of this. I promise there won't be any more of this stuff."

"I hope you mean that." He seemed sincere, and truly sorry. "Mom, I have to talk to you about some things and I need you to listen to me. I've been doing a lot of things I shouldn't with people I shouldn't be with. I'm going to meet with them tonight and tell them I'm not going to be a part of all of this anymore."

"What are you talking about?"

"Well, I just want to get on with my life. I saved enough money working for them to buy a car; they've been keeping it for me, and they owe me money. I want to settle that and just get out."

"What people, Scott? What do you mean you have a car? Why haven't I seen this car? This doesn't make any sense to me."

"Mom, if you had seen the car, you'd have started asking a lot of questions that I didn't want to answer. You didn't need to know. I don't want my family involved with this." He was right about that. I would have been asking questions and wouldn't have stopped until I got the answers.

"Scott, this just makes no sense to me. Where are these people from?"

"The people I need to meet are in Boulder. I want you to drop me off in Louisville, and I'll call them."

"Scott, I'll stay with you. I'll just drive you there and you tell them what you have to say, and we'll go."

"No, Mom, I don't want you involved. Let me just handle this, and then it'll be over. I promise you."

What kind of people could he be involved with? My mind was filled with the things Scott had just told me the rest of the way home. How could all these things be happening without me even suspecting it? Our lives used to be so easy, so much fun.

When we pulled up to the house, Scott's brother was waiting. He adored his brother. Dave was an adorable child; blonde, blue eyes, with not a mean bone in his body. He was always happy and smiling. He didn't have a care in the world, except when his brother got in trouble.

"Hey, Dave, what's up?" Dave came running into his arms. Seeing the two of them together again felt so good. Dave helped Scott get his things downstairs to his room.

"Dinner's ready kids."

"Mom, it's so good to eat real food again."

"I can't imagine; what were you eating in jail?"

"I don't know, something they called food."

We all laughed. I couldn't help but think about what Scott had told me on the ride home. I was worried and uncomfortable with the secret life he appeared to be living, and kept trying to remember any clues to his activities. I couldn't remember any.

Steve and I cleared the table while Scott and Dave talked. They had a lot of catching up to do, but Scott kept glancing at the clock. It was obvious he had an appointment to keep with someone.

"Mom, I'm going to go take a shower and then you can take me."

"Take him where?" Steve asked. I filled him in on what Scott had told me in the car. Steve, too, was concerned. Although he was of age, if he wanted to live in our home he had to live by our rules. Before Scott had come home, we had established rules and we expected him to follow them. When Scott finished his shower and was ready to go, Steve reminded him he had rules to follow and limitations.

"Scott?"

"Yeah, Steve?"

"I want you in by 11. You just got out of jail and you don't need to be out late."

"OK. This won't take long. I'll be home by then."

We drove towards Louisville. I didn't like Scott's plan at all, but Steve and I agreed, though, that at least Scott was going to put an end to the mess he had gotten himself into. We believed in him and wanted to give him every opportunity to get back on the right track.

"Steve, there's a 7-Eleven right off the exit, that's where you can drop me off."

"OK, Scott, but remember what I said: In by 11." We pulled off the exit to the 7-Eleven. Scott gave me a kiss after he got out of our car.

"Mom, don't worry. I'll be home on time." As we pulled away, I glanced back. Scott was on the pay phone talking and laughing with someone.

"Steve, I don't like this. Who can he be involved with?"

"I don't know, but at least Scott realizes he has to make some changes in his life."

I tried to imagine every possible scenario using the limited information Scott had confided. I wanted so much to believe in him.

I glanced at the clock on the console. It was almost 9 p.m. At least he would only be gone a couple of hours. We drove home in silence. I've always wanted to know everything and everybody involved in my children's lives; I don't like the unknown. Steve felt I was way too protective of my kids; maybe he was right.

When we got home, I changed into my pajamas and got into bed. It was a warm fall night and all the windows were open. Our bedroom window faced the street, so I could hear when Scott pulled up. I looked at the clock again; it was 11 on the dot. Where was he?

The phone suddenly rang as if to answer me.

"Hello?"

"Mom, this is Scott. I know I'm running a little late, but I needed to stop for gas."

"Where are you?"

"I'm close to home. I'll be there soon."

"OK, Honey, I'm glad you called."

"See you soon." The dial tone replaced Scott's voice after he hung up. Steve rolled over and leaned up on an elbow.

"Was that Scott"?

"Yes."

"What did he say?"

"He said he needed to stop for gas and he would be home soon."

Scott sounded so cheerful on the phone. Through the years I had trained myself to always listen for anything "different" about my sons' voices. With what Scott had told me he was going to do tonight, I was listening hard for anything I could pick up on; anything that would tell me things weren't OK. There was nothing, now I could relax. He was keeping his word, living up to our agreement. Even though he'd be a little late, he'd called to make sure we knew he was OK. I propped myself up so I could listen better for any cars outside.

Ten minutes passed. Where was he? Something started gnawing at me. My family had always made fun of my "gut feelings." I tried to dismiss the uneasiness I was feeling. Finally, I heard a car outside. It stopped; a car door slammed and then the vehicle sped away, kicking up gravel in the road.

"Steve, Scott didn't go get a car, someone just dropped him off." Steve gave me a quizzical look, then we heard the front door open and close.

Scott appeared in our bedroom doorway, covered from head to toe in what looked like grease.

"Mom, help me! I've been stabbed!"

"Oh my God; Steve!" I jumped out of bed and grabbed Scott. As we moved down the hallway, I opened the linen closet and grabbed a pillowcase to use as a tourniquet to stop the bleeding. I tied it around Scott's arm and grabbed the telephone to call 911. My God, there was blood everywhere. Scott's arm looked like a split sausage on a grill. Blood was spurting from his arm and hand. There were so many wounds.

"Scott, what happened?"

"I was at a gas station and I was jumped by three men and one of them stabbed me."

By this time, Dave had woken up from all the commotion and was standing in the living room in horror.

"911, may I help you?"

"Send an ambulance…my son has been stabbed!"

The dispatcher asked so many questions. I was shaking, but tried to keep calm so they could get the information they needed. While I talked to the dispatcher and tried to stop Scott's bleeding, Steve told me there was a car parked in front of the driveway. Where did it come from? I knew someone had dropped Scott off.

The emergency medical technicians arrived with two police officers. Scott was very pale and ashen-colored. As the ambulance personnel started to take him out the door, I remembered that my car was in the shop. I didn't want to leave Steve without a vehicle.

"Scott, where are the keys to your car?"

He mumbled, "They're in my pocket." I reached in his pants pocket and pulled out a set of keys.

"I'll be right behind you." The medics left with Scott. Dave was still standing in the living room horrified and crying. The look of pain and fear on his face was terrible; I'll never forget the look on David's face. I gave him a hug and told him not to worry.

"Steve, I'm going to the hospital. I'll call you from there." I glanced back at the two of them. Steve was trying to clean up the blood that was all over our house. As I was driving to the hospital, I glanced around the strange car. Something was wrong. There was a car phone, and the car was cluttered with toys, papers and clothes. "This can't be Scott's car," I thought. I locked the doors and dismissed the question, concentrating instead on Scott's injury and the trip to the hospital.

Thank God the hospital was only five minutes from the house. I was scared to death. When I reached the emergency room, Scott was already on a stretcher. His whole body was shaking. There were medical personnel and police officers all around. I felt like I was going to pass out. There was so much going on around Scott. I leaned over and gave him a kiss. More police had shown up at the hospital and began asking questions about the car that I had driven there. One of them wanted me to point the car out to him; I did, and left them.

I went back into Scott's room. He and I were alone for a moment. I leaned over him and whispered, "Scott, what happened? Has anyone else been hurt?"

"I don't know, Mom. I tried to stop them; I tried to stop them."

"What do you mean, Scott? You have to tell me the truth, what happened tonight?" My God, what had happened from the time he called me and the time he got home?

"Mom, he was into them for a lot of money. I tried to stop it." More nurses came into Scott's room to attend him. He? Who was he? I put my finger up to my lips, gesturing to Scott to stay quiet. Terrified, I went to the telephone and called home. I was crying uncontrollably now.

"Steve?"

"How's Scott?"

"Steve, there's something very wrong here, there's something very wrong, please come to the hospital."

"I'll be right there." I could tell Steve was angry but I couldn't worry about his mood. I went back into the room with Scott. Some of the police officers were asking me questions about Scott, but I was only interested in how he was doing. "I love you, honey, it's going to be all right. Just take it easy."

I was pacing back and forth waiting for Steve to arrive. I kept walking to the front doors to see if Steve was there. When I saw his car approach, I ran outside to him. I was afraid to talk in front of the police, with all that was going on and the way they were asking me questions.

"What's going on?"

"I don't know, they're asking a lot of questions about the car I drove here. Something isn't right, Steve. Something just isn't right." I had never been so scared in my life.

"Eve, Dave is scared to death and home alone right now. Find out what is going on with Scott and let's go home to Dave."

I could see how annoyed Steve was getting with all this. I needed his support right now but he wasn't giving much of it. I stepped back from him; he turned and walked back to his car.

I found the doctor attending Scott and asked what they were going to do.

"Your son has extensive knife wounds. We've called in a surgeon. It's going to take awhile."

I went into Scott's room to let him know that he would be there awhile and that I would be going home to Dave. I was so torn. Dave needed me too and Steve obviously wasn't going to help with any of this. I couldn't be in two places at once. What to do; stay at the hospital with Scott or go to Dave, who I knew was scared beyond belief. Steve took me home. I paused at the door of Scott's room. I turned and stared at him; he was dosing in and out. My God, what had happened tonight?

The drive back to the house was in complete silence. When I got in the house, Dave was sobbing. I did my best to comfort him, and finally got him to settle down on the couch. He didn't want to go to his bedroom. My mind was racing. Things were happening so fast. When Dave was calmed, I called the hospital to check on Scott.

"Hello, may I have the Emergency Department?"

"Emergency room, may I help you?"

"This is Eve Meyer, My son, Scott, was brought in with stab wounds and I'd like to check on his status." I was put on hold. "Mrs. Meyer? Scott needs extensive stitches and it's going to take some time."

"All right, I'll call back. Please let Scott know that I called." I hung up the phone. God, please, please don't let anything more be wrong.

After several hours, Dave and Steve were asleep but I needed to talk to someone. My sister lived in New Jersey. There is a two-hour difference, and I knew she would be sleeping, but I really needed to talk with her.

"Hello?"

"Sherry?"

"Eve? What's wrong?"

I began to cry uncontrollably.

"Eve, what's wrong?"

"Sherry, Scott came home tonight and was stabbed. He was bleeding all over the house."

"What are you talking about? How did this happen?" I went through the story with her, what I knew of the story, anyway.

"You're kidding?"

"Sherry, there's something wrong, I know there is."

"What do you mean?" I told her the story that Scott had told me earlier that day. My sister couldn't believe it.

After talking to Sherry for an hour, I called the hospital to check on Scott again; I placed a conference call and kept Sherry on the line.

"Hello, this is Eve Meyer again, I would like to know how Scott Mutchler is doing?"

"He's almost done, you can come pick him up soon."

"How long?"

"About half an hour."

"Is there any way we can speak with Scott?"

"Yes, I'll take a phone in to him." There was a pause.

"Hello?" Scott sounded terrible.

"Scott, are you all right?"

"Scott, honey, it's Aunt Sherry."

Scott was crying. Sherry did most of the talking, trying to find out what had happened. Scott was incoherent and not making sense.

"Mom, are you coming to get me?"

"Yes, honey, I'm coming to get you."

"Scott, is everything OK?"

"I just want you to come get me."

"OK, honey, I'll be there soon. Put the nurse back on the phone."

"Hello, Mrs. Meyer? There's a detective who wants to talk to you."

"OK." There was another pause.

"Mrs. Meyer, do you know anyone by the name of Shaw?"

"No I don't. Why?"

"You don't know anyone by that name, Shaw? Or Sharp?"

"I know someone by the name of Scharf. Evan Scharf."

"Yes, Evan Scharf." The detective had a menacing tone to his voice; his questions were confusing me. What did an old neighbor have to do with Scott's injuries?

"Look, detective, I'm not going to play games with you. Either tell me what's going on or don't, but don't play games with me."

"Evan Scharf is dead."

"Oh, my God! Oh, my God, no! This can't be happening. Sherry, Sherry, my God, no! This can't be happening!"

I dropped the receiver and crumpled to the floor, leaving the phone dangling. My horrific screeching brought both Steve and Dave out of a dead sleep. Steve came running out of the bedroom. I couldn't stop screaming, but I could faintly hear Steve in the background talking with my sister and the detective.

The Horror Begins

There was a knock on the door. A tall, well-dressed man in a suit introduced himself as Alex Ragulsky, a detective for the Louisville Police Department. His demeanor was surprisingly kind. My friends, Lauren and Mona, and my mother-in-law were with me.

"Mrs. Meyer, I have some questions to ask you, may I come in?"

I led the detective to the living room. I was shaking. What more could he possibly tell me? I had never cried so hard, I had never felt so much sorrow.

When the boys and I first moved to Colorado, we lived on a small cul-de-sac in a wonderful neighborhood next door to the Scharfs. Evan was a single parent raising one of his children – it always seemed strange that he had the custody of only one of his children. His son

Robbie and my youngest son Dave had been friendly. Scott had baby-sat Robbie and done many odd jobs for Evan.

The detective asked many questions. I was numb, but tried to answer him the best I could. Finally, I asked a question.

"Where is Scott?" I couldn't control the tears.

"He's at the Boulder County Jail."

"Is he OK?"

"As far as I know, he's fine." I needed to know more about what had happened. If Evan was dead, what had happened to Robbie? Part of me didn't want to ask, but I had to know.

"What about Evan's son, Robbie?"

"He's dead."

"Oh, my God! No! No, no, no! This can't be happening!" Everyone around me started to move. I remember hearing the detective tell another officer to get a victims advocate to the house immediately. I was losing control and I didn't know how to get it back. "God, please take this away," I thought.

I wanted everyone out of my house. A woman from the victims advocate arrived, but didn't have much to say. It seemed obvious I wasn't her idea of a victim. She didn't seem to want to help the family of the accused. We weren't really victims in her eyes.

Scott was a suspect in the murder of two people whom we had known, and there was nowhere for us to turn, no one to turn to. My soul had been taken. My child was in the Boulder County Jail; he had been brutally stabbed and two people were dead. I asked God "Why?" again, and again He didn't answer.

I went to my husband. It was amazing the comfort I had always felt when I was near him, but that feeling wasn't there now. I couldn't imagine how he was going to handle all of this. All Steve and I ever wanted was a happy life together, and now all of our lives were in turmoil. Steve looked into my eyes and told me things would be OK; we would make it through this. How could he be so sure?

"Eve, you need to know I'm not letting this thing change my life. I'm a coach, and this is what I have to do. I'm going to practice."

"What do you mean, you're going to practice?" My heart sank. How could he leave me at a time like this?

"I have to cope with this, too, but I have to handle this my way. I need to clear my head. I'll make sure someone is with you so you're not alone."

I couldn't even speak. I didn't want someone else with me. I needed my husband to be with me. I needed to feel safe with him. Steve's mother and my friends left shortly after he did.

I paced the house in a daze. My eye caught a glimpse of the cross that hung in our entryway. "How can there be a God?" I thought. "God is supposed to protect children! If there were a God, these things would not be happening." The rage inside me was frightening. I glared at that cross and walked towards it. I grabbed the cross off the wall and threw it across the room. It broke in several pieces.

There was a knock at the door. As I opened the door, I could see television reporters and cameramen everywhere. My eyes darted from microphone to microphone. Every television station in the Denver area was on my doorstep!

"Mrs. Meyer, we would like to ask you a few questions about your son."

"If you don't leave my property I'll sign a complaint against you." I closed the door and locked it. I pulled all of the blinds and kept the house dark so no one could look inside. I was terrified.

The phone rang. Now what?

"You have a collect call from the Adams County Jail."

Adams County Jail? Who could this be? I accepted the call to see what was going on.

"Mrs. Mutchler?" Who would call me by Scott's last name?

"Yes?"

"My name is EC; I'm a friend of Scott's. I called to let you know there is no way that Scott could have done this. There were two bad asses that got out of jail who were supposed to meet Scott when he got out."

"What do you mean?"

"I just want you to know Scott didn't do this." He explained how he knew Scott and all about this meeting Scott had planned with two other inmates.

"I will stay in touch, I promise. Try not to worry. Remember, Scott didn't do this."

This was maddening. What was he talking about? Who were these other two people? How did this inmate get my phone number?

Of course I believed Scott could never have done this. I knew he was involved somehow, but I knew he couldn't be guilty of murder. So, whoever Scott was with that night was still out there, and they knew where we lived. We could be in danger.

Three days after this nightmare began, I still hadn't heard from Scott. Dave was afraid to go to school. He stayed home, clinging to my side. While Steve went on with his regular routine of coaching football, Dave and I felt different. We were hiding. Reporters and so-called "friends" who wanted to know what had happened kept the telephone ringing constantly.

Steve's family was not taking the publicity very well. There was a terrible strain between us. His mother called me to bemoan "what is happening to the Meyer name." All she was concerned with was what was happening to her family's name and to Steve.

When Steve came home from football practice, I told him what his mother had said. He told me not to worry about his family, that all I needed to worry about was what he thought and said.

"I'll be back later." He was gone quite a while. When he got back, I asked him what happened.

"I told Mom that either she was with us or against us, but to get on one side or the other. She chose to be with us." Thank God, I really needed her then.

Scott finally called. He sounded so lost.

"Mom? I'm sorry for all of this."

I was at a loss for words. We both cried and cried. What was there to say? My heart was aching for him.

"Scott, how's your arm and hand?"

"I can't move my fingers, and I'm in a lot of pain."

"What are they going to do for it?"

"They're going to take me for surgery. They say there's a lot of damage."

"Do you know when?"

"No, they won't tell me. They say for security reasons, they can't let anyone know.

"I'll try to find out and be there for you."

"Mom, they've assigned an attorney to me, his name is Sam Shaw. He came to see me. Mom, I didn't do it; I didn't do it, Mom. Will you come see me?"

"Yes, I'll be there. Who do I call to set it up?"

"Call that Sam Shaw. Write down this number and call him." I jotted the phone number on a scrap of paper.

"OK, I'll call and have it set up. Everything is going to be all right, Scott." I tried to sound reassuring.

"Mom, I need you to do something for me. There's a package in my room in a large brown envelope. I want you to call my attorney and give it to him, OK?"

"What's in the package, Scott, and why does your attorney need it?"

"Mom, I have something in there I want my attorney to have."

"OK, Scott. I'll call him and tell him to come get it."

"Mom, we're only allowed 15 minutes on the telephone and then they'll disconnect us."

"Scott, call me back when you can."

"OK, Mom, I love you."

"I love you, too, honey." I hung the phone up slowly.

Over the years, my boys and I never ended a call and never went to sleep without saying "I love you." There was silence. Overwhelming silence.

I went down to Scott's bedroom to get the envelope he wanted me to give to his attorney. I looked inside. There were some papers, none of which made any sense to me. I closed the envelope and sat down on his bed. I looked in Scott's closet where his clothes were hanging. I took one of his shirts off the hanger and put it to my face. I could smell his presence. I lay down on the bed and cried, clutching his shirt. My heart and soul had been torn out of me.

I glanced around his room where all his track medals and ribbons hung; all his football trophies were laid out around his room. How could this be happening?

I had called everywhere looking for a private attorney. They wanted money I just didn't have to defend Scott. I offered them my home and business, but they all wanted cash up front. We were forced to rely on the court-appointed public defender.

The next day, I started planning Dave's birthday party. Everyone told me I needed to keep the family going, especially for Dave's sake. I had received many calls from parents saying they didn't want their children at our house, considering Scott's situation. The friends who did stand by us, though, would be there with their children. I had to find a way to help Dave through this. While I was making my plans, the phone rang.

"Mrs. Meyer?"

"Yes?"

"This is the principal at Dave's school." I knew what was coming.

"Yes?"

"Why has Dave not been in school for four days?" The tears welling in my eyes began to sting. I couldn't answer her. I didn't know how to answer her.

"Mrs. Meyer, why has he not been in school?" I couldn't control the tears any longer, and began to tell the principal what we were going through.

"Mrs. Meyer, I'm sending Dave's counselor and the school psychologist over to your house immediately. I want you to know we're here for you." I couldn't stand the thought of anyone else coming to the house, but I knew I had to make things right with the school. Dave needed to go on, too. Within 20 minutes the doorbell rang. A woman and a man were standing at the door.

"Mrs. Meyer, we're from the middle school. May we come in?" I led them to the living room. Dave had come upstairs to see who was in the house.

The counselor put her arms around Dave and hugged him. The two of them cried. It was killing me to see how much Dave was suffering.

Scott was his whole world, and he was shattered. The counselor and psychologist let Dave and I know that we had all the support we needed from the school. The counselor said Dave had a very good team of teachers, and that Mrs. Knight, the head of that team, adored Dave and they would all be there to support him. She also let him know that, if at any time during school hours he needed to get away, to come to her office and she'd be there for him. I thanked them both and let them know that I appreciated their help.

Football season was beginning and Dave needed to get back to his routine instead of hiding out in the house. I knew that I had to get back to some kind of routine, too. I went into the office that I had in our home and began working. A half hour or so went by before a figure standing in the doorway caught my eye. Dave was there dressed in his football gear, tears pouring down his face.

"Honey, what's wrong?" He walked over to me and dropped to his knees. He laid his head on my lap and began sobbing. His soul had been taken, too.

"Mom, I need my brother. I need him." He could barely choke the words out. I stroked Dave's hair.

"I know, honey, I know." I needed him, too.

The next morning was Saturday, Dave's party. Steve had a football game to go to and would be home in time for the party. I was trying so hard to give a small piece of happiness to Dave right now; but I was numb.

"Dave, let's go pick up the last minute things we need for your birthday."

"OK, Mom." I didn't want to talk about Scott today. We filled the ride with idle chitchat about football, school and how fast he was growing up. It was nice doing something other than hiding in our home. Funny, though, I still felt everyone was watching me, that anyone who looked in my direction knew who I was, what Scott was accused of. I just had to shake this.

With all of our shopping done, we headed home. As we were approaching the house, I told Dave that I needed to make one more stop, to get his birthday cake, and would be right back.

"Dave, when you get in the house, lock the door and don't let anyone in. If anyone calls asking questions about Scott, just hang up."

"OK, Mom." I watched until he got in the door and turned to pull away. Suddenly, there were cars surrounding me from everywhere. Police jumped from every car and I jumped out of mine. I recognized Detective Ragulsky among the officers.

"What is going on?" I demanded.

"Mrs. Meyer, we have a search warrant to search your house."

Tears stung my eyes. I was so humiliated. The neighbors were all looking out their windows; some had come out to the curb. I needed to get back inside, away from their stares.

"This was not necessary. I've cooperated with all of you when you've asked. Why did you have to do this?"

Apologies were being made as we entered the house. I was becoming angrier and angrier at what my family was being made to go through. As we came down the hallway into the dining room, Ragulsky noticed the decorations.

"Mrs. Meyer, whose birthday is it?"

"It's Dave's. Everyone told me to try to keep my house going, I took that advice and I'm trying to give Dave a birthday party!" I was becoming hysterical.

"We didn't know, Mrs. Meyer. We'll do this as quickly as possible and get out, I promise."

The lead detective gave instructions to all of the officers to restrict their search to Scott's bedroom only and to do it as quickly as possible so they wouldn't be there when Dave's friends arrived. Ragulsky stayed upstairs with me, asking more questions.

"Eve, my wife is making food for you and your family. I'll bring it back to you later today."

I couldn't understand why he was being so kind to us. He was trying to convince everyone that my son was a killer, yet he appeared to have compassion for what we were going through.

"That is very kind of you. but really not necessary."

He smiled a warm smile. "No, it's something we want to do. I want you to know something: If you or Dave need anything, just call. I'm so sorry for what you're going through."

They kept their promise and were gone by the time the guests started arriving, but my nerves were raw.

I could barely keep my mind on Dave's party. People talked to me, but I couldn't focus on what they said.

Dave's best friend, Rich, went up to him and put his arm on his shoulder. "Dave, I'm your best friend," he said. "If you need anything, I'm here for you."

"Thanks Rich."

It helped to see Dave's best friend reach out to him and let him know he really cared. Not long after we cut the cake, all of Dave's friends except Rich began to leave. Our friends Lauren and Ron stayed into the night. Steve played some music and tried so hard to pretend it was just another night, but my mind couldn't block out the pain and reality of what we were dealing with. Things were never going to be the same. Everything was out of control.

The days started to blend together. I had more and more difficulty focusing. In a short time, I had built incredible walls around me. I was learning how to live in a state of numbness. Steve tried to deal with all of this too, but his way was to not be home. The nights he went out he would come home later and later each time. I couldn't blame him; I didn't even know who I was anymore and I started to push him away, too. Our relationship was deteriorating by the minute. It felt like he was never home. And when he was home, all we did was fight. I felt so very abandoned; so very lonely. I was becoming increasingly withdrawn and more depressed.

I couldn't get the call from EC, the inmate at the Adams County Jail, out of my mind. I was terrified to be in my own home. Steve's father loaned us a gun to keep in the house and, at night when Steve was gone, I sat in the dark, curled up in a ball holding that gun, shaking. I guess I felt someone would charge through the door at Dave and me.

As if things weren't bad enough, I received a call from Steve's youngest sister. She called to inform me that she and her parents were concerned that Steve wasn't happy. She told me her parents hated me like they did her ex-husband. Why did she tell me that? What was wrong with her and her family? I had never done anything to them to deserve this. I didn't know how much more I could take.

My thoughts drifted back to when I first met her. We had become friendly and did a lot together, but things changed quickly. It seemed the closer Steve and I got, the more jealous she became. She, too, was a single mother raising an only child. She felt Steve was the most important person in their lives, and I imagine she felt the kids and I were a threat to her since we were taking up his time now.

Over time, things went from annoying to downright ugly. Steve was always caught in the middle of whether to believe my word or hers in our disputes. It became one of the biggest problems in our marriage.

I glanced at Steve. Thank goodness, Steve was home when she called this time. He never would have believed me if he hadn't been there. He was in the living room when she called and overheard my part of the conversation. Finally, he got up and took the phone from me. I stood there watching as an argument broke out between them. I had never heard him speak with her in this manner.

I couldn't understand why all that was happening. I knew his sister hated me, but I just couldn't believe she would attack me at a time like this. I felt like I was losing my mind and Steve's family was pushing me over the edge.

I walked back to my office, my mind filled with my growing anger and hate for them. Only one member of Steve's family didn't turn her back on me; one person stood up to the hatred of her family. Steve's sister, Norma, was one in a million. Her love and guidance helped me keep my sanity. She, too, paid a heavy price with the hatred from the rest of her family because she wouldn't turn her back on me. They didn't like her loyalty to me, and they let her know it.

It didn't help that I felt my own family had abandoned me. My sister on the East Coast openly said she didn't want anything to do with this mess. My other sister was out of the country, and my brother, too, wanted nothing to do with our problems. Although each of them was there if I needed to talk, I felt terribly alone. I prayed for the exhaustion to set in at night so I would fall asleep. It was my only escape from all of this.

Ring…

"Mom?" It was Scott. "We need to talk about something. When the trial does start, I don't want you there."

"What do you mean? Of course I'll be there for you. Why would you not want me there for you?"

"Mom, listen to me. There isn't anything you can do to help me in there. The courtroom will be packed with reporters and other people that will bother you. I know you are alone with this mom. I know no one is there for you; not Steve not anyone and I can't help you in there. I have to concentrate on what's going on, not worry about who's bothering you."

"But, Scott, you can't go through this all alone."

"Mom, I'm not alone. You'll be with me every second. You don't have to be there physically for me to know you're with me. Just be there when they say you have to be. Please do this for me."

Scott asked how his brother was doing and I tried to fill him in on what was going on at home, but my mind was consumed with what Scott had just said to me.

"Mom, they're going to disconnect us. I'll call you soon."

My heart was breaking. With all he was facing, he still was trying to protect me. "Dear God in heaven, I can't stand any more of this pain," I thought. I hung up the phone and went to my bedroom. Behind the headboard was a bottle of Valium. I stared at it for a long moment, closed my eyes and fell asleep.

"Eve, I'm going to head back to the room for a while. What are you going to do?" Steve's voice brought me back to the present.

"I think I'll sit here and go through more of these trial transcripts. How about if I meet you for lunch?"

Steve stood up and pulled me close. "I'll see you then." He kissed me and started walking back to our hotel room. I watched as he walked away. So much had happened between us.

I sat back down and pulled out the first volume. I needed to read the transcripts, to find out what was said, to understand what happened in that courtroom. I looked out toward the ocean and began to pray out loud.

"God, if you can hear me, I need to find a way to help Scott. If he's truly not guilty of what they say, help me find a way."

I began reading the pre-trial transcripts that I'd been studying before leaving for vacation. So much of this I didn't understand. It was hard enough accepting the outcome; it was harder now knowing what really went on in the courtroom. I turned back to the discussion of DNA testing. DNA testing that might have proven Scott wasn't alone in the Scharf's home. DNA testing that wasn't allowed.

The Insanity Continues

JUDGE MORRIS SANDSTEAD JR.: "Enter your appearances please."

ASSISTANT DISTRICT ATTORNEY PHIL MILLER: "Phil Miller for the People, Your Honor."

PUBLIC DEFENDER SAM SHAW: "Sam Shaw, Linda Cooke and David Wymore for Mr. Mutchler, who is present in custody. Judge, this comes on our request for the Court to consider a motion that we wanted to have you consider yesterday. That's the motion, which we entitled, Request for Access to All Testing Procedures and Physical Presence of Defense Experts During Testing.

"We also filed a motion for discovery and an order for appointment of DNA expert. And I put those on the bench. I think you got those."

JUDGE: "Yeah. Do you have other orders, because I'm going to let you appoint experts in just about anything you got. We're going to have so many experts here the jury will forget what the trial is about. Maybe, that's a tactic somebody used. I'm not sure which."

MILLER: "Your Honor, I'm in receipt of the motion filed earlier about access. And I have just received copies of the discovery motion and request for a DNA expert.

"It appears the Court is inclined to grant the expert motion forthwith, and I have no objection to that. We need time to digest the several pages of discovery request and that will involve contacting the technician or technicians who are conducting the test in Washington D.C.

"As far as the…likewise with the motion for access. I'll need to have some time to determine what access, if any, is afforded defense experts or defense representatives."

JUDGE: "What does that mean? What if I sign this order and then when the defense expert gets on an airplane and flies to Washington D.C. and in order to save money, takes the …flies into National instead of…"

"Dulles."

"…Dulles. And he takes the subway into town and he gets out at the FBI labs. And he goes up there and they say, 'You can't come in here. Who are you?' Then what happens is he gets back on the subway, goes all the way back to the airport, flies all the way back to Denver, drives all the way back to Boulder, comes to see Mr. Shaw and says, 'They won't let me in there.' "

MILLER: "I agree. If the Court suggests that, we can find out what the access is or what access, if any, is afforded. Then we can report back to the Court rather than have you sign an order that may not carry any effect. I'd like the opportunity to do that.

"Mr. Shaw asked me yesterday about coming in here today and I have talked with the CBI experts. I have not reached the FBI technicians. So I could respond to the access motion probably as early as tomorrow. I'd like a little more time than that to evaluate the discovery motion."

JUDGE: "Well, are you…I guess…let me see if I hear you correctly. It appears to me that you're saying you either don't know or you're unclear or you don't believe the defendant's arguments that they…that your expert, if done by FBI labs, won't...won't grant all these things. You just want to confirm that. You don't know it already."

MILLER: "Which motion? Are you now referring to discovery?"

JUDGE: "I'm just saying I don't know what I'm referring to. The defendant argued yesterday, and I've heard on prior occasions, that their position is that they think...and I don't remember the source of their thoughts...that your expert won't let them have any of these procedures and protocol and such."

MILLER: "Well, Your Honor..."

JUDGE: "If that's true, then we're going to have to come back here and resolve this issue. We keep trying to make it so we're not going to have a trial on the 20th and I'm going to make it so we are. In fact, I'm going...not even going to try; I'm going to have it then, period. I'm going to have a trial on the 20th no matter what. And then to tell me you're not ready or you don't have something is...is not an argument I'm going to hear from anybody on either side."

PUBLIC DEFENDER DAVID WYMORE: "Judge, I think our position needs to be made a little clearer concerning the entire scope of what's happening. We're not...the whole issue on asking the People whether or not we can be present, I think, is a false issue because I think that in Colorado, we have a constitutional guaranteed right to be present.

"If the Court looks at the case of People versus Garries, which I have a copy of for the Court. And I don't know if it's been tendered...well, of course I only have one copy, Your Honor. But..."

MILLER: "Your Honor, may I say that I have no objection to the...to the Court's appointing a DNA expert. But on both the motion received today and the access motion, I'd like to have it set down for some kind of hearing so we can digest the contents, particularly the new motion that...and also my efforts to contact or confirm or argue whether or not access is in fact denied. I can't confirm some of these facts.

"I can confirm that the FBI does reveal the protocol that they used in the testing; that the sample...the test that is run, it can be rerun by other experts. The membranes, which are used for the probes in this testing, are also available, as well as, I think they're called the x-rays or photographs of the autorads. That's my understanding of the terms to argue that we heard yesterday. And some of what might be in the long motion which I haven't read in its entirety…I may be incorrect about what the FBI will and will not do."

JUDGE: "Well, let me read this case because I've got a great idea, just a great idea. We let them do whatever they want to do, whatever they think they should do and then we let your…we let you cross examine their experts about everything they did and how they did it."

WYMORE: "That doesn't work."

"Well, it might work. I like the idea. I think it's a great idea. And the more you try to argue against me and interrupt me about it, the more I'm going to be set in my ways."

"But…"

"And you'll get to say to this jury that this is the little procedure they used that clearly leads to false…leads to false positives or whatever all the time. And you'll just destroy that guy on cross-examination."

"Well Judge, that's…"

"And vice versa, they get to cross-examine your expert, too."

"All I want to do is have an opportunity to be heard here today."

"You're going to get plenty of time. But I need the opportunity to be heard, too. You know what I'm thinking? Why, I'm thinking you want to get this case pushed off so that it never happens over some petty issue that probably doesn't…"

WYMORE: "Excuse me, Your Honor. I'm not trying to delay anything. I'm not trying to raise a petty issue. And I am a little bit taken aback that the Court is even insinuating that. What I'm trying to do is show the Court what is happening, what we want and what we think is the position of the constitutional rights of the defendant. And I don't think constitutional rights are a petty issue.

"The issue is, we filed these motions over a month ago, almost two months ago. So it's not as if notice hasn't happened. But the issue is...is that we're saying that Mr. Mutchler has a right to have an expert present at testing. And that's what Garries says. Garries is an FBI case. Garries is a case where they sent blood samples to the FBI and…"

JUDGE: "Tell you what. Let me read it. Just everybody be quiet and I'll read it."

After a pause, Sandstead continues the hearing.

"Let me ask a question of the prosecution. If I don't let the defendant refer in argument to the failure of the prosecution to do DNA testing in order to pin down their case, then why doesn't that eliminate the necessity of doing DNA testing?"

MILLER: "It could. Could you restate that again, what you would consider?"

"Sure. Enter an order that the defendant cannot argue to the jury that in order to…there is other methods of further proving the attendance of the defendant at the scene of the crime by suggesting to the jury that they could have done more in their investigation or testing, such as having DNA testing done on the blood."

WYMORE: "Your Honor…"

JUDGE: "And so that this...they're sort of saying DNA testing would have done this. They're admitting that DNA testing by that argument is good, but that's the only thing, the only reasoning they would have to suggest it. If I prohibited them from doing that, then why do we need to go through this whole process?"

MILLER: "Well, Your Honor, I think that's a step in the right direction. I think…I think what we would be interested in…and I'd like to consult with co-counsel on this before I respond directly. "But argument to the jury is one thing. I suppose cross-examination of other witnesses, too…it's the same drift.

JUDGE: "Right. 'Isn't it true, Officer, that you could have saved that blood and done DNA testing on it? And you, Mr. Blood Spatter Expert, you could have photographed those blood spatters and had them sent to the FBI and that would have even been a better way of…of pinning down your testimony than this hypothetical posed by the prosecution.' "

MILLER: "Your Honor, I would like the opportunity to consult...I mean, that's a remedy that I think…I believe the prosecution would consider. I need to consult with at least one or two other people before I make a definite response to it. Could we have until later this afternoon at 5 or 9 tomorrow morning?"

JUDGE: "Well, let me see. Maybe the defendants now decide that it's important that we have some information with regard to testimony from a DNA expert."

WYMORE: "Judge, we're...we were addressing the motion of having an expert present during testing. And accepting stipulation such as that because it's…this evidence might be potentially exculpatory also. It's kind of…"

JUDGE: "Let me ask that question. 'Tell me how…' "

SHAW: "Well, what if it shows that it's not Mr. Mutchler's blood or that the test performed is…becomes inconclusive?"

JUDGE: "What if it shows it's not Mr. Mutchler's blood? So what does that mean? What does that mean?"

SHAW: "It shows that it's not Mr. Mutchler's blood that was present at the scene if it shows…"

JUDGE: "Maybe he didn't bleed at the scene."

SHAW: "No, I can't tell you exactly what that would show…that test would show that that's not Mr. Mutchler's blood or whatever inference or argument arises from that. I can't foresee at this point in time. So I don't know what that means."

JUDGE: "Nor can I. I don't see the possibility of it being exculpatory anyway."

SHAW: "Mr. Wymore…I suppose it could suggest that there were other people at the scene besides Mr. Mutchler. And…"

JUDGE: "Who bled."

SHAW: "Yeah, who bled, besides the two victims in this case. We're certainly not ready at this point to reach an agreement with the prosecution that our cross-examination or argument in the case is limited by not raising the subject matter DNA.

"And, I don't know that if we didn't make that kind of agreement, if the Court would have the authority to limit our argument in that way.

"The prosecution has a burden of proving their case beyond a reasonable doubt, and I don't think we can be foreclosed from making certain arguments that might raise a reasonable doubt."

JUDGE: "But isn't it true that you filed a motion to prohibit DNA testing? Is that true, yes or no?"

SHAW: "We filed it and it's been denied."

JUDGE: "But if I were to deny that now, then do you think I would permit you, in closing argument, to say, 'Well, why didn't you do DNA testing?' And then they have to bring…say 'Well, you asked us not to and the judge ordered us not to.' Then the judge goes off on some tangent that has nothing to do with this case."

SHAW: "We'd be in a position...in a different position if the Court had granted our motion for sure. But we can't have it denied both ways."

JUDGE: "Well, the district attorney wants a little recess so he can consult and decide whether or not if I...which is the same thing. I could just change my mind with regard to whether or not I'm going to permit DNA testing and change my mind by saying 'No, I will not, because of the reasons set forth in the defendant's motion.' And then I will tell you that the order must be and will be the law of the case that no one can raise the issue of 'Why wasn't DNA testing done?' Because that's my responsibility and that's not relevant to the jury. Or it takes care of it the same way."

SHAW: "Assuming you deny them the opportunity to test."

JUDGE: "Right."

MILLER: "Well, whatever the Court would permit me. I'd like time..."

JUDGE: "Well, how about ten minutes?"

"How about 3:30?"

SHAW: "What's this for?"

JUDGE: "It's a meeting..."

SHAW: "For us to talk about what we're..."

JUDGE: "No. No. For Mr. Miller to discuss with some other of his colleagues if they think this is a good decision to make at this stage, but might not lead to error or inability to prove their case or something; all those things that lawyers think about in presenting their side of the case."

MILLER: "3:15."

JUDGE: "All right."

After a 45-minute recess, the hearing resumed at 3:30 p.m.

JUDGE: "Back on the record in the Mutchler case."

MILLER: "Your Honor, Phil Miller again for the People. I've filed a motion that expresses the People's position and provided a copy to the defense. I guess now I would ask that...request that the Court inquire of the defense whether they persist in that motion. And if so, we've stated our position on this."

JUDGE: "The Court having reconsidered its mind…"

SHAW: "Whoa. Whoa. Are you all set to rule, Judge?"

JUDGE: "What's your position? Are you going to change your mind?"

SHAW: "I guess I don't have any problem with them not testing. That's your decision. As was said yesterday, you can't control whether or not they test. But what I have a problem with them doing is manipulating DNA testing in this case, manipulating this Court into prohibiting us from raising defenses in this case."

JUDGE: "What's the defense? What defense, that…"

SHAW: "One of our defenses is to argue inferences from evidence that they present. And if one of those inferences is that they haven't foreclosed the possibility of other people being in the residence when the victims died. Then I think the Court is basically helping them out of a jam.

"Some time ago, they decided 'Maybe we've got a problem here, because we don't have any evidence that there wasn't a third party in there. And there are a couple of ways that we can reduce that. We can do DNA testing or we can simply argue to the jury from our forensic evidence that there's not a reason to believe that.'

"Well, they didn't do the DNA testing and I don't know if they've even started it yet. But it was sent off, I think. And they picked a vendor that won't let us observe what they're doing.

"So, essentially, the Court is saying, 'Well, you really can't do that. I mean, you can do it.' This is as of yesterday. 'You can do it if it can be done by the 20th, our trial date.' But that's not going to happen.

"And today, we come here to discuss whether or not Mr. Mutchler's constitutional right to observe the testing would be protected by the Court. And I'm assuming that that…"

JUDGE: "Wait a minute. Wait a minute. I'm not going to hold that the defendant has a constitutional right to observe all testing done by the prosecution. It's only under the narrow circumstances defined in the case of Garries. But…"

SHAW: "Fine."

JUDGE: "Anyway…"

SHAW: "The point is that they have manipulated us into not having a defense by messing around with the DNA. When this case started, we had the right to argue the defendant might not have been there. And we can argue that from any evidence they didn't -- did or didn't -- present. And if they had tested DNA back then, they wouldn't have this way of getting the Court to order that we couldn't do it.

SHAW: "I don't care what they do with their DNA testing as long as they do it and we can observe it. And if they don't do it, that's OK. But the Court can't here today say, that 'I have the power now to deny them to do the DNA testing and I'm going to renew your motion and now let you argue reasonable inferences from the…not let you argue reasonable inferences.' "

JUDGE: "Now so ruled. Anything further?"

SHAW: "You didn't have the power to grant yesterday and I don't know where it comes from today."

JUDGE: "I just granted your motion to deny DNA testing."

SHAW: "But you…yesterday you said you didn't have the power to do that."

JUDGE: "I just granted your motion to not grant DNA testing. I told you I changed my mind. And based on that change of mind, had I done that originally, I would have not permitted you to argue the failure of the prosecution to use DNA testing.

"Now, that does not, in my view, deny you any defense at all. It only denies you the opportunity to argue that, for some reason, this prosecutor didn't do DNA testing because you're the one who didn't want it done in the first place. And I will not let that be part of this case at all, in any way, period.

"That's my ruling. I don't think we need to make any further record on that."

SHAW: "Well, you know, I don't know what else to say, other than I've already said it, Judge. But basically what's happened is they have manipulated us out of a defense we have in the case."

JUDGE: "No, that is not true. And you can file anything, you can say anything you want, make any record you want. Put it in writing. I'll make it part of the file. Anything further? Any other issues going to come up tomorrow that we can deal with today?"

MILLER: "I just want to make sure I'm clear on...we asked you to reconsider the motion, the defense motion that was handled yesterday. And I wanted the Court to inquire of them. And I'm not sure if it came out directly or not. Do they persist in that motion or not? Because if they...if it's not been before us, I'm not sure what you can say or do about it."

JUDGE: "They have never withdrawn their motion to prohibit DNA testing."

SHAW: "It was denied. It was decided, I assumed."

JUDGE: "Well, and do you now persist now? Do you want to change your mind? I did ask that question. I said, 'Do you want to now change your mind and not object to DNA testing?' "

SHAW: "I don't care if they do DNA testing, as I said, so long as Mr. Mutchler's constitutional rights to a speedy trial and to observe the testing of evidence are protected."

JUDGE: "Right. And that's now moot, because there's not going to be any DNA testing evidence, nor will there be any argument by either side of why or whether or when or if it was done or could have been done or should have been done. That's irrelevant in this case."

SHAW: "Well, I don't think it's irrelevant because they have to prove their case beyond a reasonable doubt."

JUDGE: "Of course they do."

SHAW: "We have the...we have the liberty to argue inference from that evidence."

JUDGE: "No. No."

SHAW: "Including the things that weren't done."

JUDGE: "The only thing you do not have the liberty to argue is 'Ladies and gentlemen of the jury, the prosecution could have done DNA testing and proved whose blood this was,' because you...you've taken a contrary position about that from the very beginning. You will not be permitted to make that argument."

SHAW: "I said that they could test as long as his constitutional rights are protected."

MILLER: "Your Honor, I just...I think I understand your ruling."

JUDGE: "Now, I understand my ruling and I don't care whether anybody else does or not. But I…I understand it and it seems absolutely clear."

MILLER: "Essentially clear on all aspects except to make sure that when we ask that a motion be reconsidered, that that was their motion and they persisted in that. Because that has to be before you. I don't think…"

JUDGE: "They don't want to tell me whether or not they still persist in that motion."

SHAW: "I answered that. And…"

JUDGE: "That is you now would like to argue that they should not do DNA testing."

SHAW: "No. I don't care if they do DNA testing."

JUDGE: "Wait a minute. Wait a minute. The question is, you filed a motion to deny DNA testing."

SHAW: "Right."

JUDGE: "And I changed my mind. Now I'm granting that. Do you want to…now that I'm…I've said I'm going to reconsider that. Do you want to still persist in not wanting DNA testing, the same motion that you filed before all this happened?"

SHAW: "No."

JUDGE: "You want to now permit DNA testing?"

SHAW: "So long as the Court will protect Mr. Mutchler's constitutional rights to a speedy trial and to observe the testing."

JUDGE: "Well, we're getting too close to trial now."

SHAW: "That's not our fault."

JUDGE: "Well, so I agree."

SHAW: "And I don't' want to have my defenses limited by the fact that we're too close to trial for them to do the testing. They could have done it."

JUDGE: "In no way will your defenses be limited."

SHAW: "Well, that's what's being suggested here."

JUDGE: "It…it is not being suggested in any way. What I will not permit is for you to lie to the jury. That's what I won't permit. Now, lying to the jury is not a defense."

SHAW: "What lie would that be?"

JUDGE: “That they could have done DNA testing but they didn’t.”

SHAW: “They could have done it.”

JUDGE: “I ordered them not to do it. Do we have to go through all this?”

SHAW: “But we’re in this position because they waited five and a half months to do it. Now, I don’t know why they didn’t do it. That’s why we’re…the Court is denying us the opportunity to bring it up, so they have manipulated us out of a defense.”

JUDGE: “Well, I’m going to...I’m going to leave this as part of the file, for sure, your motion to deny DNA testing. Anything further that we can take care of today that might come up tomorrow? Are you…you’re going to present orders with regard to all of the other experts?”

WYMORE: “Your Honor, on the other experts, we have a separate budget. DNA is the only budget where we’re obliged to seek Court approval or Court access into that budget. Otherwise, the Public Defender has their own budget that covers expenditures with the intention of experts for fibers, ballistics, things like that. So I don’t think we’re going to need orders from…for that particular order. We can handle that ourselves.”

JUDGE: “All right. Well, I guess I am anticipating what he had said yesterday with regard to all of my orders that you may hire experts if you want to counter their experts. The only one I would be interested in having a Frye-test hearing over would be blood spatter. And we may have set that up or not. I don’t know, because I don’t know what they’re going to offer if they’re going to offer it, and if so, why and what the testimony would be.”

SHAW: “On blood spatter?”

JUDGE SANDSTEAD: “Right.”

SHAW: “I think, you know, sometimes so we don’t get in the situation they put us in with DNA…”

JUDGE: “That’s right. We’re going to have a hearing on blood spatter evidence.”

SHAW: “When?”

JUDGE: “The week before the trial.”

SHAW: “Fine. But what if…so far as I know, they haven’t done any blood spatter testing.”

JUDGE: "Well..."

SHAW: "What we keep running into, Judge, is they try to foreclose us from effectively assisting Mr. Mutchler by delaying testing until we don't have the opportunity to do anything about it. We run up against whether or not we waive a speedy trial by asking the Court for a continuance, which the Court might deny or not; being able to have our experts test their evidence; or not being able for them to introduce such evidence. Then you tell us we can't raise the issue, so they close us out."

MILLER: "Your Honor, I think CBI efforts on blood spatter is available to them in this. It's in discovery, which has been provided to them. So the testing has been done to date."

SHAW: "So we have results from..."

MILLER: "You have a report. I'm not sure. There may be a final report. He has an interim report."

SHAW: "I don't remember seeing any of that. But..."

JUDGE: "Well, let me ask you this. If you...if it's there...assume for the moment that there is some testing results report which an expert...then what is it you do? Don't you...based on what Mr. Wymore just said, it looks like a tactical decision. Should I go out and find somebody who has expertise in the field of blood spatter to review those reports and tell me what I need or if I need anything or if he really does have the qualifications as the other side for being an expert or if it's relevant to anything?

"And then, if you have information in that regard, you bring it here and I decide whether or not I will permit them to call a blood spatter expert. And if I do, then you get to have your blood expert testify to see if he qualifies as an expert, and if he has something to say that would counter that. I mean, am I...is that scenario correct?"

SHAW: "Right. I think that's right."

JUDGE: "And you could tactically decide that you don't care what their evidence is. It isn't relevant to your defense."

SHAW: "We need full discovery beyond the typical CBI printout."

JUDGE: "Well, that's what I am assuming. I assume blood spatter requires some sort of photographic evidence or preservation of the...of the actual spatter."

SHAW: "Right, and notes of whoever this expert is and what happened."

JUDGE: "Right."

WYMORE: "And his bibliography and his references."

JUDGE: "Now, I want everybody to sit and think just a minute before we leave because I'm…although I may be available for a few minutes tomorrow, I'm going to run out of available time to have a daily hearing in this case."

MILLER: "Can you give the prosecution one minute?"

JUDGE: "Sure."

MILLER: "Your Honor, at the risk of...well, let me make some request because I think key to what you…what you're proposing in what you've ruled, or apparently are prepared to rule on DNA, is the status of the defense motion and the response to the Court's question, you know, 'Are you persisting in that motion?' The answer…the response that I've noted is that we don't care, or they can do it if they want to without speaking to his motion. And I guess I'd like a little less equivocation if the Court is inclined to obtain that, because I think that's some…I think that's a key to the Court's ruling or intended ruling in this case is where they are on that motion."

JUDGE: "Well, I've pushed them as far as I think I need to. I think the record is clear about the alternatives that, had I granted the motion in the first place, I clearly would have entered exactly the same order. Tell you what. I didn't get my thinking cap off in time, but let me just say this. This motion with regard to sequestration of the jury during deliberations, I won't rule on until voir dire."

SHAW: "Now wait a minute Judge. I'm going to have to get out a legal pad and stuff."

JUDGE SANDSTEAD: "Make sure you write this down. I'm not going to decide whether or not to sequester until I hear the voir dire. I'm not going to presume that a jury could be somehow tampered with by whatever means.

"With regard to the motion for additional preemptory challenges, you're entitled to ten each side. I guess I'll rule on that at the time of the voir dire based on how it's going. If I think the length of the voir dire and the questions and answers being handled require extra preemptories, I'll make that decision at that time."

SHAW: "Judge, at the motions hearing we contemplated presenting some evidence on some of these motions. And I think that one would conclude, I think, that evidence we would present concerning publicity in this case might affect the Court's decision. So I'd ask you not to make a ruling on the one you just did and others of that nature."

JUDGE: "All right. I reserve the right to change my mind in that regard based upon some evidence that you present. I've already instituted a process for making a record of the jury service excuses and postponements for the jury summonses for the 20th.

"The motion for individual voir dire, I'm very likely to deal with individual voir dire for the purposes of prejudice, pretrial publicity."

MILLER: "Hardship."

JUDGE: "Hardship. And those are likely to be done in camera. Well, there's never been any limit on voir dire that I've ever imposed, so I don't know what the thrust of this motion for enlargement of time is."

SHAW: "Good."

JUDGE: "I mean, I reserve the right, of course, to limit it when I think it...I mean, in my experience, when I see a juror sort of...their eyes roll back in their head, I have some responsibility..."

SHAW: "Call an ambulance."

JUDGE: "...towards the pubic to prevent that from happening. If it means limiting voir dire, I will do so. And I presume you're going to have a whole lot of information here on the motion to quash the information or is that just one of those numbers on the computer that was..."

SHAW: "That was a well thought out motion."

JUDGE: "At one time, I'm sure it was."

MILLER: "Your Honor, you have one motion for enlargement of time. Apparently, I didn't get that one."

JUDGE: "It was some motion to enlarge the time for voir dire."

MILLER: "I'm checking the court file."

JUDGE: "All right. And I've said I've never limited voir dire and opening statements. That doesn't mean I'm going to let somebody pass out from boredom. These are citizens forced to come here and sit on the jury. Court is in recess."

I closed the book and rubbed my eyes. It was draining to read through all of this. It was more draining to realize what had really gone on. How could Judge Sandstead not want to know exactly what happened? Why did he not want to allow enough time for everyone to gather all the evidence they could to prove or disprove Scott's innocence? Why was he in such a hurry to get this trial over with? These are all questions that need to be answered. There has to be someone who can look at this behavior and do something about it.

I'll never forget when they had sent Scott to the State Psychiatric Hospital for evaluation. I had received a call from the physician who was attending to his case. He wanted me to know that they had not finished their tests and assessment with Scott but Judge Sandstead had ordered them not to continue and to send Scott back to Boulder. Why?

I laid my head back on the chair, enjoying the warmth of the sun. As much as I wanted to bask in this warm feeling, I forced my mind back to the events leading up to Scott's trial. I closed my eyes and drifted back to the day before jury selection.

The Set Up

The phone was ringing again.

"Hello?"

"You have a collect call from the Boulder County Jail." I accepted the call, but a strange voice was on the other end of the phone. It wasn't Scott.

"Mrs. Mutchler, Scott wanted me to get word to you that he was thrown in the hole."

"The hole? What's the hole?" I didn't understand what this person was telling me.

"They have him in solitary confinement."

"Why?"

"He said to tell you he's under investigation."

"For what?"

"That's all he told me to tell you. He'll call you later."I was in shock. "What could be happening now?" I wondered. An investigation? I just didn't understand.

It seemed like an eternity before Scott called later that day to say he was being charged with having a "shank" – a homemade knife.

"An inmate named Ciserelli turned me. He said that I grabbed him and said, 'I'll slit your throat like I slit theirs.' This is such bullshit, Mom. I never did anything. They wouldn't listen to me and charged me."

I couldn't believe what I was hearing. "Why are they doing this, Scott?"

"I'm being set up, Mom."

The incident was breaking news on every major television station. The reports made it seem that Scott was guilty of killing the Scharfs and trying to kill an inmate at the Boulder County Jail.

I couldn't stand any more. I called the jail and spoke with a Sergeant Cunning, who said guards found a knife on Scott's person and there would be a hearing within 72 hours. That was it. The story was all over the news for the rest of the day. I knew this story had to be a lie. I wanted some answers.

The next day, I called the jail and spoke with Sergeant Haas, who said there had been an investigation. Scott already had been brought before a judge and formal charges were filed, but then dropped. This was just bizarre! They accused him of something so very serious and, the next day, the charges were dropped? Nothing was making sense to me.

I opened my eyes and shook my head. I could feel the anger rising again as I remembered the events leading up to Scott's trial. I remember feeling then, and I feel more strongly now, that the prosecution had deliberately planned the charges against Scott while he was in jail. There could be no other logical explanation for that kind of lie to be generated and leaked to the press. The prosecution wanted to win this case no matter what it took. It was insanity. How could those people do this to another person? How could our system work like this?

I stood up, stretched, and looked around the beach. I stared at a family close by, watching as the children played in the water and smiling faintly as I remembered the days when I had shared such wonderful times with my own children. I started to walk along the beach, letting my mind drift back to the pretrial events.

Things were crazy. Scott didn't trust or like his attorney, and I had to try and do something. The attorney, Sam Shaw, wouldn't return my calls.

His assistant, Toni, finally did. She was wonderful. On first impression, she seemed to be a very warm and caring woman. She proved to be just that in the years to come.

She filled me in on what was happening with Scott's case. Finally, someone was telling me something! I asked her why Scott's attorney wouldn't return my calls, and she said Sam Shaw didn't want to talk to me. I couldn't understand this. Why would he not want to talk to me? I was Scott's mother and just wanted to do everything I could to help.

"Eve, I'd like to come over and get as much information from you as I can to help Scott."

"Anytime you want to come is OK." I was anxious to talk with anyone who wanted to help Scott. We set an appointment for her to visit, even though she wasn't Scott's attorney.

"Eve, there's one more thing you should be aware of."

"What's that, Toni?"

"It's a reelection year for Alex Hunter."

"Alex Hunter? Why would that make a difference?"

"It will. Believe me, it will." After briefing me a little more on what the procedure would be for Scott, she gave me her home phone number.

"If you need anything, call me."

"Thank you, Toni." I began to cry.

I didn't understand what she meant about this being an election year for Alex Hunter, the district attorney. It's more clear to me now.

I opened the yellow pages and started calling around for a private attorney again. There had to be someone out there that would help us. Finally, I found a lawyer willing to help, Larry Sather. When he got on the phone, I introduced myself and started to explain Scott's situation. He said he'd been following the case and wanted to meet with us.

The next day, Mr. Sather came to our home. Steve and I told him everything we knew. We didn't have to tell him about all the publicity.

"Mrs. Meyer, I'm appalled at the public defender's behavior. Your son's being railroaded and I want to help. I'll go see Scott on Monday." Finally, I felt some hope.

Scott called that evening and I told him about our meeting with Sather. We both felt that now, maybe, we'd get some real help. I also let him know that Shaw wouldn't return my calls.

"I'll take care of it, Mom."

What we didn't know was that Scott's every conversation was being listened to and recorded by the District Attorneys office. They knew what we were planning.

And the Judge Laughed

Funny how word gets around so fast. I received a call from Scott's public defender, Sam Shaw, soon after my conversation with Sather. He told me there would be a hearing Thursday at 9 a.m. and I had to be there.

"The district attorney doesn't want Scott to have the court approve a private attorney; they'd rather deal with us."

"What did you say?" I was shocked.

"How do you know we want another attorney?" I didn't wait for his reply.

" 'The district attorney doesn't want…' What difference does it make what they want?"

"I don't have answers for you. Court is Thursday morning at nine." If they were so sure Scott was guilty, why did they care who represented him? I was trying to make sense of what Scott's attorney just said. 'The district attorney would rather deal with us.' What the hell did that mean? Scott didn't have a prayer!

I called Sather to tell him about my conversation with Shaw. It didn't surprise him, since he felt there was a conspiracy going on.

Sather and I appeared together in the courtroom. Scott was in the jury box alone and handcuffed. Shaw was there with a team of attorneys from the Public Defenders' Office. The prosecution was there with a team of attorneys. This was a circus. Sather stood and addressed the judge.

"Your Honor, I'm here today on behalf of the defendant and his family to request a change in counsel. "

The judge began to laugh out loud. "This court does not recognize you are even in this room. Sit down."

I couldn't believe what I had just heard. I can't believe the judge actually laughed! How could he have thought any of this was funny? Scott looked at me in horror.

"Your Honor, I want this man as my attorney!"

The judge was still laughing, "You have an attorney. What's next?"

That was it. Sather was ordered to leave the courtroom. Scott looked at me with a hopeless expression. I didn't know what to do. The judge presiding at my son's trial was literally laughing at everything that was going on. It was clear to me; Scott would never receive a fair trial. This case had already been decided.

Shaw's assistant had warned me we were in trouble because it was a reelection year for Alex Hunter. I kept hearing those words in my mind.

I called the jail to schedule a visit with Scott. I spoke with Officer Haas, who said I could have a contact visit. I asked him if there was any word about the knife incident. He said the captain was very unhappy with the way the investigation was conducted. There had never been a knife; the whole story was nothing but a lie.

"How could this happen?" I wanted answers from this man.

"I don't know. Sometimes things leak out of the jails."

"Leak out? What do you mean leak out? This was an out and out lie!"

"I'm sorry, I don't know how this happened."

I couldn't believe it. The damage had been done. A jury hadn't been selected yet and every television station and newspaper had reported that not only had Scott been accused of murder, but also that he had tried to kill another inmate. All lies.

I waited for the DA or the jail to tell the television stations and the newspapers that the incident had been a fabrication; that Scott never had a knife. I wondered if the media would suspect, as I did, that this was a publicity stunt set up by the District Attorney's Office. Nothing. Not one word of retraction was made. I thought at least one of the television stations or newspapers would have followed up on this story. Nothing.

They did have something, though…they had Judge Sandstead pose for a picture for the newspaper, which appeared beside a picture of the prosecuting attorneys. I had never in my life seen anything like it! What kind of judge would pose for a picture before a murder trial?

I was beginning to feel Scott was right, he was being set up. We were in trouble.

"Steve, did you see the papers today?"

"Not yet. What's in them now?"

"My God, Steve, the judge that will be hearing Scott's case posed for a picture next to the prosecutors! I can't believe this!"

"Eve, I can believe anything at this point. What does it say?"

"Basically, it talks about their personalities. It says 'the cast of characters will be led by Judge Morris "Moe" Sandstead.'

"Boy, they summed that up right. 'Characters' is the word! It then says that he's a friendly judge with a sense of humor; that he gives lectures during sentencing; that he runs a tight courtroom and won't allow trials to drag on.

"It says he was appointed to the bench in 1982 and that he is 49 years old. It then goes on to describe the prosecutors. It says Phillip Miller is 51; that he graduated from law school in 1965 and he used to be a public defender. For that Pickering, it says that he's 45 and he describes himself as a 'drummer with a day job.' The paper says that he's the most interesting of all the lawyers; that he 'comes across as a puppy dog and is as tough, unyielding, and as bruising as a pit bull.'

"My God, Steve, what are they doing? What kind of people would allow themselves to be photographed and described in this manner? This is a damn joke!"

"Doesn't it say anything about Scott's attorneys?"

"Let me look." I read through the article. "Yes, they have a very, very small mention on them. It says Sam Shaw is 44 and 'the perfect defense lawyer for this case.' I bet they think he's perfect!"

"What else does it say?"

"It says he has 'a calm and reasonable courtroom style.' They say that Linda Cooke has a reputation as a good, solid lawyer and they predict that the jury will not ignore her pregnancy. They're saying that with her being pregnant, it will show the jury that she isn't afraid of Scott."

"Do they have any pictures of Scott's attorneys?"

"No, no pictures. Steve, this is just so unbelievable! Scott doesn't have a chance!"

I stopped walking and turned to look out at the endless sea. The water looked so inviting. I kicked off my sandals and walked out into the water to meet the breaking waves. As I swam around in the cool water, I remembered how much Scott loved the ocean. Once he was in the water, he was hard to get out. He just loved riding the waves. He laughed at the way I did it. I hated getting all that salt water in my eyes.

I turned in time to catch a good wave coming in and rode it to back to the beach's edge. I sat there and let the waves break over my legs, remembering all the times I'd done this with Scott and David.

Why did this judge do this? Why did he get to decide who represented Scott? I don't know the law, but so much about Scott's case doesn't seem right. The pictures…I had never seen a judge and prosecuting team pose for pictures before a trial started. What was their purpose behind all of this? Why did they need the publicity?

I stood up and began walking back to my chair. I needed to get back into the transcripts. I needed to find the answers.

I toweled myself off and sat back down. I opened the transcript where I'd left off. Apparently, Scott had been doing some reading from the law books available at the jail. He was trying desperately to help himself, since his court-appointed attorney didn't seem to be helping.

Scott Addresses the Court

MILLER: "Phil Miller, John Pickering and Bill Nagel for the People."

SHAW: "Sam Shaw and Linda Cooke for Mr. Mutchler, who is seated at the defense table. Judge, Mr. Mutchler advised me that he'd like to address the Court. Normally I wouldn't encourage that. Apparently, it has to do with his representation. I assume it's going to be fairly brief and he probably has a right to do that."

SCOTT: "Your Honor, I would like to make an oral motion to discharge Sam Shaw and Linda Cooke from the Public Defenders' office under the grounds that Sam Shaw turned over a packet containing incriminating evidence to the prosecuting attorney. In doing so, he broke the lawyer-client privilege. I believe you will find that Rule of Evidence, Article V, 501(2), lawyer-client privilege.

"The second reason being is Sam Shaw or Linda Cooke turned in a false motion of alibi that they never consulted with me about. In fact, it's not the correct alibi concerning my case."

JUDGE: "Well, I happen to have with me, just by pure luck, all of the research I've collected over the years. I have here a memorandum of defense attorney's motion to withdraw or defendant's request to discharge appointed counsel.

"Mr. Mutchler, the issue with regard to the surrender of what you claim to be incriminating evidence was dealt with in late September. The reason I know that is that, number one, the reason I know the date is that I read last night all of the Defendant's Exhibit B in the motion with regard to newspaper articles. The date of September 21st appeared in an article with regard to the appointment of Michael Enwall to represent you. That issue was dealt with and findings were made and conclusions made. That would be insufficient grounds."

"Your Honor, that subject was dropped because it was my understanding the district attorney was not going to admit that evidence at that time. Since then, I've learned that he is going to admit it."

JUDGE: "Well, am I right? Didn't I completely deal with the issue of whether or not there was any conflict of interest between court-appointed counsel ..."

SCOTT: "I don't believe the Court ever..."

JUDGE: "Just a minute. I'm talking. I thought I dealt with that issue in its entirety. Mr. Enwall represented you, and the matter was taken care of."

MILLER: "Your Honor, if I could address the Court. My recollection is that Mr. Enwall was appointed for the specific purpose to talk with Mr. Mutchler to review the developments that occurred surrounding the evidence that he discusses. And that following consultation with Mr. Enwall, at least my understanding or recollection is that.. that it was reported back to the Court by Mr. Enwall and/or Mr. Mutchler that he was content. The issue rolled down to, 'Do you want to stay with the Court-appointed lawyer or not?' And at that time, he was content to stay with them and agreed to do so. Probably could look at the record to find out the exact statements.

"But that's...it was an issue that was considered an outside counsel appointed for that purpose. And the matter was brought to some resolution. I don't remember the exact order."

SHAW: "Judge, this takes me by surprise. I mean, just prior to you coming in, Mr. Mutchler indicated to me that something like this was going to happen. But before that, I didn't know. And I didn't know that it was going to be based on this evidence packet in which the Court is aware we turned over to the prosecution.

"So I'm just relying on recollection like Mr. Miller. And I guess the rest of my recollection is that we got beyond that. We got beyond in part because Mr. Mutchler indicated through Mr. Enwall he no longer wished to urge the conflict, if there was one.

"The other thing that I recall from that was that it was Mr. Mutchler's position at that point…well, prior to that point, prior to withdrawing his complaint, that he wanted the Court to appoint different counsel to represent him. That's my memory of that."

JUDGE: "That was the day when Mr. Sather was here?"

SCOTT: "Yes."

SHAW: "That's correct."

JUDGE: "All right. Well, to go on, I think it's dealt with. I find that there is no conflict. Let me read you what the law is, and then you can respond.

"I can refuse a motion to withdraw or request that your lawyer be discharged only if I have a reasonable basis to believe that the attorney-client relationship has deteriorated to a point beyond effective assistance of counsel. And I have nothing on which I can make such a finding.

"I then balance my primary concern being the orderly administration of justice with the fact of some irreconcilable conflict, which I can make no finding. And, I may consider the timing of motion, the inconvenience to witnesses, the time between the trial…crime and trial, and the possibility new counsel have the same conflict.

"So if you have anything to say to me on why you think that there…that you should be permitted to discharge your lawyer, I will hear it.

"In the alternative…by the way, should I make appropriate findings and grant your wish, you would have to go on trial on Monday and represent yourself. If I do that, I need to give you all kinds of advice and cautions with regard to the possible penalties.

"I'm fairly sure that although I could do that again if necessary, that you're already aware of all those possible consequences and you're probably aware of the severe admonition that it would be a very, very silly thing for you to represent yourself."

SCOTT: "Well Your Honor, I believe going to trial myself pro se, I believe the Court would have to give me a sufficient amount of time to look over the evidence, since I haven't been allowed to, or have not viewed any of it, basically."

JUDGE: "The trial is going to start Monday. Now, is there any other record you want to make with regard to your motion to discharge counsel?"

SCOTT: "Not at this time."

JUDGE: "All right. There are no facts, none in any part of the record at any time or place, which would permit the Court to find a reasonable basis that the attorney client relationship has deteriorated to the point beyond effective assistance of counsel.

"In fact, I would make the finding that your lawyers have done an absolutely spectacular job of raising every remotely possible issue in this case. I have nothing upon which I could base the finding of irreconcilable differences; that the relationship deteriorated beyond the point of effective assistance of counsel.

"I find beyond any doubt that your lawyers will represent you to the fullest possibility and represent every right that you possibly have in this case. Anything further on that regard?"

SCOTT: "No, Your Honor."

JUDGE: "Well, Mr. Shaw, Ms. Cooke, do you want to make any record with regard to some statement by your client that…it was something about a false motion of alibi which is withdrawn and the issue is moot. There is no…there's no pending claim of alibi that the prosecution is supposed to be made aware of by your pleading."

SHAW: "Well, Judge, we filed a response to their motion for discovery and their motion for disclosure of alibi in a timely fashion and did indicate an alibi in that motion."

JUDGE: "And that is the alibi which you intend to present if necessary at trial?"

SHAW: "Well, I guess I could adopt that. I think probably my vocabulary would have been it's a defense that we may use."

JUDGE: "Tell me what the pleading says. What are the words?"

SHAW: "Judge, it says that the defendant appears through counsel, Colorado State Public Defender, and subject to constitutional limitations, replies as follows to the People's Motion for disclosure: 'Paragraph A through H addressed a variety of defenses. For example, things like general denial, lack of specific intent. Mr. Mutchler maintains that he was not at the scene of the crime alleged in this case and that for part of that period which these crimes are alleged to have occurred, he was in the area of 120th and Perry or Federal Blvd. In support of his alibi defense Mr. Mutchler may call the following witnesses. I've indicated Steve Meyer, Eve Meyer, Officer Hartmann, Officer Schuler, Ron Pollard, Robert Yusko, Ronald White, James Baldwin, Scott LaFleur, Dr. Schmidt, Dr. Carp, Paula Gutzmer, Toni O'Brien, and Frank Weigle. There should be a copy of that on file with the Court, Judge."

MILLER: "That conforms with the copy I received, Your Honor."

JUDGE: "All right. Anything further? Anybody want to make any further record? All right. Let's talk a moment about some of these motions. There is a motion for enhanced, expanded media coverage. And I'm required to make findings…make…enter the order on the record.

"Any record you want to make with regard…I think…did Mr. Shaw file an objection?"

SHAW: "I believe I did, Judge. And if I could just have a second to find it so I could see what I said in the matter."

MILLER: "Your Honor, while he's looking, I'll make People's response, which is that the People really take no position on the matter. We leave it to the Court's discretion to consider the request."

JUDGE: "Well, my sense is I don't have any discretion unless I make specific findings that it would either turn the matter into a circus or substantially impair the rights of the defendant. I don't have any record yet. That's why I'm waiting to hear their position."

SHAW: "Judge, I don't have anything to add to what I've alleged in paragraphs one through four of my motion except by way of offer of proof.

"I can tell the Court, for example, that Mr. Mutchler's mother Eve was very concerned about cameras being in the courtroom and thought that it would intimidate and confuse her. I think that that's probably not an illogical notion that this Court couldn't accept.

"I'm concerned, of course, for all the reasons one through three. But I believe that it's my experience and anyone can imagine that witnesses who aren't used to testifying at all, not to mention in front of live or still cameras, are going to be distracted. It's going to affect their ability to recount what happened and concentrate on the questions asked them. I'm very concerned about the jury being intimidated by the presence of cameras and their fear that either personally they're going to be identified in the press or that this being a relatively small community, people will know anyway and they'll consider that they have some responsibilities in their verdict beyond that which the law requires.

"I'm concerned about what the community at large might think about their verdict one way or the other. Those are my arguments to expanded media coverage. I know the Court indicated that you'd likely grant it. I have comments about what we do if you do that. But in the first instance, I object to expanded media coverage."

JUDGE: "Well, it's my believe that I, in order to deny your motion…deny the motion I would have to make findings which somehow impair the rights of the defendant to a fair trial or somehow interfere with the dignity of the Court.

"What I would like to do is grant the motion, not permit either…did we get a request for television? We did, did we not from…"

MILLER: "There was a media representative that filed on behalf of several portions of the media. But I don't know if they…"

JUDGE: "I think we got both television and still cameras. What I'd like to do is say that television, if and when it's permitted, will be only after seating of the jury."

SHAW: "Judge, I only have one motion. It's from the Daily Camera. It's signed by Vern Walker, chief photographer."

JUDGE: "I thought there was a letter."

SHAW: "It is a letter. It says, 'Please accept this as a formal request for camera coverage of the murder trial of Scott Mutchler in your courtroom beginning March 20. Because of the widespread interest in this case, we will act as pool photographer for print media if you so request'."

MILLER: "That is the only contact I have, too, Your Honor."

SHAW: "Judge, it's going to be my position that if any of the television stations want to have a live camera in the courtroom, at this point it's too late. I'm going to ask the Court to deny it if it should come in."

MILLER: "Your Honor, my recollection is that sometime during the early days of the motions hearings, you told counsel that you had been contacted by, I believe, a print media representative. You had directed them to either Judge Richtel...it was Judge Richtel and someone was..."

JUDGE: "That was last week. That was during...following the Peters sentencing. Ms. Hutchinson left a message with the division clerk and said would I meet with her to talk about expanded media coverage. I said no, I would not meet with her. She needed to talk...I would only talk to her after she had talked with Cliff Dodge, who happens to be the director of the Colorado Broadcasters Association. I had...I'd like her to talk with Judge Richtel, who happens to be either past chair or present chair of the American Bar Association Commission or Committee on expanded medial coverage and televisions in the courtroom and such.

"I had reviewed the law. This made me think I didn't have any discretion in that regard as long as it wasn't going to interfere with a fair trial, and I had some control and they would comply with Canon Eight, which said that if I have to engage in any way in disputes over expanded media coverage and pooling that I just get to deny it. If they want to engage me in who gets to be the photographer, then I just say 'Sorry, no deal.'

"And that's...that happened since last Tuesday or Wednesday. But I thought before that I'd received a letter from..."

SHAW: "Well, Judge, based on what you just said, if you can...and it doesn't sway that Vern Walker of the Daily Camera is going to be the photographer for them. I'd say there's a dispute about who is going to be the photographer at this time. I would just deny it all."

JUDGE: "Well, I don't care. There's not a dispute that I know of there. Somebody is going to pool and come in here and do that. That's fine."

MILLER: "Well, Vern Walker is representing he's going to do it."

JUDGE: "Well, maybe he will. I don't know. Let's come back to that because I hear there's…some motion was filed."

MILLER: "Your Honor, may I ask respectfully that we return to the alibi. I think later someone may look at this and determine we left it somewhat open-ended because what the defendant said in three parts was that a false motion for alibi was filed, it was not the correct alibi and he wasn't consulted on it. All I'm saying is I don't want the defendant to be cheated out of asserting an alibi and if he wants to change that alibi he should be…we're the ones that are going to be prejudiced by it. But we need to know if there is one now, and what it is. I wouldn't want him to go on trial having determined…or having the appellate court determine that he was not permitted to assert his alibi."

JUDGE: "He's represented by counsel. If they want to assert a different alibi, they must do it or they won't be permitted to present the alibi."

MILLER: "Hearing no revision or change…I understand that the alibi before us is the one that was being…or may be asserted."

JUDGE: "Well, let's come back to that one."

SHAW: "We're coming back to the expanded media coverage?"

JUDGE: "Yeah, we're going to come back to that later tomorrow if necessary, Saturday if necessary. Then let's talk about some of the motions. Reservation and remedies due to pretrial publicity. Do you have anything you want to say about that? I mean, I don't think you're restricted from raising that issue during the jury selection process if it becomes necessary. Are there some facts that you want to present to the Court with regard to pretrial publicity?"

COOKE: "I'm sorry, Judge. On reservation and remedies, we have not moved to change venue up until this point based on the pretrial publicity, and we do not intend to. But what the purpose of filing this motion was is that, in the event of, during the course of voir dire, there are a number of jurors that indicate extreme familiarity with the publicity in this case. So far, that is not apparent that he cannot get a fair trial in this jurisdiction. We certainly would like to reserve our right to request a change of venue at a later time if that becomes necessary."

JUDGE: "I wouldn't have any grounds for change of venue until we get to that. But that could still happen."

The hearing continued with a discussion of the trial's anticipated length. I closed the book. My God, if I had only known this was going on in the courtroom. I could have done something: Gone to the press, something. There was no one there to stop this judge.

I folded my hands across the volume still closed on my lap. How could anyone expect to get an impartial jury after what had happened? The media had gone wild with the publicity. The public trusts the media for complete truth; they only got a shred of that truth; Scott had been arrested for a double homicide; just about everything else was insanity. The next volume dealt with jury selection.

Part 2

The Jury

The Jury

JUDGE: "This is out of an over abundance of caution. There is sometimes a fear that, even though you don't think you have any knowledge about this case, that after you start hearing some of the evidence, something goes off in your head and you think 'Well, maybe I did read something about that in the past,' or something, so we want to briefly jog your memory with not much more detail than has already been read to you but the allegations that I read of a number of counts of first-degree murder. Hearing those things, they are alleged to have occurred last September 10. They are alleged to have occurred at Van Buren Court in Louisville, which is somewhere in that area, near the...off McCaslin Boulevard, I think.

"The victims of the crime were a man, 48-years-old, and his 10-year-old son. Do any of those, you know, facts give you any thoughts that maybe you do have some prior knowledge about the case? Four or five of you. Well, I don't want to know what it is you know about it because I don't want you to tell me too much of the details and then all of us will know what it is you know.

"Let me ask the question this way. Those of you who now maybe had your memory jogged a little bit; can you give me a hint of the source of the information that now has been brought to your mind?"

JUROR ERIC FRENETTE: "Television."

JUDGE: "How long ago was that?"

"Quite a while."

"Did you form any opinions at the time or have any thoughts about it at that time?"

"No, because it really didn't influence me."

"So you think that, at least with regard to the issue of that knowledge about the case, it won't influence you, you haven't made up your mind about the case or anything like that?"

Sam Shaw stood. "I ask the people to raise their hands that have been brought in for individual voir dire?"

JUDGE: "Your name is Frenette, 479?"

FRENETTE: "Yes."

JUDGE: "All right, and I believe your name is…"

JUROR MARCUS SWEET: "Marcus Sweet, 371."

JUDGE: "OK, I want to know the source of the information."

SWEET: "Television."

"And how long ago was it?"

"When it first came out."

"Have you formed any opinions about the case?"

"No."

"Do you think that knowledge of the case would have any effect on your ability to sit fairly and impartially in this case?"

"I don't think so."

"All right, William Smith?"

JUROR CANDIDATE WILLIAM SMITH: "Television, probably around the time it came out at first."

JUDGE: “I will ask you the same questions, do you think…did you form any opinions about the case at the time?”

“No, sir.”

“Do you have any current opinions about it?”

“No.”

“Do you think just having seen that or heard something about this on television in any way will affect your ability to be fair and impartial in this case?”

“No.”

“Will you decide the case based on the evidence here?”

“Yes.”

“Somebody else? Mr. Scheirman, 398.”

JUROR CANDIDATE SCHEIRMAN: “It was television, about the same time, the middle of September.”

JUDGE: “And did you form any opinions about it?”

“No, we were in the process of moving and I was pretty much preoccupied with the move.”

“Yes sir, Mr. Wasserman, 255.”

JUROR CANDIDATE WASSERMAN: “I seem to recall seeing newspaper headlines around that time.”

JUDGE: “Newspapers about that? I will ask you the same questions, did you form any opinions about it at that time.”

“No.”

“What I will do is permit counsel to ask you questions after you come back tomorrow at 1:30 if they want to further inquire and we’ll bring you back in at 1:30. I think if you will remember the admonitions very carefully, do not read the newspaper headlines or articles or watch any television about this case or listen to the radio. I know it’s hard to do, but it’s fundamentally important to having a fair trial.”

(The panel is excused).

JUDGE: “Bring in juror 234.”

SHAW: “Before the juror is brought in, I propose that with these individual voir dires, we alternate: the prosecution, the defendant. I am sure there are different theories and goals on how they want to voir dire the people and it’s been my experience in the past, sometimes if the defense doesn't get to go first, sometimes they can't bring jurors back to what we, of course, would say is their honest opinion about some things.

"I think the prosecution's position is opposed to a continuance or change of venue. If permitted to lead every single juror into saying they can be fair and the publicity they heard, can be put aside, we'll have to dig everyone out to the point where they can say what is on their mind rather than what they are led to.

"I ask the Court to let us alternate with the individual voir dire. The other thing I would like to say concerns the reiteration of my motion to continue and the motion for change of venue.

"I won't take up a lot of the Court's time, but by our rough calculations, at this point we have 95 percent of the jurors that have heard or read something about this case. In my opinion and in my experience, that is an overwhelming amount and that in and of itself is enough for the Court to grant the continuance.

"We request and I ask the Court to take the time, sometime between now and when we reconvene this afternoon, to read People vs. Botham, 629, p. 2d 589 and People vs. Bartowsheski, 661 p.2d 235 and the fair trial and free press guideline statute 8-3.3, concerning granting of continuance and motion for change of venue. Botham pretty much lays out what I think the status of the law is, Judge, but point one is that where a defendant has demonstrated massive, pervasive, and prejudicial publicity which would create a presumption that he was denied a fair trial, the motion for change of venue or continuance should be granted.

"The other standards, if the Court will deny that, are further found in the Botham case but I think we are at point one now and I think the Court would be totally in accordance with the law if the Court at this point, based on the number of jurors and percentage of jurors that have heard something about this case, grant our motion for change of venue."

JUDGE: "The motion is denied. Bring in juror 234."

COOKE: "Ms. Reynolds, do you recall how many newspaper articles you read at the time about this?"

JUROR CANDIDATE REYNOLDS: "I probably read five or six."

"Do you remember whether you read the entire article when you read it or whether you read just part of the article?"

"Sometimes I read all of the article. I think I read all of the article right after it happened and then the later ones that followed up, I didn't read all of them."

"In terms of the…you indicated that you also saw this on Channel 4 and Channel 9, do you remember how many times you saw coverage of this on TV?"

"I believe once or twice is all."

"Do you recall whether you sat through their whole piece on this thing or whether or not you got up and left to go…?"

"I usually sit through the whole thing. I am not sure how much attention I am paying to all of it."

"OK. At the time that you first learned about this back in September, either from the newspapers or from the television, did you discuss the case with anybody, anybody else in your household or from work or something?"

"My mother and my sister."

"Can you recall just as briefly as you can the nature of your discussions with them?"

"Well, we all sort of agreed that he was guilty, that is why I came up with that opinion, I guess."

"That was an opinion that was held not only by yourself but by some other members of your family?"

"Yes."

"Do you recall whether you discussed it with them not just on one occasion or on more than one occasion?"

"Usually every time it came up either in the newspaper or on TV. I don't think just normally."

"OK, do they live in your household? Is that how you came to discuss it?"

"I live at my mother's house, yes, and we are a very close family."

"So it's fairly common for you to discuss things that you see on the news, for instance?"

"Yes."

"You indicated that you thought…you told Judge Sandstead you thought the case was pretty well made and by that you meant that the person that was arrested was probably guilty?"

"Yes."

"Can you recall what led you to that conclusion?"

"Well, there seemed to be a lot of evidence in the papers...as I say, you can't always believe everything you see in the papers, but they seemed pretty sure."

"So even though you may not recall the exact details that you read, you do recall that what you read was enough to convince you pretty well that the person that they had in custody was the person who had committed the offenses?"

"Yes."

"What about your discussions with your mother and your sister, did that serve to reinforce your opinion?"

"Yes."

"Do you recall how long or how in depth your discussions were? Did you talk about the details for instance, that had caused all of you to reach that opinion or did you just…could you characterize the nature of your discussions with them?"

"Well, I can't remember the details of the case but my mother tends to be real cut-and-dry about everything and she was saying he was definitely guilty and my sister, I just sort of listened to all of them say, 'Well, I don't know.' "

"OK, but you had basically reached the conclusion on your own he was probably guilty?"

"From reading the newspapers."

"The judge and the district attorney both asked you if you could put aside anything that you learned from the newspapers in deliberating on this case and just limit yourself to the evidence that is presented at the trial and you indicated that you thought you could do that."

"I think I can, yes."

"Do you think that…what I guess I am asking is sort of a super human effort to ask people to put aside anything they ever knew about something and approach something in a vacuum because I think it's real hard for us when we are looking at something?"

"Yeah, I can't say that it wouldn't have something to do with it for sure, I don't think that anybody can."

"Right, that is just asking too much of us almost, would you agree?"

"Yes."

"Do you think that it's possible if you were sort of not sure about how you were going to decide this case if you were sitting as a juror if it would be natural for whatever opinion that you formed at that time to sort of come in and pry into the background that you tried to put that down but that it might have some influence even subconsciously in your decision?"

"I don't know. I would pretty well have to go by the facts that you are giving. I think the trials are very interesting. I have read a lot of them. We print the Colorado Lawyer Magazine and I read a lot of trials. "

"I am asking if it's still possible on a subconscious level that your prior knowledge and prior opinion that you formed way back when this happened and you read about it or heard about it on the news, if that might have some subtle influence on you that you wouldn't be able to control because it's a subconsciousness?"

MILLER: "I object. I am not sure that any of us knows what effect our subconscious has on us, and I think she answered that as fairly as she can. She would be governed by facts."

JUDGE: "If she has an answer, she can give it."

REYNOLDS: "It's true, sometimes I am not very particular about what I really think, but I try to be truthful in what I do and say and I try to not guess on that about people and stuff like that."

COOKE: "OK. I think you are trying very hard to be very truthful about what you know and how you think that would affect you here today, but if I can summarize and you can tell me if you agree or disagree with this. I think to summarize, you formed an opinion about this case at the time that it happened. That that opinion was formed based on details that you no longer recall but that you read about at the time."

"Right."

"That you discussed it with other family members and all shared similar opinions and that you would try very hard to put those things aside and decide the case but you can't guarantee us what influence, if any, because none of us have control over our subconscious. That might happen?"

"I don't think anyone can guarantee it."

"Would that be adequate?"

"Yes."

"Thank you, no further questions."

JUDGE: "Next juror."

SHAW: "Before the next juror comes in, we need to address the Court briefly. I challenge Ms. Reynolds for cause based on her prior knowledge of the case, the fact she formed a strong opinion at that time.

"She discussed it with others who held similar opinions and that, although I think she has been very honest and indicating she would try to put things aside, that she can't deny her prior knowledge may have some subtle influence on her decision."

JUDGE: "Denied. Next juror. Ms. Friden, please take a seat. Did I pronounce your name correctly?"

JUROR CANDIDATE FRIDEN: "Friden."

JUDGE: "You have indicated that you have some prior knowledge about the case. Could you give us an idea what you know and where you learned it?"

"Well, through the papers and television. I am also a secretary at the Boulder County Sheriff's Department. I put criminal reports into the sheriff's computer, so I am pretty familiar with everything."

"OK, that sounds to me like a disqualification."

"I am not paid, I am a volunteer."

"Oh, you are a volunteer?"

"But I have done it for six years."

"You do not have to return tomorrow. Bring in the next juror, Ms. Beno. Is it Ms. Beno?"

JUROR CANDIDATE BENO: "Beno or Bino, whatever, that is the way I feel about my name."

JUDGE: "Ms. Beno, you indicated to us that you have some pretrial knowledge about the case?"

"Yes."

"Can you give us an idea of what you know, what you remember, and where you learned the information?"

"Well, as early as this morning on KOA, the early morning news. They said something about the defendant being released from the hospital and shortly after, going over and doing the accused crime. Then I remember from reading it last summer in September when it happened at the time because I live in Boulder and it's local news and I read it in the Camera."

"Let me ask you this. Having read the newspapers and listened to the radio, did you then or have you now formed an opinion about the guilt or innocence of the person charged in this case?"

"I have to be honest with you, yes, I feel like he is guilty and I also feel that I don't believe in rehabilitation of this particular person that may have had a troubled young life."

"All right. Let me ask you this because the real question is, I have got to make a finding that because of your pretrial knowledge in having formed an opinion, you would be able to base your verdict totally and only on the evidence you hear in the trial. Are you telling me that outside influence would prevent you from doing that?"

"Yes, and you may say I am prejudiced."

"No, you are entitled to have those feelings. A lot of people do but I am trying to pick a fair and impartial jury who tells me they can base their verdict just on the evidence that comes in the courtroom and you are telling me you think that wouldn't be possible for you?"

Why was Judge Sandstead trying so hard to qualify this juror?

BENO: "No, because I have a deep-seated feeling…"

JUDGE: "OK, well, that I think disqualifies you from sitting on this jury. Thank you.

The jury selection continued, with almost every prospective juror acknowledging they had formed some opinion, or at least had seen some media coverage of the case. The transcript made it obvious Judge Sandstead would not be swayed by the pretrial publicity. One candidate, Hoffman, went to the same church as the victims. He told the Court he believed Scott was guilty, but Sandstead argued that he was not prejudiced. I reread part of his selection questioning, still unable to understand the judge's reasoning:

SHAW: "OK, in the discussions you had about this case with people, have you ever discussed whether or not you or they thought Mr. Mutchler was guilty of the charges?"

HOFFMAN: "In most discussions, I will expand your questions, the assumption has been that he is guilty."

"Why did you say that, why was the assumption that he was guilty?"

"I feel like the press, the newspaper articles have made that assumption and that was just carried over in the conversations."

"So that the sources of information that you have relied on for what happened in this case, in your opinion, have presented the opinion that Mr. Mutchler is guilty of those charges. Is that a fair characterization?"

"Yes. I mean the term may be used, alleged or accused, you know, the correct terms, but then the discussions, in my mind, didn't leave any real doubt."

"So, in the discussions you had about the publicity or just about the case, is it fair to say that it has been assumed that Mr. Mutchler was guilty?"

"Yes."

"And you assumed that too?"

"Yes."

"And have you harbored that assumption since then?"

"I am not exactly sure what you mean by harbor."

"You don't have to use my…"

"I haven't changed my opinion, you know."

"Your opinion has been since the date of the offense that Mr. Mutchler was guilty?"

"Yes."

"And of course, since the date of the offense to today's date, you have been saddened by the death of the Scharfs. Is that correct?"

"Yes."

"Judge, I challenge the juror for cause. I understand from Mr. Miller that he won't object."

JUDGE: "Well, I heard Mr. Hoffman say that he thought he could be fair. I heard Mr. Hoffman say that he thought he could set aside previous knowledge that he might have read in the newspaper. Did you think that what the newspaper said was evidence at all? Is that what you are saying you changed your mind about?"

HOFFMAN: "I haven't changed my mind about being able to be fair."

JUDGE: "What that means is that you must base your verdict solely on the evidence that you hear at the trial and you may not use anything that you learned elsewhere in arriving at a verdict and I guess that may be a hard question, but I think the fact that you are sad, it's OK to be sad. It's a sad thing. There is nothing wrong with reading the newspapers. What I need to know is, I need to be assured that in spite of the fact that you are an aware citizen and read the newspapers and are sad at the sad things, are you able to base your verdict in this case on the evidence that you hear in the courtroom and follow the instructions of the law of the court?"

HOFFMAN: "Yes."

JUDGE: "OK. Motion is denied. Any other questions?"

After more questions from both attorneys about Hoffman's ability to set aside his presumptions about the case, Judge Sandstead asked Hoffman to return the following day. Then he told the lawyers that knowledge of the case didn't necessarily prejudice potential jurors. The discussion became an argument between the Court and the public defender.

JUDGE: "I will not permit either lawyer to argue with these people or demean them or make fun of them in any way, challenge them because they are saddened by death, whether they are saddened by crime. Just because somebody reads the newspaper does not make him or her prejudiced. Just because they form opinions does not make them prejudiced.

"I would prefer a fair trial from people who are living in the community and not putting their heads in the sand and avoiding it. I mean, let me read you from a case called People vs. Roy, 'It is the duty of the trial court to determine the competence and credibility of a juror. The test is one of a nature and strength and opinion formed or the information learned from pretrial publicity are such as necessarily raise the presumption of partiality or of the inability of the potential juror to block out the information from his consideration. This question is essentially one of fact, which lies within the sound discretion of the trial court.' Bring in the next juror."

SHAW: "I have a response to that."

JUDGE: "You don't need to make a response."

SHAW: "I cite People vs. Botham, page 599. You know it says 'In the examination of the effect of pretrial publicity on the jury panel, a juror's assurance that he can lay aside his impression or opinion of partiality is not dispositive of a defendant's claim that he was denied his constitutional rights to a fair trail.'

"This court can't just ask people who have invested the last year of their life in feelings about this crime and developing opinions about this crime whether or not they can be fair and think that is the end of the issue."

JUDGE: "You are telling me that you think, based on this record, that they lied to us, and I do not, so, fine."

SHAW: "I am not saying that."

JUDGE: "You did."

SHAW: "You missed the point."

JUDGE: "I did not so, fine."

SHAW: "You missed the point. I am not saying they lie."

JUDGE: "You are, too."

SHAW: "I am saying…

JUDGE: "Are too."

SHAW: "I think you are missing the point of these questions, Judge, and I will continue to ask those questions until you tell me to shut up and sit down because I think they go to issues this court has to decide in determining whether or not we get a fair trial."

JUDGE: "Bring in the next juror. Robert Arvidson, 452. Mr. Arvidson, you indicated this morning that you have some knowledge about this case and we would like to inquire as to what you know and where you learned it?"

JUROR CANDIDATE ROBERT ARVIDSON: "OK, I believe I have limited knowledge. I had heard...I remember vaguely hearing news, like a radio news report, even like a traffic report type of thing when they had found the two bodies in Louisville and then after that I really hadn't heard too much or read any articles until Friday or Saturday. I heard they would make selections this week for that case, but I am really not any more familiar with it than that."

"Did you read the articles you saw on Friday or Saturday?"

"No. I heard about it yesterday at a family event going on and I kind of did want to stay away from it if that was indeed what I would be hearing."

"So you suspected maybe yesterday that you would be called for this trial."

"Possibly. I knew there were two different things going on today, so I knew 50/50."

"OK, if you were chosen as a juror, would you be able to base your verdict solely on the evidence that you hear from the witnesses and exhibits introduced at trial?"

"Yes, absolutely."

"Mr. Miller?"

MILLER: "Mr. Arvidson, if I heard you correctly, your only knowledge about this case is from the first one, certainly, a radio report?"

ARVIDSON: "Yes."

"OK, and that was a short report?"

"Right, just saying like, 'Stay clear of this area,' or..."

"Did that include any names?"

"No. Either my wife or mother-in-law, someone this weekend when I said, you know, that I would be in for jury duty Monday and they said that such-and-such case comes to trial or selection this week. I asked what it was because the name didn't click in my head. In fact, I still don't know the defendant's name, but I asked, like, 'Which case was that?' and they said 'The two murders in Louisville.' "

COOKE: "Do you recall, for instance, how many people were killed or ages of the people killed?"

ARVIDSON: "I know that there were two, and I believe it was a father and son, I am not sure."

"OK, so there really wasn't that much in that article other than what you just discussed?"

"Right."

"You don't recall having read anything about this case in the newspaper at all?"

"No."

JUDGE: "All right. We need to see you tomorrow at 1:30."

ARVIDSON: "OK."

JUDGE: "Dennis Teursch, 473. Mr. Teursch, you indicated this morning you had some prior knowledge about the case and we would like to inquire as to what you know and where you learned it."

JUROR CANDIDATE DENNIS TEURSCH: "Well, I remember reading about it in the papers and also seeing it on the news, but last night, we were at a friend's and we talked about it and they said that they had heard he was found with the car and gun and that is about all I know."

JUDGE: "All right. You haven't read anything recently?"

"Well, I read the Daily Camera, yes."

"So, you read the paper yesterday too?"

"Right."

"I guess we need to know if you can base your verdict solely on the evidence you hear in the trial?"

"Right, I think it would be difficult."

"Well, I know it's difficult to say, 'Don't look at the elephant on the ceiling because…don't look up there!' but what it really boils down to, you know, you have to say in order to be a person who could sit on the jury, that 'I think…that difficult as it may be, can I set aside, in fact, I might have learned elsewhere and base my verdict only on the evidence I hear at trial' ?"

"It's going to be difficult for me because my friends indicated they felt that he was guilty and I will have that in the back of my mind so I would try to be fair."

"Have you formed an opinion about his guilt or innocence?"

"Not really, no, but…"

"Would you be able to follow the law that unless the evidence presented in this courtroom proves beyond a reasonable doubt each and every element of the offenses with which the defendant has been charged, that he is guilty, that you would be able to follow that law?"

"Yes, I think I would."

"If you were to be convinced that maybe the state had not met the burden of proof, would you feel…would there be anything going on in your mind that you somehow would be disappointing your friends or that you might want to reconsider because your friends may be dissatisfied with what you did here if you were to find him not guilty?"

"Well, I wouldn't be dissatisfied or anything like that but I would be feeling like I would have to…"

"Can you do that?"

"Well, I could if I felt there was proof or wasn't proof, whatever the case may be."

"If you follow the law and make findings that the state had not made their case beyond a reasonable doubt of each and every element and you felt comfortable with that, do you think you can walk out of here and…"

"Oh, sure."

"And feel OK even though your friends may be dissatisfied?"

"I don't know if they would be dissatisfied."

"Well, or even angry with you?"

"No, I don't think so."

"Ms. Cooke?"

COOKE: "Mr. Teursch, what newspapers do you read?"

TEURSCH: "The Daily Camera on the weekend and the Denver Post on the weekdays."

"The source of whatever news article, you would have read those two papers?"

"Right."

"You also saw it on the news?"

"I do remember hearing it on, we watch Channel 9 normally, you know, back whenever, in September. I don't recall any specifics from that."

"OK, let me ask you. Let's back it down one at a time. Tell me what you recall about what you heard about the case either from the newspapers that you read or from the TV station back in September?"

"From the paper or from the TV I really don't recall much at all."

"Tell me what you do recall."

"Just that, you know, a father and son were killed in Louisville and I live right outside Louisville."

"Any other details?"

"That it was a younger gentleman that was arrested."

"OK, do you remember anything about what evidence they felt linked this gentleman to the case?"

"Not from the paper or from that."

"You indicated that you heard they found a car and a gun, is that right?"

"Yes."

"Do you recall what the source of that information was?"

"Well, it was, we were at a friend's for dinner last night and their neighbors were neighbors of the murdered victims originally and they said they had found him in the car with the gun and a knife, I think they said."

"OK, so you gained a lot more knowledge about the case when you were with these friends last night?"

"Right, because they knew I would be a juror and they kind of put two and two together and told me that they had heard…"

"Do you remember what else they told you about, what else they heard about the case?"

"That is essentially it."

"You said that they formed an opinion about whether or not Mr. Mutchler was guilty and that that was an opinion they shared with you. Do you know how they formed that opinion?"

"They expressed, 'Well, the guy was found in the car. He must have been guilty…he must be guilty with that kind of reasoning.' "

"So, their opinions seemed to be based on what they knew about the evidence that they read in the paper or heard from some source?"

"Right."

"And how many of the people that you were with seemed to have this opinion?"

"I guess it was unanimous. Everyone kind of agreed. No one said, 'Oh, yes, I agree' everyone kind of goes, 'Yeah, uh huh.' "

"Nobody disagreed so you sort of adopted that opinion based on the information you heard at that point?"

"Yes, I guess that is true."

"Mr. Miller?"

MILLER: "Now, yesterday you were around some people who expressed an opinion about guilt or innocence to you?"

TEURSCH: "That is right."

"You even kind of went along with it at the time or at least didn't disagree?"

"Right."

"You understand, and of course, my question is today now that you are a potential juror, are you telling us that you now have an opinion of your own about the guilt or innocence?"

"Yes, if I had to make a judgment at this time without any evidence, yes."

"But you understand that the oath you would take, I think the judge indicated this, to become a juror in this case, there would be an oath that says whatever knowledge or opinion or information you have about this case you must set aside and decide the case in the courtroom on what comes in here?"

"Right."

"Could you do that?"

"Yes, I think I could."

JUDGE: "Mr. Teursch, you said that you adopted more or less the opinion last night but still had an opinion. You haven't heard any evidence. What is your opinion about guilt or innocence now?"

TEURSCH: "At this point, I would go along with the guilty."

JUDGE: “OK, I need to see you tomorrow at 1:30.”

SHAW: “Judge, we challenge Mr. Teursch for cause. I don’t think he is able to accept the presumption of innocence based on his own answer to questions.

“Everyone, including the Court, has asked him. Furthermore, he has fairly close connections to the actual facts of the case having gotten his information from neighbors and neighbors of the victims.”

JUDGE: “The motion is denied.”

The rest of jury selection followed much the same pattern. Jurors acknowledged varying degrees of knowledge about the case, the defense objecting in some cases and being denied by Sandstead. The tension between Shaw and Sandstead continued, as well.

SHAW: “Before the next juror comes in, I will ask the Court to excuse Mr. Blackburn. He has a fairly detailed, thorough-quality recollection of the facts in this case and a recollection of the article yesterday in the paper talking about personalities and tactics and the best he has been able to tell the Court is that he will try to put that aside. It’s clear from what he said that he harbors reservations about his ability to do that, and I ask the Court to excuse him.”

JUDGE: “Well, I will make a finding. I think to do so would mean that we don’t want anybody who is intelligent or completely honest on juries and I don’t happen to believe that.

“The challenge is denied.”

Several jurors later, Shaw tried again.

SHAW: “Judge, I would like to renew my motion for change of venue and or continuance. I think that the more we talk to jurors, the more we find out how persuasive the publicity has been in this case.

“The concerns I indicated to the Court about jurors being honest even though they are trying to be or knowing their innermost attitudes about the case in spite of what they say….

"I guess that an example is the juror who submitted to the Court a note after assuring us she could be fair and impartial and thinking about it overnight and deciding that was far from the case, she was actually fearful of the defendant.

"I think what the Court needs to do is insure that Mr. Mutchler has a fair trial and that means an impartial jury and a jury that hasn't been exposed to all the publicity in this case and some bad publicity concerning opinions about the quality of evidence and restatements of the evidence, the kind of news reporting that many of the jurors have said seem to lead the reader to a conclusion of guilt in this case.

"The only way to make sure that that happens is to move it out of Boulder County and/or to continue the case and that is what I will ask the court to do."

MILLER: "Your Honor, if I may respond briefly. I think that what we have learned from the jurors that have been talked to yesterday and today is that there exists no massive persuasive prejudicial publicity. A lot of jurors have heard about it but, in our inquiries, we are not finding the kind of deep and bitter prejudice throughout the community that appears in some of the cases, the reported cases where change of venue issues are discussed.

"I believe that we found that we have, by my count, some 56 jurors that can come in here and form the pool from which we may pick a jury in this case. I think the Court should deny the motion for change of venue or continuance if that is also included."

JUDGE: "Well, while I am concerned about a lot of things with regard to the First Amendment, and while I am aware that the media really has no professional standards whatever, they don't care about the kind of things that I care about, but they are not in the business of court administration. They are not in the business of efficient provision of fair trials for citizens...They don't care about privacy of anybody; they don't care. That is not their job and they will, frankly, tell that to you but I haven't felt that the citizenry has the same standards and the same beliefs.

"I am convinced that having heard this jury and in spite of the fact that they have each heard or read about some details, much of which opinions they learned, if not from the newspapers, from my having read the charge to them at the beginning of the trial. I have an abiding belief in the fairness and justice of our citizens and of these citizens who I am convinced, can provide in Boulder County, Colorado, and a fair trial to Mr. Mutchler and the motion is denied."

The trial continued the next morning.

SHAW: "Sam Shaw from the public defender's office and Linda Cooke for Mr. Mutchler. I asked we have a hearing…"

JUDGE: "I'm sorry, Mr. Miller."

SHAW: "…for the motion…the few motions related to press coverage. I would like to move to introduce into evidence yesterday's Daily Camera which I thought we had but I guess we didn't, April 21, 1992, and today's, which is Section C of the paper article of the 22nd, 1992."

JUDGE: "It's admitted. All the newspapers will be admitted into evidence."

SHAW: "What I want to talk to the Court about is the comments that this Court has been making in court and comments that the District Attorney's Office is making to the press, which I think calls for, at the very least, a gag order but probably more appropriately, granting my motion for change of venue and a continuance.

"We can start with this morning's paper where it says that I moved or was discharging jurors who knew anything about the murders because they could not judge the case by only the evidence presented at trial. I never said that, and that is not the law, and I never claimed that it was.

"I have cited Botham for change of venue and I stressed heavily to the Court the section of the case that says the Court can't rely just on representations of the jurors. When I have talked about the amount of publicity that calls for change of venue, I referred to the standard in that case which is massive and pervasive. I have never said that jurors that have read anything about the case should be excluded, and that is not the law.

"The article goes on to quote you, Judge, and it says that you were angry. I can tell the record that that was my perception of the way you were responding as well. 'I have an abiding belief in the sense of justice and fairness of our citizens,' and it said, adding, 'too often the public wrongfully believes what the Court wants are empty-headed jurors.'

"The Court was ruling on some motions that I never made and it certainly gives anyone who read that a negative impression of the arguments I am making and a negative impression of the defense.

"I don't know why the Court has to get angry when I make lawful objections.

"If the Court is trying to intimidate me, I don't think you will succeed, but if you do, then we'll need to get a new lawyer for Mr. Mutchler who isn't intimidated because I am trying to protect his right to a fair trial and I am making motions that I think the law supports.

"Mr. Miller is still talking to the press. We have here, 'Phil Miller, the lead prosecutor who says he hopes to finalize jury selection today' and that plays nicely into the expert covering the case, Mr. Caplis, who says in response to a question apparently posed from Ms. Hutchinson of the Daily Camera, 'Will all this extra time spent on jury selection help one side or the other?' 'Yes, it will help the defense.'

"So, the clear message there that they are playing out is, 'I want to get it done today and if it doesn't get done today, it's because of the defense's strategy and that is why you jurors are being inconvenienced' and then we get the district attorney involved. Where did he get into this?

"Alex Hunter, why are we talking to him and why is he talking to them?

"This is where they want to try cases. He says, I guess he is referring to us, 'This county has a reputation for bright and fair juries.'

"Well, I'm sorry, I never said it didn't, but it sure is getting shoved in my face.

"I open the paper, someone is suggesting that I think Boulder County jurors aren't fair and what do you know, right down here at the bottom, 'District Attorney Alex Hunter will run again in November.' Is that a coincidence?

"The bottom line, Judge, is this is a circus and this side show is going on that doesn't have anything to do with Mr. Mutchler or whether or not he can get a fair trial and it's going to continue to go on because the press is covering it unless we move it out of this county.

"At the very least, I think the Court has to order that the prosecution not talk about the case at all, in any respect, and in addition in their office to the press at all, because whether they intended it or not it gets turned into a little scenario that has the defense trying to delay this case and the defense thinking that any juror that has read a paper or has a thought in his head shouldn't sit on this jury.

"That is wrong and I never made such a statement, but it doesn't matter. We need to control this case and it's not being done. I am going to ask the Court to enforce a gag order and I will ask the Court to rule simply on the motions I make."

JUDGE: "Motion denied. Let's go back in and pick a jury."

Another juror, another confrontation between Shaw and Sandstead:

SHAW: "Judge, I'd ask the Court to excuse Ms. Elges. It's clear that she's having a great deal of difficulty in making a decision in this case. The Court needs to understand…you probably do…that that's the backdrop of everyone telling her she's got to be fair and impartial and follow these instructions. Still…I didn't look up at the clock, but I think it took her over 15 seconds to respond last time I asked her whether or not she could be fair. She's indicated in the past she's read about the case, discussed the case with her husband and they both expressed their opinions that Mr. Mutchler is guilty of the charges. Even if we ran out of jurors she would be the last juror for Mr. Mutchler to have sitting on this case."

JUDGE SANDSTEAD: "You know, I can be brought to tears when I say many times about the jury process. I mean, here is a woman who was about as honest as you can possibly be in discussing some difficult and important issues. She's indicated to me, and I would find, that she is not only honest but sensitive, intelligent and willing to admit that decisions jurors are required to make, as does everyone else in their lifetime have to make, are sometimes made with difficulty.

"But, she makes me proud and happy to be an American. I think that this is the kind of person…based on what she said, I have a totally different perspective about her answers than you have, Mr. Shaw. I'm willing to admit that I may be wrong but this makes me feel…gives me chills to think that citizens can come in here and tell us this is important and this is difficult and I'm going to do everything I can…I possibly can to follow the law, which I believe in and accept. And I will, for that reason, deny the challenge for cause."

SHAW: "It's not my point that these aren't good, honest people. That misses the mark. My problem is they've been exposed to too much and developed opinions that they can't let go of and they've been honest about that."

JUDGE: "I too often get the sense that the public thinks that what we want in jurors is empty-headed, non-reading, non-caring, unintelligent people with, quote 'empty minds'. I don't happen to believe that to be the case."

I slammed the transcript closed. "Damn that judge!" No matter how many times I read this section, I couldn't believe this actually happened. What was wrong with this judge? Wasn't he supposed to make sure Scott received a fair trial? How could he let some of these jurors sit and decide Scott's fate after what they'd said? There was no doubt in my mind that this judge wanted Scott convicted of this crime, whether he was guilty or innocent.

I glanced at my watch. It was time to go meet Steve. I packed up all the transcripts and headed to the hotel room.

Steve was waiting for me. I looked at him and smiled. "Let me grab a quick shower to get the sand off me and we can head out for some lunch."

"Where do you want to go?"

"You pick it."

One of the hardest things I had to do was keep switching gears with my emotions. I tried desperately not to let what I was going through with Scott interfere with my relationship with Steve, but for the most part, I failed miserably. It was always with me.

Steve had selected a great seafood shack for our lunch date. We ordered lobster and wine.

"Eve, you're so different when you're around the ocean. You come alive here. You have a glow that you don't have anywhere else. I wish you could bring that feeling back home with you."

I looked into my husband's eyes.

"I wish I could, too. I don't know what it is about the ocean that makes me feel so good."

We finished our lunch and headed back to the hotel.

"What are you going to do the rest of the day?"

"Just stay on the beach, soak up the sun and keep reading these transcripts. I hope you don't mind...I've got to try to find some answers. What are you going to do?"

"Just relax. I can't handle as much of the sun as you can."

Back in our hotel room, I changed into my bathing suit. I grabbed the beach bag with the volumes of transcripts.

"How about if you meet me down there later and we'll watch the sun set together."

"Sounds great. I'll see you then."

I gave Steve a kiss and headed out the door. I turned back and looked at him. He smiled a reassuring smile.

I found my deserted spot on the beach again. After oiling down, I pulled out the first volume of actual trial testimony.

Part 3

The Trial

It Begins

JUDGE: “On the record is People versus Scott Mutchler. We are outside the presence of the unsworn jury panel.”

SHAW: “Sam Shaw and Linda Cooke of the Public Defender's office and Mr. Mutchler appears to my left.”

John Pickering was an evil-appearing man to me. I felt he was unnaturally driven to win, no matter the cost to anyone else. Before the trial, law students that worked in the prosecution's office told me he was taking home pictures of the deceased and staring at them to keep focused. I just couldn’t comprehend the mind of this individual.

MILLER: “Phillip Miller and John Pickering and Bill Nagel for the People, Your Honor.”

SHAW: "I have a few things that I'd like to bring up prior to commencing trial. The first has to do with publicity.

"I have here two sets of articles from the Daily Camera Newspaper, one from yesterday, which is a copy, and today's paper, which includes the article by Julie Hutchinson and the expert's view from Dan Caplis. I'd like to admit those into evidence, and I'd like the Court to (hands to Mr. Miller)…Mr. Miller had a chance to see them.

"What I'm going to ask the Court to do, Judge, is poll the jury as the case goes on to make sure that nobody has read these articles. And then, if they have, take the next step to see what effect, if any.

"My authority for that…I'm sorry. With the press of business, all I have is the Brief Times Reporter and Harper versus the People case. It was a case that came from Grand Junction where there was publicity in the course of the trial. And I can give you a copy of that if you want to review the Brief Times Reporter. It's from the Supreme Court. Would you like my copy?"

JUDGE: "Sure."

SHAW: "What's the cite on that before I give it to you, Judge?"

JUDGE: "I'll just tell you what I understand the case to say. First, if there's publicity in the course of a trial, the Court should first determine whether the coverage has a potential for unfair prejudice.

"Second, if the Court determines that it does canvas the first, to find out if any of them have been exposed to it.

"And thirdly, examine the jurors individually. And I get that from page 1273 of the Brief Times Reporter, the opinion.

"I won't rule on that yet, but I'll read the case."

SHAW: "Just a little argument that I'd like to plug in the Court's consideration at this point. I think that concerning the initial hurdle is probably where the Court -- where I'm concerned the Court won't agree with this. And I'd like to indicate that the articles that have been reported yesterday and today on first reading are not extremely prejudicial, although yesterday it does contain the…I'm not sure how it's termed. And you've got in front of you a rehash of Mrs. Wesson's opinion on the evidence. Obviously, that's potentially highly prejudicial to the defense case.

"And today's paper, what I can comment on concerning prejudiciality is the article by Dan Caplis where he reports what he anticipates opening statements will be and what he thinks the defense ought to do. And my concern there is that the jury might not hear what Mr. Caplis thinks they ought to hear in order for us to prevail in this case.

"So I'd ask the Court to consider the articles from yesterday and today in the Boulder Camera in light of those arguments.

"The other thing I'd like to do is yesterday, you know, I moved to continue until this afternoon at 1:30 to get Edith Greene to Court. At that point, I couldn't lay my hands on her. I'd like to introduce her CV in, to supplement my arguments.

"The third thing I have, Judge, is we had filed long ago a motion for additional preemptory challenges. And I know the Court granted us one. And I don't know if by implication it thought we were satisfied with that and didn't want more. The Court has reserved ruling on that motion. And at this point, I would like to urge the motion on the Court and have the Court rule on that motion."

JUDGE: "Denied."

SHAW: "That's all I have. I don't know if you want to take up pictures at this point or not."

JUDGE: "I do in a second. The person who has a camera is in the courtroom seated to the far left. That's probably about as appropriate a place as he can be. It prevents him at all from photographing the jury. The problem is, from there, he may not be able to see the witness stand. But he can't move so…"

MILLER: "It occurs to me if he shoots from there, he might be shooting through the…I don't know if it's a good spot or not. My point is you made a commitment to the jurors that they wouldn't be photographed."

JUDGE: "Well, they're not going to be photographed."

SHAW: "Well, I share Mr. Miller's concern in that regard. Last time I heard one of those cameras, they were…"

JUDGE: "I haven't been able to hear the camera. I've never been able to hear a camera in the courtroom. Can you give us a demonstration of its noise?" (The camera was demonstrated).

"I heard them quieter than that."

"I'll turn up the hum."

SHAW: "I think that's a distraction. The jury is going to look around when they hear that and they're going to be worried about being photographed. So I don't find that positioning acceptable at all."

JUDGE: "Well, it's OK with me."

SHAW: "Your Honor, we're not going to be addressing the Court from the table. You could turn this microphone off. Apparently, you have the power panel up there. Do you know where it is?"

JUDGE: "There's actually a switch right on the mike with…all right. With regard to the photographic evidence, let's make a record. Let's start making a record with regard to photographic evidence. As soon as all the jurors get here, I want to start with the jury."

SHAW: "Judge, our position on the pictures is that they have to demonstrate to the Court's satisfaction … and I'm talking just now about pictures of the victims in this case. We don't have objection to the pictures of the residence, or if memory serves me, the pictures of what the prosecution claims is blood in the house. Last I recall, those that they intended to offer, they were not prejudicial.

"However, concerning pictures of the bodies, it's our position that none of them are necessary for the prosecution to establish the elements in this case and not necessary to assist witnesses in testifying.

"This Court has heard a fair amount of evidence at the preliminary hearing and motion hearings, and you yourself can be a judge of how important it was for you to see pictures in this case. I think you saw a few at the preliminary hearing.

"But there's no difficulty in understanding Dr. Meyer's testimony or anyone else's report of what they saw when they arrived at the scene or how these victims died.

"At the preliminary hearing, we had a chart, which was fairly benign, that Dr. Meyer used to demonstrate location of injuries and type of injuries. It's our position that that's more than adequate to explain to the jury what happened in this case to the victims.

"So I'd ask the Court to not permit any pictures of the bodies of the victims in this case, autopsy or otherwise."

JUDGE: "Well, let me tell you what my concern is. I'm going to reserve the right to…as the exhibits are offered to make a 403 finding.

But at this stage, I don't think...I'm not concerned about any but the autopsy photographs. What are the..."

MILLER: "The reason autopsy photographs...the law is pretty clear that photographs are admissible to allow a witness to refer to demonstrate with. And the autopsy pictures themselves are not gory, bloody pictures. Fact is, there is no blood in the autopsy pictures. They are, in fact, clinical exhibits in and of themselves that Dr. Meyer has selected to demonstrate the nature and the depth and the location of the wounds that caused the manner of death. And in the case law, there's certainly ample authority for the Court to allow those autopsy pictures. "

JUDGE: "Well you know, you run the risk that I will find them cumulative, and therefore unfairly prejudicial. But at this stage, you may introduce all of the photographs that I've observed here. But if I think that you're...that they're cumulative, I won't let the jury see them."

SHAW: "Judge if it will satisfy counsel and he'll withdraw those exhibits, we will stipulate to the cause and manner of death."

MILLER: "We won't accept that stipulation. If I could have the photographs back?"

JUDGE: "You may. Anything else?"

SHAW: "Judge, I've got a problem if you intend to...on not polling the jury on publicity this morning. I think if the Court can't decide on whether or not those articles are potentially prejudicial, the easy step is to just ask them if they've been exposed in any way to those articles in the last two days. And then, if anybody raises their hand, maybe we've got a problem. But if they don't, we can get on with it."

JUDGE: "Well, I'll tell you what. I might at some time in this trial ask them if they've had any exposure to any pretrial publicity. But after four days of having it pounded and pounded and pounded into their head, having read in...I am apologizing now for reading that instruction over and over again. I will still do so. And I might ask them. But to ask them now, in my view, is to challenge them that they've been lying to me for the last four days, and I do not find that they have."

SHAW: "Well, I don't think it would be. Judge, somebody could be exposed accidentally to publicity, as the Harper case points out. And they're not sequestered. They're out there in the world where other people who haven't had the admonishment are around them and could have accidentally even exposed them to something from the press. So it isn't suggesting that they're lying. They're not sequestered. Anything can happen out there. I think the Court can phrase it that way so they aren't offended."

MILLER: "Your Honor, I agree that it will be relatively benign to simply pose the question about whether any publicity has made contact with him by any means to insure a clean record. I don't think they would be insulted if you put it in those terms as well."

JUDGE: "I'll think about it. Are we ready?"

The Prosecution Presents Its Case

JUDGE: "Are counsel ready for opening statements?"

MILLER: "Yes, Your Honor."

SHAW: "Defense is ready, Judge."

JUDGE: "Mr. Miller."

MILLER: "Thank you. Ladies and gentlemen, through the reading of the charges and through the voir dire process, you've received a hint of what this trial is about. However, during opening statements counsel for both sides have an opportunity to make an opening statement, which would outline the evidence they expect to see in this trial. It's intended to give a background for what is to come.

"Ladies and gentlemen, witnesses during this trial will testify and tell you that in 1989, the defendant, Scott Mutchler, lived on Van Buren Court with his mother, his brother and his stepfather; in fact, that he lived just a few doors away from Evan and Robbie Scharf who resided at Van Buren Court.

"You'll learn that they came to know one another; that is to say, Scott Mutchler knew Evan and Robbie Scharf. They were neighbors. And on occasion we learned that Scott Mutchler baby-sat for young Robbie Scharf and did some lawn work for Evan Scharf, and in fact other neighbors.

"You'll learn that Scott Mutchler, of course, had been in the home of Evan and Robbie Scharf; been in the home and knew the inside of the home. And he knew where Evan Scharf kept his keys to vehicles.

"In the summer of 1989, Scott Mutchler and his family moved away from Van Buren Court. But ladies and gentlemen, the evidence will show that in the summer of 1991, Scott Mutchler planned and carried out a return to the Scharf residence.

"You will hear that in the summer of 1991...you will hear witnesses that knew Scott Mutchler. And that during that summer, June and July of 1991, he told them of plans to get a car and other valuables from a man and his son in Louisville.

"Specifically, you'll hear from Eric Peterson who will say that in 1991, in the summer, Scott Mutchler told him of his plan to break into a person's house in Louisville; that that person had a kid; that there was a lot of computer equipment in the basement; and that he had a Honda Prelude. Peterson will tell you that he was...Mutchler said he was going to knock out these people with some kind of a drug, and he even asked Eric Peterson to assist him in getting or making such a drug, and to assist him in taking their valuables. Mr. Peterson declined.

"You'll also hear from a Mr. Scott Seppers, another acquaintance of Scott Mutchler's. The defendant told him that he was going to use chloroform to knock out a man who lived alone with his son, for whom he used to baby-sit, and his plan was to steal their credit cards.

"You'll hear from Samuel Schafer that in July of 1991, he was planning to rob a house where a father and son lived, and where he had once baby-sat. He planned to use a drug that he remembers as "chloro-something" to knock them out. Mutchler told them he was going to take the car and the VCR and the TV.

"Andrea Tyson, a young lady acquaintance of Mr. Mutchler's, will tell you that in mid-July of 1991, Scott Mutchler stayed briefly in the trailer that was located behind her family's home, and that she found a piece of paper or list or something that puzzled her. And she confronted Mr. Mutchler about it in July. And she was told by Scott Mutchler that he was going to rob a neighbor he used to baby-sit for. He told her he was going to tie the man and his child as well and use some chemical to knock them out.

"Andrea Tyson will also tell you something else. She'll tell you that on the occasions…or an occasion when she was with Scott Mutchler that summer, and that the two of them sat down and apparently wrote separate notes that they were going to make to a mutual friend, Zac Page. Indeed, Scott Mutchler asked Andrea to send his note along with hers.

"Andrea Tyson never did mail that note. She never mailed her own, apparently, either. But she kept that note, police officers in the investigation of this case asked her for that note, and we have that note. And you'll hear and you'll see it. It is in his own words, the letter that says, among other things, to his friend, 'I'm breaking into this house at 1 a.m. The only people who live there are this man and his kid. Anyway, I'm going to put chloroform on his mouth and his nose and tie him up so he can't move, ever. Then the same for his kid. Well, then his money, credit cards, and car with the cell phone are mine since he'll be all tied up. Then I'm moving after I buy all this good stuff. And the car won't be reported stolen because he'll be busy. I told you I was going to do one last big job.'

"You'll see that letter in the defendant's own handwriting. You'll learn also that the defendant was in the Adams County Jail from a period of July 23rd, until September 10, 1991. While in that jail, Scott Mutchler told a fellow inmate that he used to live in Louisville. He had been in a neighbor's home. He will tell you that Mutchler told of a car, some kind of a Honda, another thing that he wanted to take for himself.

"The evidence will show that on September 10, 1991, the defendant was released from the Adams County Jail. His mother, Eve Meyer, picked him up in Brighton and brought him home. This was around 7 p.m.

"You'll learn that the defendant came home, showered, changed his clothes, and had dinner with his family, or had dinner at the home at least, and then asked to be dropped off in Louisville. This is September 10th.

"He told his mother and his stepfather that he wanted to pick up his car. You'll learn that he hadn't owned a car or had a car before he went into jail earlier that summer. And then the defendant directed his mother and stepfather where to go, where to drop him off.

"And you'll learn that about 9 p.m. on September 10th, Scott Mutchler was dropped at a convenience store near Louisville off the Boulder Turnpike, about one mile from Van Buren Way.

"Meanwhile, you'll hear evidence that on that same evening Evan and Robbie Scharf apparently had been shopping, but they stopped off at about 6:30 to visit Joyce Underwood, a friend of Evan Scharf's. You'll hear her testify that both Evan and Robbie were very tired that night, and that when they left around 8 p.m. to go home, they were going to go home and go to bed soon.

"Sometime later that night, an intruder entered the Scharf home through a basement window where a screen had been pulled away from its frame. The intruder entered a window that apparently had not been secured. There's no breaking other than the screen removed.

"The evidence will show that the intruder carried about a 3-foot piece of two-by-four with him into the home. Once inside, the intruder went upstairs from the basement level to the middle level of the home. There he abandoned the two-by-four and obtained a fireplace poker from the set in the living room. The intruder then went into the kitchen and removed a butcher knife from the butcher block that had other knives of similar kind.

"Then the intruder went upstairs into the darkened bedroom where Evan Scharf lay sleeping on his stomach, apparently, and nude. The intruder swung the fireplace poker at Evan Scharf, at the sleeping form of Evan Scharf. With one blow the head of the poker came off, exposing the threads that held the tip of the poker onto the shaft. The intruder struck Evan Scharf. The force of one of these blows after the head of the poker came off was with such force that the thread around the tip of the poker left a brand-like impression in the back of Evan Scharf. You'll see that. You'll see a photograph of that.

"The evidence will show that the intruder struck Evan Scharf many more times with the fireplace poker on the…elsewhere on the body. Then the attacker used the butcher knife to continue his assault on Evan Scharf in his own bedroom.

"You'll hear from the coroner of the defensive wounds to the hands and arms and fingers of Evan Scharf as he tried to repel or deflect the blows and the stabbings that were occurring.

"You'll hear of the large amount of blood consistent with the blood of Evan Scharf that was found in his bedroom, and you'll learn that Evan Scharf only was able to cover the distance between his bed and the threshold of the door between his bedroom and his bathroom. That's where Evan Scharf fell to the floor, and that's where he was found dead a few hours later by police.

"Dr. Meyer, the county coroner, will testify that a major wound to the back of the neck of Evan Scharf was inflicted after Evan Scharf's heart had stopped beating, after Evan Scharf was already dead.

"There on the floor between his bed and bathroom is where Evan Scharf's body was found by Louisville police a few hours later.

"In the frenzy of this attack on Evan Scharf, the attacker was also cut; you will hear that blood other than that of Evan Scharf is found in the bedroom. You will hear that only one type other than that of Evan Scharf was found in the bedroom. You'll learn later that it's the same type of blood as that of Scott Mutchler.

"Through photos taken by the police at the Scharf home, you will follow or see a trail of blood from Evan Scharf's bedroom and bathroom where his body came to rest down the hall to the other upstairs bedroom where Robbie Scharf normally slept. You'll see that trail of blood go into his bedroom. You'll see it on the floor of his bedroom and on his bed.

"The blood drops leave a trail out of Robbie's bedroom down the stairs to the main floor, where a bloody shirt is found at the top of the stairs, down to the basement level and down the hall to the door of the bathroom on the lower level where another bloody shirt is found.

"The trail of blood leads into that bathroom to where Robbie Scharf's slim, lifeless body was found by the police, too. He was dead as a result of knife wounds to his neck.

"You'll hear testimony about a lot of blood in the home of Evan Scharf and Robbie Scharf, how that blood was tested, and how the results of those tests were consistent with the blood of three people; Evan Scharf, Robbie Scharf and Scott Mutchler.

"The trail of blood goes back upstairs to the main floor into the living room where there were drops on a chair, from the living room to the dining room, into the closet near the kitchen, into the pocket of a trench coat that hangs in the kitchen closet, and then into the kitchen to the kitchen telephone. You will see the picture of that bloody kitchen telephone, and you will be told that blood on the Scharf's kitchen phone is also consistent with that of Scott Mutchler.

"Also on that phone is a blood fingerprint. And you'll hear testimony that on that kitchen phone in the Scharf kitchen is a fingerprint that is the fingerprint of Scott Mutchler.

"Eve Meyer will say that about 11, she got a phone call from her son, about two minutes before 11. She was expecting him at 11. She will say that her son sounded normal, he sounded like Scott. He said he was going to get gas and be home shortly.

"Mrs. Meyer will testify that her son, Scott Mutchler, did arrive home 15 or 20 minutes later. He was wearing the same clothes that he had on when they dropped him in Louisville at 9. But Mrs. Meyer will tell you that the clothes were not the same because, in her words, they were covered with blood.

"She will tell you that her son was injured and that his left hand and arm were injured; that he had something wrapped around it. She will also tell you that she gave him a pillowslip or pillowcase for him to hold over the wound as well.

"She called 911, and a few minutes later emergency personnel responded and Adam County police officers also. The paramedic, the first paramedic, was Robert Yusko, a witness in this case. He was told by Mr. Mutchler that he had been attacked by three unknown men somewhere on 120th Street.

"Police officer Rick McNair, who responded with the ambulance people, will tell you that Mr. Mutchler told him that he was assaulted by three unknown assailants at a gas station on 120th Street. He gave minimal details. And when he was advised that there was no station at 120th, he said west of that.

"Deputy McNair and Officer LaFleur, a Broomfield officer, who comes into play later, will tell you that Mr. Mutchler's mother followed the ambulance to the hospital in an automobile. She wasn't immediately behind them, but she followed them. And she was there a few minutes later. When she arrived, she pointed out to the police a car that she had driven. And she referred to it as quote, 'her son's car.' This car was secured by police officers, and later you'll hear about the testing and examinations that were made of them.

"Office LaFleur of Broomfield police will tell you that when he responded to the hospital to investigate the assault at 120th Street and Perry Street inside the city of Broomfield was the jurisdiction of Broomfield officers. He will tell you that Mr. Mutchler, who had reported himself as a victim, told him that he was assaulted after calling his mother on the telephone at a gas station as he returned to his car.

"Officer LaFleur will also indicate that Mrs. Meyer pointed out her son's car to him in the hospital parking lot.

"Other police detectives and personnel and hospital personnel will tell you of their dealings with Mr. Mutchler and his car that night. Emergency room nurse Paula Gutzmer who treated the wounds of Scott Mutchler, Detective Dan Schuler from Broomfield who came in to try to apprehend or find the three males who Mr. Mutchler blamed for his wounds; also Detective Tom Hartmann who came from the Broomfield Police Department to assist in the investigation of the assault reported by Mr. Mutchler.

"You'll hear that Mr. Mutchler told all of these people the same basic story that he told the other officers earlier; he'd been attacked by three men in a gas station after calling his mother.

"These and more police officers will tell of...of their efforts to find the scene of the assault that he had reported so they could apprehend the attackers and protect the public from them; how they could find no evidence of any assault at the gas station as he described it or any gas station or convenience store up and down 120th Street.

"They will tell of their conversations with Mr. Mutchler and report how they continued to inquire of him about the details so that they could do a better job. I can tell you that they'll testify that he didn't eagerly discuss the assault and did add details to what he said before, but none of the details could be confirmed. No blood was found on 120th Street.

"The detectives will then tell you how their investigation turned when they learned that the car driven home by the defendant, then driven to the hospital by his mother, was not his car. You'll learn how the police checked with the Department of Motor Vehicles, found that this car was actually listed to Evan Scharf, Van Buren Court in Louisville, in the County of Boulder.

"Upon learning that, the police officers will tell you that they decided to make a personal contact. And they asked Louisville police to make a personal contact with Mr. Scharf to see if there was an explanation of why Mr. Mutchler would be driving his car.

"Louisville officers will tell you about their grisly discoveries at the scene; that they found Evan Scharf, the owner of the car driven by Scott Mutchler, dead in his bedroom from the vicious stab wounds, and how they found Robbie dead in the downstairs bathroom.

"The trail of blood has come in a full circle. It encircles Scott Mutchler. The trail started in the attacker's wounds from where it dripped as the bleeding attacker went through the Scharf home; Evan Scharf's bedroom, Robbie's bedroom, downstairs to the bathroom where Robbie was killed, back upstairs to the living room, dining room, into the kitchen and to the fingerprint, the bloody fingerprint."

SHAW: "Judge, counsel's opening statement is getting repetitive and, therefore, argumentative. I'd ask the court to restrict him to opening statement."

JUDGE: "Don't argue. Go ahead. Overruled at this time."

MILLER: "The fingerprint is the blood of Scott Mutchler. The trail then leads to Evan Scharf's car, then to Scott Mutchler's home, to the ambulance, from there to the emergency room where the wound was treated. The trail leads back to the car, and from the car, we learn that the officers find the dead bodies in the Scharf home.

"As clear as that trail of blood is to follow from the victims to the defendant and then back to the victims again, the evidence in this trial will also show you that there's another trail of blood which links Scott

Mutchler as the killer of Evan Scharf and Robbie Scharf. Because the blood of Evan Scharf and Robbie Scharf also follows Scott Mutchler to the emergency room.

"The testimony of experts will show that Scott Mutchler's clothes were covered not only with his own blood, but also with blood of Evan Scharf and Robbie Scharf.

"After the discovery of the two bodies in Louisville, the police at the emergency room acted quickly and seized Scott Mutchler's bloody clothes; his pants, his shirt, his socks, and his wrestling shoes as well as the items that had been wrapped around his arm. And we learn not only was the blood on Scott Mutchler's clothes consistent with his own blood, but also on the drenched clothes was blood that would be tested as consistent with that of Evan and Robbie Scharf. Although Evan and Robbie Scharf never left their home, their blood did. It was on the clothing of their killer, Scott Mutchler.

"Following the discovery of the two murder victims, officers and detectives of the Louisville police continued their investigation and called in the Boulder County Coroner and the Bureau of Investigation to assist them in the examination, the collection and the testing of items of evidence from several sources. Investigators and Dr. Meyer, the Boulder County Coroner, went to the crime scene while the bodies were still there. And Dr. Meyer will testify to you about his own observations at the scene and how he found the bodies and how he observed…how that assisted him in making his conclusions later about cause of death.

"In a more clinical setting, he will tell you about the postmortem examinations, the autopsies that were conducted on both Evan and Robbie Scharf. You will see pictures of those two lifeless bodies and the circumstances in which their killer left them. Those pictures of the death scene and the wounds, which caused those deaths, will demonstrate to you the deliberation with which those two people were attacked and killed.

"Dr. Meyer will tell you as he learned of the wounds suffered by the victims, the defensive wounds, and the wounds inflicted after Evan Scharf was dead. Dr. Meyer will give you his opinion that the knife wounds caused the death of Evan and Robbie Scharf. Once again, you will see pictures of that autopsy so you will appreciate the full nature of the killer's conduct and the effect of that conduct.

"Police investigators will tell you of what they found at the scene. You'll hear a lot of evidence about how this crime scene was gone over from top to bottom. They will go into great detail about the collection of evidence, and the evidence collected from the defendant himself and the care with which they preserved the evidence and examined it.

"They collected blood samples, fingerprints, shoe prints, hair, and sections of the kitchen floor, the kitchen telephone, clothing, bedding, the two-by-four, the fireplace poker, and the knife. You will see much of this evidence. You'll see pictures of other evidence.

"Police obtained samples of Scott Mutchler's blood and compared it with the trail of blood throughout the home; found them to be consistent. They have obtained Scott Mutchler's fingerprints. Scott Pratt of the Bureau of Investigations compared them with the fingerprints found on the phone in blood in the kitchen, with another fingerprint found in blood on a coupon in the kitchen. Those fingerprints they found in the blood in the Scharf home to be those of Scott Mutchler's. He will tell you the other fingerprints in the home were those belonging to Evan and Robbie Scharf, who lived there.

"Dr. Meyer will tell you that he found on Evan Scharf what turned out to be a hair that was seized. You will hear that the sample was given to Andrew Olinger. Mr. Mool Verma is a Bureau Investigator expert on hairs and fibers. You will learn that the hair that Dr. Meyer took from the hand of Evan Scharf was compared with other hairs that were taken from Scott Mutchler after his arrest. You will learn from Mr. Verma that his conclusion was that the hair in the hand of Evan Scharf in death was a hair from the arm of Scott Mutchler.

"You'll hear that the blood samples from Evan and Robbie Scharf taken by Dr. Meyer were tested by Ted Davelis, the blood or serology expert from the FBI. He will tell you that he took the samples of the blood of the two victims. And he will tell you that blood on the clothing of Scott Mutchler…"

SHAW: "Judge, here we go again. We've already heard about this. How many times are we going to go around?"

MILLER: "I think I'm permitted…"

JUDGE: "Overruled. Well, you're arguing. Don't argue."

MILLER: "I'm permitted to outline the case. Blood on the clothing that Scott Mutchler was wearing the night his mother took him to Louisville, that clothing was seized from him in the emergency room. Ted Davelis will tell you that blood, Scott Mutchler's blood...blood consistent with Scott Mutchler's blood was found on Evan Scharf's hands; that a drop of blood consistent with Scott Mutchler was found on the heel of Evan Scharf. Scott Mutchler's blood was found on a shirt, which was over the slashed throat of Robbie Scharf as he lay in the tub.

"You will hear that handwriting exemplars or samples taken from Scott Mutchler were compared with handwriting from the Zac Page's letter that I talked to you about. That expert will conclude that the letters...the samples were written by the same person, Scott Mutchler.

"Scott Pratt will testify that shoe prints found on the Scharf kitchen floor matched prints of the wrestling shoes recovered from the defendant at the hospital emergency room.

"Scott Pratt will also testify about a bloody knife that he found in the bedroom adjacent to the downstairs bathroom where Robbie Scharf was found dead. The testing on the knife by Agent Davelis disclosed that the blood on the knife was blood consistent with Robbie Scharf.

"You'll also hear about blood consistent with that of Scott Mutchler's being found on the gearshift knob of the Honda and on the steering wheel cover of the Honda.

"Ladies and gentlemen, you're going to hear a lot of evidence, and a lot of it will be very unpleasant, but it will prove beyond a reasonable doubt -- any reasonable doubt -- that Scott Mutchler obtained and exercised control over Evan Scharf's vehicle without authorization; that Scott Mutchler entered and remained unlawfully in the dwelling and occupied structure of Evan Scharf with the intent to commit the crime of theft; and that Scott Mutchler, being armed with a knife, entered and remained unlawfully in the building or occupied structure of Evan Scharf with intent to come commit the crimes of murder and theft; that Scott Mutchler committed or attempted to commit first-degree burglary and in the course or furtherance of that crime he was committing, the death of Robbie Scharf was caused; Scott Mutchler committed or attempted to commit first-degree burglary and, in the course and furtherance of that crime he was committing, the death of Evan Scharf was caused; that Scott Mutchler after deliberation and with the intent to cause the death of Evan and Robbie Scharf. Ladies and gentleman, Scott Mutchler carried out his plan to return to the Scharf home. He returned to the Scharf home on September 10. He returned not as a neighbor or friend…"

SHAW: "Judge, this is clearly argument."

JUDGE: "We're getting into argument."

MILLER: "Your Honor, I'm summarizing the People's case, and I'm nearly done. I understand that this is unpleasant, that the defense doesn't want to hear this."

SHAW: "That's not the problem. The problem is we've heard three times what it's going to prove. He's arguing his case."

JUDGE: "This is evidence. I mean, this is not evidence. This is your attempt to tell what you…you think the evidence will show. But don't argue the case."

MILLER: "All right."

JUDGE: "You will be permitted to at the close of the evidence."

MILLER: "The evidence will show that Scott Mutchler returned not as a neighbor or friend, but as a burglar…"

SHAW: "Are you permitting this Judge?"

JUDGE: "Yes."

MILLER: "As a thief, as a killer. Scott Mutchler was that intruder in the home. He was the knife-wielding attacker. He was the killer of Evan Scharf. And based on the presentation of the evidence, which I've summarized, the prosecution will ask you to return verdicts, which match the evidence presented here. Ask to return verdicts of guilty against Scott Mutchler on all counts: theft of the automobile, burglary of the Scharf home and the murders of Evan and Robbie Scharf."

The Defense Speaks

JUDGE: "Opening statement? Do you desire to make it or waive?"

SHAW: "We will make it now. Ms. Cooke will do that."

JUDGE: "All right. Ms. Cooke."

COOKE: "Ladies and gentleman of the jury, you're about to begin a process which will result in the decision of a lifetime for this young man, Scott Mutchler. While you may make more important decisions in your own lives, chances are that you won't be making a decision that more profoundly affects another person than the decision you'll be making in this case.

"There's no doubt that a terrible thing happened at Van Buren Court last September. A man and his son were stabbed to death in that home. And it's natural for you to feel any number of emotions about that: sorrow, anger. Those are a couple that come immediately to mind.

"But while it's OK for you to experience that strong emotion, and indeed we expect that in a case like this, you need to set that emotion aside. You need to look at this case objectively."

PICKERING: "Your Honor, I'm going to object to this as being argument."

JUDGE: "Let's move to present evidence...what you expect the evidence to show and not argue the case."

COOKE: "You need to determine whether the prosecution has proved all of the elements of the charges against Scott Mutchler beyond a reasonable doubt.

"The prosecution has told you in their opening statement that the evidence will show you, first of all, that Scott Mutchler planned to burglarize the Scharf home. Well, the evidence, ladies and gentlemen, will also show that it was not Scott's plan to harm the residents of that home.

"The prosecution has told you that the evidence will show that the intruder's first move was to hit Mr. Scharf with a fireplace poker. It makes no sense for an intruder to strike a sleeping person."

PICKERING: "Objection, argument."

JUDGE: "Sustained. You may tell what the evidence is, but it can't be in the form of an argument."

COOKE: "The evidence will show you that it makes no sense for an intruder to strike..."

PICKERING: "Objection, argument."

COOKE: "...a sleeping person on the back. The burglary or theft is the intent of that person. The prosecution has also told you in their opening statements that Scott was at the Scharf home soon after being dropped off at the convenience store in Louisville, and that he was there until he phoned home to his mother to say that he would be home soon.

"But ladies and gentleman, the evidence will also show that it doesn't take two hours, from 9 p.m. until 11, to cover the short distance to the Scharf home from the convenience store and to cause the mayhem that they say Scott did. Something more was going on.

"To understand this case from the prosecution's side and from our side, you need to look at this case the way you look when you go to buy a diamond. The jeweler will tell you how to look at the stone and evaluate its worth."

PICKERING: "Objection. This is argument unless we're going to hear evidence in the case about buying a diamond."

COOKE: "What the prosecution is holding out to you in this case, what they have told you the evidence will show in this case, is that it will show you a sparkly diamond.

"What you need to do is to take the evidence in this case, grab it the way you would grab a diamond, and look at it the way a jeweler would. And while the prosecution's case appears to be the genuine article, you need to look at it. You need to look to see if it's the real thing, or if it's flawed."

PICKERING: "Objection, argument."

JUDGE: "Sustained."

COOKE: "You need to listen carefully to the questions and answers the prosecution will elicit from the witnesses they call. Think about the differing ways the evidence can be viewed.

"Let's take the knife, for instance. There are no fingerprints on it. There's no blood on the handle, no blood consistent with Scott Mutchler.

"Take the screen in the basement window they talked about. No one will be able to tell you whether that screen was removed from the inside of the window or from the outside.

"And although there are trails of blood throughout the house, as the prosecution has told you, the evidence will show you that there are no trails of blood in other places that you would expect to find them; no trails of blood from the Scharf home to the Honda, no trails of blood from the Honda to the Meyer home where Scott returned at some time after 11 p.m.

"In listening to the evidence in this case, give equal attention to the questions that Mr. Shaw and I ask of the witnesses. Most of the time we'll be going second. We may have fewer questions, but the witnesses' answers to those questions are equally important as those asked by the prosecution.

"Resist temptation to form a conclusion about this case before you've heard all of the evidence in the case. Look for anomalies or unexplained facts in the evidence; questions like, why are there shoe prints around the Scharf home that don't match Scott Mutchler's; why did Scott's mother hear a car door slam and a car drive off just before Scott entered the home.

"Those are just a couple of examples, but these are the types of things you need to be alert for in listening to the evidence in this case in determining what it tells you about the elements that need to be clear to you.

"Don't place undue emphasis on testimony concerning facts that aren't in dispute. For instance, you're going to hear an impressive array of experts whose testimony will place Scott in the home that night. You've heard about a few of them; the fingerprint expert, a blood expert, and there are a couple of others.

"Well, Scott was in that house that night, but that's only one of the elements that the prosecution has to prove in this case.

"You need to also listen to what the experts have to say about facts that are in dispute. For instance, listen to evidence that they tell you, evidence from the home that cannot be traced to either Scott Mutchler or Evan Scharf or Robbie Scharf.

"I don't need to remind you of the gravity of the charges in this case. You know as well as anyone that the decision of a lifetime rests in your hands. And, although every criminal case that's brought to trial is important, surely this case of all cases requires that you apply the legal principles we've discussed with the greatest of care.

"So we ask you in listening to the evidence to listen carefully and critically, and to keep an open, inquiring frame of mind, and to grab that sparkly stone and look at it with a jeweler's eye. Thank you."

The Witnesses

JUDGE: "Your first witness."

MILLER: "Robert Yusko. Good Morning Sir."

"Good morning."

"Mr. Yusko, how are you employed?"

"I'm a paramedic for Emergency Response Company in Denver."

"And does your company provide services to Adams County?"

"Yes, we do."

"And on September 10th, were you working for the ambulance service?"

"Yes, I was."

"And what was your assignment? Where in greater Denver were you assigned to work?"

"Southwest Adams County fire department district."

"And late on the evening of September…excuse me, September 10, did you have a call from your dispatch or communicator directing you to respond to an address at Oakwood Street in Westminster?"

"Yes."

"What information did you have from the dispatcher about why you should respond there?"

"Adams County Communication dispatched to that location on a stabbing."

"Is that…is there any kind of code or information that comes out that assists in knowing before you get there what's going on, what you might expect?"

"Additional information aired that the call was to wait in the area for a code four for police to be on the scene."

"Any other information?"

"No, sir. That was it."

"OK. What did you do upon receiving that call?"

"We proceeded about a block from the actual address and waited for Adams County Sheriffs to give us a code four."

"Did they respond shortly?"

"They were already there, yes."

"What happened next?"

"We proceeded to the residence and entered the residence."

"Did you eventually contact…make contact, see and then make contact with the person with an apparent injury?"

"Yes. Directed to the kitchen area where I met my patient."

"Is that person present in the courtroom?"

"Yes, he is."

"Would you indicate where he is seated and how he is dressed?"

"He is sitting on the right side of the…my right side of the court dressed in a pink shirt."

"I ask that the record reflect identification of the defendant. Mr. Yusko, tell us what you saw when you first entered the home, in terms of your patient."

"My patient was a young gentleman sitting in a chair in the middle of the kitchen area with his left arm wrapped up in a white towel."

"Let me back up a minute and ask a little bit about your training so that the jury has an understanding of that."

"OK."

"How do you define yourself?"

"I am an emergency medical technician paramedic."

"And is there a hierarchy of training and classification of paramedics that you can place yourself into by telling us a bit about that?"

"Yes. The health department of the state defines three levels of emergency medical technician training as basic, intermediate, and paramedic in that order."

"And the most accomplished of those three is the paramedic?"

"Yes, sir."

"And are you in that category?"

"Yes."

"How long have you been in the field generally?"

"I've been in the field for six years."

"So based on the training that you obtained in your six years of experience, what do you look for…what did you look for in this case when you're sent to where someone has an injury? What is it you're trained to do?"

"The first thing is I look for a life-threatening emergency. And I'm trained to stabilize or correct those problems, and transport the patient to the closest emergency department."

"Let's take that first thing about…what about life-threatening emergencies in this case? What did you determine?"

"There were no life-threatening emergencies."

"What, in fact, did you determine from or about Mr. Mutchler?"

"I did a quick visual examination on the scene. I determined there were no life-threatening injuries. There were at that time…I did not know the exact number, but there were multiple lacerations on his left forearm and hand."

"OK. What did you do upon making those observations? What course of action did you take?"

"At that time, I asked what appeared to be his mother or a female in the room what had happened."

"And what did you learn?"

"I learned…"

SHAW: "Objection Your Honor hearsay."

JUDGE: "Overruled."

MILLER: "What did she say?"

YUSKO: "That her son, the patient, was supposed to be home at 11. And I don't remember the exact time. It would be about 11:30."

SHAW: "Judge, why isn't this hearsay?"

JUDGE: "The objection is overruled. We can discuss the reasons for my rulings outside the presence of the evidence."

SHAW: "Well, I'd like to do it then."

JUDGE: "All right. It's not offered for the truth that…it's offered to show why he was doing what he did."

SHAW: "Well, I don't know. I mean, they ought to have to make an offer of proof without you telling them."

JUDGE: "The objection is overruled. Go on."

MILLER: "What background or what information did this person say?"

YUSKO: "That the patient was supposed to be home at a certain time. He arrived late in this condition."

"Did you yourself speak with Mr. Mutchler about his injuries?"

"Yes. At that…after reviewing that, I started talking to the patient, yes."

"Was there a question asked and answered? Tell us what you said and what he said."

"I asked him where was he hurt at, and he indicated the same location. I asked him if there were any other injuries, to determine if there was some that I had missed right off."

"Were there any other questions or responses…questions and responses?"

"I can't recall verbatim what else was said, but it was a brief history."

"OK. Did he describe…did you ask or did he tell you how this happened?"

"Not at that time, no."

"OK. So after making your initial observation and getting some background, what did you do with your patient?"

"I asked the patient if he was able to stand and walk to the ambulance."

"What did he say? What did he do?"

"Yes, he got up and walked with me to the ambulance."

"Did Mr. Mutchler appear to understand what was being said to him?"

"Yes."

"Were you in turn able to understand what he said to you?"

"Yes."

"Was there any disorientation?"

"No."

"Are you trained to make observations of apparent intoxication or drug involvement?"

"I am medically trained to identify, yes."

"What observations, if any, did you make along those lines?"

"I observed his gait, his speech, pupillary response, you know, physical response."

"What did you determine?

"That he was not showing any signs of alcohol or drug use."

"Now, you have him walking towards your ambulance vehicle?"

"Yes."

"What happened? What happens next?"

"It was the patient, me and the Adams County Sheriffs officers walking him out. And we were stopped in the front lawn by his mom to make sure where we were going. And she asked for the…for keys to his car so she could ride to the hospital."

"What did you see, if anything, concerning that?"

"He gave her a set of keys and said, "I'll meet you at the hospital."

"Now, did you go to the ambulance?"

"Pardon me?"

"Did you go to the ambulance?"

"Yes. After that we took the patient in the ambulance, yes."

"Did you have more conversation with him about the injury?"

"Yes."

"And what is it that…what conversation?"

"I asked him how these injuries occurred. And he stated that he was jumped by three males, which happened at an unknown gas station. He did not know where it was at. I asked him if there were any other weapons, if anything else had happened. I was trying to determine if there was anything that I was missing, trying to get more of a detailed report."

"Was there any details?"

"He denied any other weapons used, denied that he was kicked or anything. He just said it was a knife."

"Back up a minute. You mentioned that while you were walking out, the mother…apparently the mother, asked about the car."

"The car keys, yes. She asked for keys to his car."

"Did you know…did you see a car that was referred to or see a car at or near?"

"There was a black vehicle parked in front of the house along with all the other police cars and my ambulance."

"What treatment…what observations, if any did you make of the wound once you were in the ambulance?"

"I did a more detailed observation, visual observation. I removed the towel from his arm to get him more…get a more definite determination of how bad his wounds were."

"Concerning the articles that were on the wound that were removed by you, what became of those? What did you do with them?"

"During transport they just sat on the floor of the ambulance. Once we got to the hospital, I gave them back to him."

"They didn't…did they remain in the ambulance? Is that your testimony?"

"No, they…well, I'm sorry."

"They were in the ambulance? What became of them? I just missed your answer."

"Once we arrived at the hospital, I picked them up off the floor and gave them back to the patient."

"During the transport…by the way, how long was it between when you first got him into your vehicle and then arrived at the hospital emergency room?"

"My trip report would have the exact time, but I'm guessing three to four minutes. It's a very short distance."

"Did your assessment of his signs or your observation of his condition change any during the transport?"

"No."

"Did you have further discussions with him or question him anymore about how or what had happened?"

"Yes. We talked the whole way to the hospital."

"What did he say on the way to the hospital about what had happened?"

"The story that he kept giving me was ever-changing; the location of the incident, the number of assailants that attacked him, the description of the assailants that attacked him."

"How would you define his speech?"

"Very clear."

"Is it within…are you trained to observe people who are in pain?"

"Yes."

"What would you say about Mr. Mutchler in that regard?"

"Pain is a quantitative thing for each individual you have to understand. But he wasn't…he was upset more about the wound and what was going to happen to him."

SHAW: "Objection, Your Honor. This is speculation."

JUDGE: "Overruled. You may answer."

YUSKO: "He was more concerned about how his wounds were going to be treated at the hospital and what was going to happen to him then."

MILLER: "When you looked at the wound during the transport, you say you unwrapped it. What can you tell us about the state of the wound or wounds?"

"He had five lacerations. My report would define that the exact locations mainly were on his forearm."

"You're indicating the left forearm, are you not?

"Yes."

"And that was the major wound?"

"All the rest of them were smaller lacerations. All bleeding was fairly controlled, other than just minor oozing of blood, which is just normal."

"What observations, if any, did you make of his clothing?"

"His…he was dressed in a white shirt and black pants with black shoes. He was covered from basically head to toe in blood, both fresh and dry."

"And when you first saw him he had something on his arm, is that correct?"

"Pardon me?"

"You said you saw something on his arm?"

"Yes, I saw a laceration on his…"

"I'm sorry. In terms of clothing or items other than his…"

"He was wrapped up in a white towel and a red plaid shirt underneath the towel. "

"Those were the items that were…"

"There were two items, yes."

"…given to the hospital?"

"Well, they were given to the patient."

"Very well. When you arrived at the hospital, what did you and the patient do?"

"I asked the patient if he would like help in to the hospital. He said, 'no, I can just walk'."

"What observations did you make from the way he negotiated walking from the ambulance?"

"Just fine."

"Didn't need any assistance?"

"No."

"What was the state of the wounds that you described, the arm and hand wounds, in terms of its bleeding when you saw it?"

"Bleeding was controlled at the time with the direct pressure from the towel, which will happen until it's completely clotted off."

"Can you tell us a bit about the location of the blood on his clothing you saw?"

"He was covered from basically head to toe in blood."

"Was there a concentration of blood in one spot more than the other?"

"He was supersaturated from about the abdomen down, but he had blood everywhere."

"Are you certain of colors of the clothing that you describe?"

"As best as I can recall."

"Are you trained in…are you able to tell whether or not…or how much blood appeared?"

"I am taught to guesstimate. There's no set rule for how much blood loss there is."

"OK. And what would you tell the jury."

"I would guess…"

SHAW: "Objection Your Honor."

JUDGE: "I think the jury can assess the weight of it."

SHAW: "Is he going to be permitted to guess?"

JUDGE: "Lay a better foundation."

MILLER: "Tell us about your training then."

SHAW: "He just said that his training permits him to guess."

JUDGE: "Let him answer the question."

MILLER: "Can you tell us about the training in that area?"

YUSKO: "We are taught to…we were given, how would I say, amounts for different articles of clothing if they were saturated with blood to a degree of how much blood it would hold. For example, a pair of jeans, each leg would hold just about 100 to 150cc of the fluid if it were soaked like a sponge. It would hold a certain amount. It's a way of estimating."

"Is that included in your training?"

"Yes."

"Is that offered by the state?"

"Yes."

"Is that part of the paramedic status?"

"Yes."

"All right then, I'll ask what is your estimate of the amount of blood that you saw on his clothing?"

SHAW: "Judge, they may want him to estimate for his job, but in this court he's not permitted to estimate. And that's all his training has qualified him to do."

JUDGE: "Overruled. You may answer the question."

YUSKO: "I would estimate the supersaturation of his blood, from his abdomen down, approximately 200 to 350cc of blood was lost."

MILLER: "And are you saying that was what he lost, or that it was present?"

"I'm sorry. That's how much was present on his clothes, yes."

"Mr. Yusko, one other question. I'd like to discuss the location of the blood that you saw on the clothing and its relationship to the wound on the arm."

"I don't quite understand what…"

"Well, I guess if you could just imagine a shirt and a pair…you've demonstrated on your own body the abdomen down was saturated?"

"Yes."

"And perhaps you could stand and just demonstrate on your person to the jury what, in fact, you mean by where you saw the blood."

"The patient was covered from head to toe, including his face, with blood, both arms, everywhere. But it was concentrated, super concentrated, from about here down."

"You're pointing to a point above your belt line?"

"Yes."

"Belly down?"

"Yes."

"I'm asking you how far down the pants?"

"Right below his knees."

"And the question is where you have any observation about the location of where the blood was on his clothing and the wound itself."

"The blood from his abdomen to his knees would be consistent if…I believe I know what you're asking about his wound. If he was carrying it in a position where he's trying to stabilize it. In other words, it would bleed down. The blood up and on his face is kind of inconsistent."

SHAW: "Judge, I don't know that he's been qualified…"

JUDGE: "Sustained."

MILLER: "Thank you. Those are all the questions I have for Mr. Yusko."

COOKE. "Mr. Yusko, you indicated that, in your approach to the home that you were dispatched to in this case, you waited for the police to be on the scene before actually going in?"

YUSKO: "Yes."

"And that's standard in assault cases isn't it?"

"For that district, yes."

"That's because you don't know whether the scene of the assault was the scene that you're being summoned to or someplace else?"

"And other things, yes."

"It's a matter of your safety primarily?"

"Basically."

"There was nothing specific about this case that required that other than the fact that this was a reported stabbing?"

"Correct."

"You indicated that Mr. Mutchler appeared to be upset about his wounds?"

"Yes."

"And in fact, he was concerned about what was going to happen when he reached the hospital right?"

"Um-hum."

"And the treatment that he was going to receive there?"

"Yes."

"And you had the chance to observe his injuries."

"Yes."

"In fact, you noticed that there were…you described the different lacerations to us."

"Yes."

"In fact, Scott was crying on and off during the time that you had contact with him?"

"Yes."

"Also in your…you treated a number of people who have been stabbed…"

"Yes."

"…in the course of your job, haven't you?"

"Yes."

"And based on your prior experience in that regard, you're able to give us an opinion, aren't you, about whether or not Mr. Mutchler's wounds appeared to be defensive wounds?"

PICKERING: "Objection, Your Honor. Foundation."

JUDGE: "She's laying a foundation."

COOKE: "Do you need me to repeat the question?"

YUSKO: "Yes, please."

"Based on your experience with prior stabbing victims, you're able to give us an opinion, aren't you, about whether or not Scott's wounds appear to be defensive wounds?"

"Yes."

"And what s that opinion?"

"I would say that they…the majority of them were defensive wounds, yes."

"Can you tell the jury what you mean by defensive wounds?"

"I'm trained to recognize defensive wounds as being if you were trying to deflect someone away from you. Injuries would happen on the backside of your arm from that. And that's where his were. The majority of his injuries were on the backside of the arm as if he was deflecting someone away."

"You also indicated that you looked at Mr. Mutchler and you questioned him about other possible injuries?"

"Yes."

"Looking for those?"

"Yes."

"One of the things that you noticed was…it was that he had a ring of blood around his mouth?"

"Yes, dried blood on his face, yes."

"One of the things that you asked him about was how he had been injured?"

"Yes."

"And that's because that's important for you to know to determine where the injuries might be an how you need to treat them?"

"Yes."

"And you indicated in response to Mr. Mutchler's question that he kept changing his story?"

"Yes."

"Let's get specific about that, what he changed. First of all, he changed the location of the convenience store, gas station, wherever that he suffered the wounds."

"Yes."

"Is that right?"

"Well, more specifically, he changed from 102nd Avenue to Federal to somewhere at about 120th Street and Federal. And then later on we determined a gas station at 120th Street and Perry Street."

"So…and those places are really all in the same general vicinity, aren't they?"

"Well, yes, within three or four miles, yes."

"You also indicated that he changed the number of his attackers?"

"Yes."

"In fact, he only indicated to you two different numbers. One time he indicated two, and one time he indicated three."

"I can't remember the exact number of times he indicated different stories."

"I'm sorry. Would it assist you to review your statement in this case?"

"Yeah, sure. I could read it."

"Judge May I approach the witness?"

JUDGE: "You may."

COOKE: "Mr. Yusko, now that you had a chance to review your statement, do you recall what information Mr. Mutchler gave you of that nature?"

YUSKO: "Yeah, he changed his story three times according to that report."

"And in terms of specific numbers of people?"

"It changed twice in those three statements."

"But the specific number of people that he mentioned was either two or three?"

"Yes."

"He didn't mention any other number?"

"According to that report, yes."

"You also indicated that he changed his description of his assailants?"

"Yes."

"And in fact, what he changed was from males to males with dark hair?"

"Yes."

"Let's talk a bit about your guesstimate about the amount of blood that you observed on Mr. Mutchler's clothing. You said that this is a guesstimate?"

"Yes."

"And a guesstimate is, in fact, a very rough approximation, is it not?"

"It's an approximation, yeah. The determination that would change it is the viscosity of different fluids. Blood is the fluid that we use. And we're taught an amount for different types of clothes. And it is nothing but an estimate."

"OK. So…and another thing that would change the amount of fluid that might…that you might estimate about would be the type of material that the clothing was made of, right?"

"That's true, yes."

"Some fabrics would reach the point of super saturation before others would?"

"Yes."

"So that's why it's still a rough approximation?"

"Yes."

"And you indicated that the estimated amount, guesstimated amount, in your mind was 200 to 350cc?"

"Yes."

"Do you recall testifying at a prior hearing in this case?"

"Yes."

"Do you remember what your approximation was at that time?"

"No, I don't."

"Would it refresh your memory to look at your testimony from that?"

"Yes, it would."

"Judge, may I approach the witness again?"

"You may."

"Mr. Yusko, what was your prior estimate at the other hearing in this case about the amount of blood that you observed on Mr. Mutchler's clothing?"

"200 to 300cc."

"Thank you, Mr. Yusko, I don't have anymore questions."

JUDGE: "Redirect?"

MILLER: "Mr. Yusko, concerning the wounds that you observed, your training wouldn't permit you to tell us how in fact they were inflicted, from which angle, or which side?"

YUSKO: "I don't get specific enough to talking angles and stuff like that, no."

"Or the wound on the hand, whether it came from the front or the back?"

"No, I'm not trained to."

"While you've said defensive wounds to the arm, you don't know for sure that's defensive wounds."

SHAW: "Objection Your Honor. He's leading his witness."

JUDGE: "Sustained."

MILLER: "Can you tell us about the forearm wound in your earlier testimony?"

YUSKO: "Other than it was a laceration to the backside of the wound -- back side of the arm. Sorry."

"Thank you. We have no other questions. May this witness be excused?"

JUDGE: "He may. You may step down. We're going to take a 15-minute recess."

A recess was taken at 10:25 a.m. and the trial resumed at 10:40 a.m. out of the presence of the jury and on the record.

SHAW: "Judge, I wanted to make a record. The argument I made at the bench after Mr. Miller's opening statement, we talked about how complete his case is. And in my opinion, that opened the door for us to cross examine witnesses on the absence of DNA testing and the late testing on blood comparisons that was discussed on…it was Friday, I guess, when we received from the prosecution lab evidence.

"My position is we're getting the worst of both cases and now it's been even made worse because he's telling the jury how complete their case is, and that's just not the truth. And your previous rulings have denied us the opportunity to point out to the jury where their evidence is incomplete in those two areas. And that's bad enough. But now, they're getting to talk about how great it all is, and I think the Court has to set us free to talk about deficiencies in their evidence at this point because the balance has been loaded against us now."

MILLER: "Your Honor."

SHAW: "You don't need to point out that that's totally inconsistent. May I just add, that the reference was to the 'painstaking effort they made in collecting evidence and preserving it.' "

JUDGE: "I am not sure that there was a reference to how thorough and complete the investigation itself or total was. It was just their efforts."

SHAW: "That's not what I heard. I don't see where it's consistent to the position we've taken."

JUDGE: "I think the record is just as clear as a bell by if I just say denied."

SHAW: "If you did say denied, now is that what you're saying?"

JUDGE: "I think I'm going to continue to say denied. I mean, I guess my patience isn't infinite. I guess judges are supposed to have infinite patience. Mine is not. I'm sorry.

"Denied. There was one other thing I wanted to…oh, let me clarify. I will clarify, not in the presence of the jury, my ruling with regard to what was referred to as estimation of amounts of blood.

"I look upon that as a 701 situation. And he was cross-examined on it. It's not a 702 issue. I think that under 701, lay people can express similar opinions that you may call guesstimates or estimations or whatever you want. It's a 701 issue. All right, anything further?"

SHAW: "So the court is saying that lay people could estimate to the number of cc that someone had blood on their clothing?"

JUDGE: "The amount, and refer to it in…you know, some people think America is still the only place that talks about quarts and things like that. We are not on the decimal system. Some people talk about cc. I don't know anything about cc. I went to school so long ago that they didn't teach me all this decimal stuff.

"I'm still having trouble with counting the money situation. So yes, they may use whatever terms they think are appropriate in expressing opinions about the amount of liquid in a pair of clothing. They probably all…and the reason for that is I think we probably all in our lives, I probably more than others, frequently spill things on my clothing and drip on my ties and things like that. I think I'm capable, as a lay person, of estimating some amount of that liquid that has fallen in those places."

SHAW: "Well, I mean, I disagree."

JUDGE: "I understand."

SHAW: "We also…the Court indicated that it was going to rule on medical privileges at an appropriate time."

JUDGE: "Yes, I…"

SHAW: "It's too late now, and I don't think that the Court should make its ruling that way because you're sort of compelled then after every witness has testified to find that the privilege wasn't waived, or we're going to have a mistrial."

JUDGE: "I'm going to make it easy for you. I will now… I've already made this ruling. I'm going to remake it for all of the reasons set forth in the People's memorandum of law on the doctor/patient privilege submitted in open court on April 8. Your objection is overruled with regard to the medical privilege. There isn't one. Of course, I don't think I need to specifically say that there is no privilege to a medical technician. But even when we get to the people who might clearly be subject to the privilege, for all the reasons set forth in this document, your motion is denied."

COOKE: "Judge, my problem with that is that the law requires you to look as to the people who clearly Mr. Mutchler would have had medical privileges with: nurses, doctors. The law requires you to look not only at statements that Scott Mutchler made to them, but also at observations that they made. And looking at the district attorney's memorandum breaks things down that specifically…"

JUDGE: "Well, I've heard all that evidence, and I find that the record is clear to me. And I think my ruling is clear to an appellate court. All right. Ready for the jury?"

MILLER: "Yes, Your Honor."

I leaned back and closed my eyes. The years that had passed hadn't erased the painful scars we all were living with. How did Scott ever put himself in a position to face this ordeal? What happened that night? I couldn't help but think if Scott had knocked on their door, it would have been opened, and he would have been asked in. Something wasn't right with all of this.

My thoughts drifted back to how terrified I was the first day of trial when I had to appear on the stand. The prosecution had called me as one of its first witnesses. I felt this was a trick to try to show the jury that I was a mother who was against my son. It worked.

The waiting was maddening. I could barely stand being out of the house, let alone in the courthouse with all these people everywhere. I was glad the detectives from Louisville had compassion for what my family was going through. They surrounded me in a horseshoe so no one could get close to me.

They were talking quietly among themselves. Dr. Schmidt, the physician who had taken care of Scott's wounds in the emergency room, was standing close to us. As I watched his nervous mannerisms, I could feel he wanted in on the policemen's conversation. I could feel the tension building. I watched him closely. I watched his jerky movements. I braced myself for what I knew was coming.

All of a sudden he blurted, "Yeah, I hope they fry him."

I couldn't stand anymore. I lunged at Schmidt, but Detective Ragulsky grabbed him by the back of the neck and took him quickly away from me. One of the detectives pulled out a pad and began writing everything down that was taking place. I was screaming at him.

"You're supposed to be a doctor preserving life, not hoping it's taken away."

I couldn't control myself. The detectives made their circle around me tighter so no one else could get close. I looked all around. Dear God in Heaven, why is this all happening? Why?

JUDGE: "Mr. Miller, next witness."

MILLER: "People would call Steve Meyer. Good morning, sir. What's your relationship to Scott Mutchler, Mr. Meyer?"

STEVE: "Stepfather."

"Is Mr. Mutchler present in the courtroom?"

"Yes."

"Where? Would you indicate where he is please."

"The right hand side."

"How long have you been married to Scott's mother?"

"About a year and a half."

"Sir, were you present on September 10 when Scott Mutchler came to the home with Mrs. Meyer?"

"Yes."

"And do you remember the approximate time that they appeared in the home that evening for the first time?"

"Probably around…probably around 7:30, somewhere in there."

"Did you have occasion to observe Scott Mutchler, what he was wearing at that time?"

"Yes."

"And do you remember what that clothing was?"

"I really don't remember exactly. It was just normal clothing, jeans, tennis shoes, and shirt."

"Did he remain in that clothing later?"

"I believe he changed, took a shower and changed.

"Did you…were you present with him in an automobile trip from the home to another location?"

"Yes."

"And approximately what time did that take place?"

"Probably between 8:30 and 9."

"And do you recall the destination of that drive?"

"Yes, it was to a convenience store in Louisville right off the turnpike at McCaslin Boulevard."

"And who was it that determined that was the destination?"

"I believe he did."

"Scott Mutchler?"

"Yes."

"And what happened when you got to the convenience store? Is it off, did you say McCaslin Boulevard?"

"Right. We just dropped him off. And when we pulled away, my wife noticed that he was on the phone."

"Were you present at a time later that evening when Scott Mutchler returned?"

"Yes."

"Approximately what time?"

"I'd say between 11:15 and 11:20."

"Sometime after that, did you have occasion to look outside the home and see…well, did you look outside the front of the house?"

"Yes."

"Did you see an automobile there that had not been there at an earlier time?"

"Yes, I did."

"What automobile did you see? How would you describe…"

"Well, it was dark-colored sedan, a newer model. I'm not that sure on makes and models, but it looked like a nice car."

"You didn't see what brand it was or what exact model it was?"

"No, I didn't."

"And were you present when the ambulance personnel were at the home?"

"Yes."

"When they left?"

"Yes."

"And at or near the time that they left, were you present when you saw or heard reference to any keys, automobile keys?"

"Yes, I was there."

"Where did that take place?"

"In our kitchen."

"And what can you tell us about what you saw concerning keys?"

"My wife asked Scott."

"I'm asking what…what you saw happen, if anything, involving the keys. Not what people said, but what you saw."

"I just saw the keys come out of his pocket."

"And where did the keys end up?"

"In my wife's hand."

"Did you get a chance to look at the clothing that Scott Mutchler had on when you left the home around 8:30 to 9?"

"Yes."

"And did you get a chance to see the clothing that he had on when he returned after 11? I'm not sure if you said the time."

"I thought it was the same clothing."

"Your witness Mr. Shaw."

SHAW: "Mr. Meyer, did you go to the hospital in the late evening hours of September 10th?"

MILLER: "Beyond the scope. The scope on direct is very limited, and this is well outside."

SHAW: "I have one question about the hospital. And if they will let me ask it, we won't have to bring Mr. Meyer back."

MILLER: "I'll hear the question, but we may have another objection."

JUDGE: "All right."

SHAW: "You went to the hospital the late evening hours of September 10th, didn't you?"

STEVE: "Yes."

"The scene there was pretty chaotic, wasn't it?"

"Well, I don't go to the hospital a lot, but it seemed like there was some law enforcement people there. I don't know if I'd say it was chaotic, but there were things going on."

"All right. Scott was at your home after 11 when he arrived home injured until he left with the emergency people for approximately 10 to 15 minutes, isn't that correct?"

"I'd say that's about right, yes."

"And during that time, you had opportunity to observe whether or not he seemed to be in pain, didn't you?"

"Yes."

"How are you employed, sir?"

"Pardon me?"

"How are you employed?"

"I'm a coach."

"How long have you been doing that?"

"Ten years."

"Do you think that your experience has qualified you to talk about whether or not somebody is in pain?"

"I think I'd know if they're in pain or if they're not."

"How about Scott when he arrived home after 11 on the night of September 10? Did he appear to you to be in pain?"

"Yes, he did."

"Why do you say that?"

"He was just fidgety and jumpy."

"Is that a symptom of pain you've observed before in your work?"

"Yes. I think most people when they get injured they don't know the extent of their injuries or how severe their injuries are. I think there's a doubt in their mind and it scares them. And they might do things they normally don't, as far as body reactions and things like that."

"You drove a car to Louisville, didn't you? It was your vehicle?"

"Yes."

"And was Mrs. Meyer sitting in the front seat?"

"Yes."

"And Scott sat in the back?"

"Yes."

"OK. In the course of that car ride Scott said that he was going there because…"

PICKERING: "Objection, hearsay."

JUDGE: "Sustained."

SHAW: "Hearsay from the defendant? The objection is that's inadmissible?"

JUDGE: "The objection is sustained."

SHAW: "When Mr. Mutchler got out of the car in Louisville he didn't have anything with him, did he?"

STEVE: "Not to my knowledge."

"You didn't see any sort of objects in his hands?"

"No."

"Did you see where he went when he got out of the car?"

"He just walked up towards the door. And then as we pulled away, my wife…"

PICKERING: "Objection, hearsay."

SHAW: "Well, he's already testified that she said that she saw him at the phone or something."

JUDGE: "Is that right?"

SHAW: "Do you remember roughly what time it was when Mr. Mutchler returned home, then?"

STEVE: "It was when he returned home?"

"Yes, sir."

"I would say 11:15 or 11:20."

"Just before that, just before he walked in the front door, you vaguely recall hearing a car door slam and a car drive off, don't you?"

"Yes."

"And right after that Mrs. Meyer said…"

PICKERING: "Objection, hearsay."

JUDGE: "Sustained."

SHAW: "That's clearly an excited utterance. It happened right after the events. I'll be happy to lay a foundation."

JUDGE: "Well, she's going to testify, is she not?"

SHAW: "Maybe so. But it corroborates her account of what she said, if he said she said it as well."

JUDGE: "Well, overruled."

SHAW: "Judge, I'd like to explain to the Court why I think that's an excited utterance. I don't know whether you want to take the jury out or not, but I can cite the…"

JUDGE: "I understand. And the objection is overruled."

PICKERING: "Your Honor, my problem is, I'm not sure how he can get excited over a car door slamming."

JUDGE: "That's not the excited one. Go ahead. Ask the question."

SHAW: "What did Mrs. Meyer say?"

STEVE: "She said that…I believe she said something to the effect that, 'Did you hear that? Scott didn't get a car. Somebody dropped him off.' "

"On direct examination, you indicated that you looked out the window at some point and saw a vehicle there?"

"Yes."

"And you reported that to Mrs. Meyer at some point that evening, didn't you, before…"

"Yes, I believe I did. I'm not sure, I wasn't…I can't remember if I looked out of my own curiosity, but I did look and see a car."

"OK. And do you recall when you reported to your wife what you'd seen?"

"Do I know when I reported it?"

"Yes sir."

"Just as soon as I saw it. I don't know when exactly that was."

"All right. Thank you."

JUDGE: "Are there more questions."

SHAW: "No."

MILLER: "No redirect."

JUDGE: "You may step down. Call your next witness."

MILLER: "Yes, Your Honor, the People would call Eve Meyer."

"Your Honor, before I begin, I would ask that sequestration of witnesses be followed here. I just noted that Mr. Meyer is still in the courtroom and is a witness and a potential witness."

JUDGE: "He testified. He may stay."

MILLER: "I'm saying that he may testify again, It's been indicated…"

SHAW: "I think we were all done. The only one was on the conversation in the car going to Louisville. We don't plan on recalling him."

JUDGE: "All right. He may stay."

"They're ready for Mrs. Meyer."

I heard the words, but I couldn't move. Detective Ragulsky came over and knelt down beside me.

"Eve, it's going to be OK. I'll be sitting right at the prosecutor's table. Just look at me if you need reassurance." My eyes were welling with tears. How was I going to get through this? Detective Ragulsky helped me to my feet.

I walked into the courtroom. My eyes searched for Scott. He turned to me and watched as I walked to the front of the courtroom. I felt like I was going to pass out.

My eyes met Scott's. He looked at me and smiled. He was trying so hard to let me know it was going to be OK. All eyes were staring at me as I walked toward the front of the courtroom. I felt so hot…I was sure I was going to pass out. I glanced at the jury and then the witness stand. The walk to the witness stand seemed endless…everything was moving in slow motion. I took my seat on the witness stand and stared at my son. He sat there trying to send his mental strength to me.

MILLER: "Mrs. Meyer, how are you related to the defendant?"

"I'm Scott's mom."

"If I may approach the bench very briefly, Your Honor?"

JUDGE: "You may proceed."

MILLER: "Very well. Mrs. Meyer, how do you feel about being a witness for the prosecution in your son's case?"

EVE: "I don't understand your question."

"How do you feel about being called by the prosecution to answer questions about your son's case involving murder charges?"

"Well, I feel, I don't understand what you're asking me to answer. How do you mean, how do I...how do I feel?"

"Mrs. Meyer, do you remember living on Van Buren Court in Louisville?"

"Yes."

"Do you remember that address?"

"No, I don't."

"Do you remember being in a cul-de-sac on Van Buren Court?"

"Yes."

"For what period did you live in that neighborhood, if you know?"

"I do not know the length, exactly, of time."

"Do you know what...for what period of time you lived on Van Buren Court?"

"No. I'm sorry. I don't recall."

JUDGE: "Mrs. Meyer, could you speak into the mike there because we're having trouble hearing you."

MILLER: "Mrs. Meyer, it's true, isn't it, that your son, Scott Mutchler, was in jail in Adams County?"

EVE: "Yes, that's correct."

"Do you remember those dates with any specificity?"

"I don't remember the exact dates."

SHAW: "Judge, I'm going to object to this. My understanding to the rule is leading questions are permissible if that's necessary to develop the testimony of the witness. And I haven't seen any foundation for this. Mrs. Meyer is an adult. As far as I know, she's competent. And I think he can ask direct questions without leading the witness."

JUDGE: "Well, you don't need to lead her right now. But you can ask non-leading questions now. And then, if I determine later, you may ask leading questions."

MILLER: "Do you remember the time that you picked up your son? Or perhaps the better…the time you arrived at home after picking him up?"

EVE: "This is when he was released from jail? Is that what you're asking?"

"Yes."

"I think, I believe it was around 7:30, somewhere in that area."

"That you arrived home?"

"That I arrived home."

"Do you remember what he had on when you picked him up?"

"No, I really don't."

"Did he remain in that clothing for a time later that night?"

"No, he did not."

"Did he change his clothing?"

"Yes."

"May I approach the witness, Your Honor?"

JUDGE: "You may."

MILLER: "Mrs. Meyer, I'm going to show you two items, one from a bag marked People's Exhibit 1, another from a bag marked People's Exhibit 2. Do you need to examine these clothing…these articles anymore closely to determine what they are?"

EVE: "I recognize the pants as being the pants that Scott wore, but I don't recall the shirt."

"When you say you recall the pants he wore when?"

"When he got changed that night."

"Later on the 10th?"

"Yes."

"Do you recognize this shirt at all?"

"No, I don't."

"You don't recognize it as one of your son's?"

"I don't recognize that."

"You don't recall seeing it that night?"

"No, I'm sorry."

"May I approach the witness again Your Honor?"

JUDGE: "You may."

MILLER: "I would like to show you items 5 and 6, and ask the witness if you recognize those?"

EVE: "Those look like Scott's wrestling shoes, yes."

"Do you remember seeing them on the night of September 10?"

"I believe those were the ones that he had on."

"At a time later that night?"

"After he changed."

"After he changed. Did you, concerning the shoes, say they were what kind of shoes? I just maybe didn't catch your answer."

"A wrestling-type shoe. I think that's what they are."

"Is this something he competed in or used?"

"They're something he liked."

"The clothes that he had on before…let me show you two photographs. If I may approach the bench again, Your Honor, these are…"

JUDGE: "You may."

MILLER: "Would you take a look at the clothing depicted in those two photographs? I'll ask you if you recognize that clothing."

EVE: "Um hum, I do recognize them."

"Whose clothing is that?"

"Well, they appear to be Scott's, yes."

JUDGE: "You know, the only thing I could hear, really, today was that rattling paper. So speak as loudly as you can."

EVE: "OK."

MILLER: "Do those pictures appear to be taken in a particular location in your home?"

"Yes."

"Where is that?"

"In Scott's bedroom."

"OK. And did…"

SHAW: "Mr. Miller, can I see the pictures?"

MILLER: "Surely." (The photographs were shown to Mr. Shaw). "Do you know whether or not those are the clothes that he had on in Boulder that he changed?"

EVE: "I really don't recall what he was wearing when I picked him up in Boulder."

"These pictures don't do anything to remind you of that?"

"I'm sorry. They don't." (The attorneys conferred with one another).

"Mrs. Meyer, were you present in an automobile trip that was taken from your home to another location at around 8:30 to 9 September 10th?"

"Yes, I was."

"Who else was present?"

"My husband."

"And who else?"

"And Scott."

"OK. And where was...do you know...what was the destination where the trip ended up?"

"At a convenience store at the Louisville exit off of the Boulder Turnpike."

"And who determined to...or who determined that destination or that location?"

"Scott did."

"Before being...before going to the Adams County Jail, did your son own or have a car of his own?"

"Not that I was...well, not that I saw, physically saw, no."

"Do you remember the time that he was dropped at the convenience store?"

"Approximately 9 that evening."

"Was there some agreement or understanding or statement even about when he was expected home?"

"Yes, he was supposed to be home by 11 that evening."

"Whose request was that?"

"My husband's and mine."

"Mrs. Meyer, did you receive a phone call from your son later that night after he was dropped at the convenience store in Louisville?"

"Yes, I did."

"And about…do you remember the time exact or…"

"It was about one minute before 11. It was right around 11."

"11 p.m.?"

"That's right."

"Do you remember the conversation that you had with your son?"

"Yes, I do."

"Let me ask first about his voice. What do you remember about his voice?"

"What do you mean about his voice?"

"Soft? Low? Loud? Harsh?"

"Scott…Scott…Scott was…had his normal tone of voice with me."

"Shortly after that phone call, did you see Scott in your home?"

"Yes."

"And about what time was it that you saw him?"

"It was between 11:10 and 11:15."

"Did he…the clothing he had on when you saw him at 11:15 or so, was it the same clothing he had on…"

"Yes."

"…when you dropped him off?"

"Yes, it was."

"Did it include the black pants and black shoes in your memory?"

"Yes."

"What about the black shirt?"

"For some reason, I felt that he had worn a button down shirt that evening."

"You don't…you remember the pants and shoes, but not the shirt?"

"Yes."

"All right. Did he have something else, some other article…did he have some other thing on his person when you saw him?"

"Not that I recall."

"OK. Did you, after seeing him, give him anything from home?"

"Scott came in and was extreme…very bloody. He was spurting blood. And when he came to my bedroom, I jumped up and grabbed him. He said, 'Mom, help me. I've been stabbed.' I got up and took him to the kitchen. I grabbed something from the linen closet to try to help stop the bleeding."

"It's true, isn't it, that you called 911?"

"That's right."

"Did emergency personnel respond shortly thereafter?"

"Very quickly."

"Did you see him leave with emergency personnel?"

"I saw them walk down the hallway, yes, towards the front door."

"Did you have contact with him before he left concerning some keys?"

"I'm sorry?" I looked at Scott again. He smiled and nodded. It was getting harder and harder to continue up on this stand.

"Did you have contact with your son about some keys before he left?"

"Yes."

"As he was leaving?"

"Yes, I did."

"And did you ask him for his keys?"

"Yes, I did."

"Did he indicate or provide you with the keys?"

"He said, 'They're in my pocket'."

"I'm going to approach the witness, if I may, Your Honor, with what's been marked as People's Exhibit 72."

JUDGE: "You may."

MILLER: "And if you need to take them out of the bag to look at them more personally."

EVE: "I wouldn't know if those were the keys or not. I would have no idea."

"So your son provided or gave you a set of keys for a car?"

"Yes."

"For his car?"

"Yes."

"And that was your understanding?"

"That was my understanding."

"Did you see a car in front of the house thereafter, or perhaps even before the keys were…"

"I'm sorry?"

"You're not hearing me? I'm sorry. Did you see a car in front of your house that you had not seen earlier that evening?"

"I had not, but my husband had."

"Did you later see a car?"

"Yes, I did."

"Did you later drive a car?"

"Yes, I did."

"And did the keys that Scott Mutchler gave you operate the car?"

"Yes they did."

"You went to the hospital after the ambulance left?"

"That's correct."

"In the car, keys for which had been provided by your son?"

"That's correct."

"Did you see any police personnel present at the parking lot or at the hospital when you arrived?"

"I'm sorry?" My mind kept reflecting back to the night in the emergency room. Everything was becoming such a fog. I looked at Scott again. He gave me his reassuring smile and nodded slowly: It's OK, Mom.

"Did you see any police personnel at the hospital parking lot when you arrived?"

"In the parking lot?"

"Well, take it there first. Did you see any in the parking lot?"

"I don't recall."

"Immediately?"

"There were police that came with the paramedics to our home. They were in our home."

"And did you see one or more of them also at the hospital?"

"Yes, I did. I saw them inside the emergency room."

"Did you indicate to any of those personnel, including the one you had seen in your home, the car you had driven to the hospital?"

"After I was at the hospital for a few moments, I had stepped outside waiting for my husband. And one of the police officers there asked me to point out the car that I had driven to the hospital, so I did."

"And you did?"

"Yes."

"Did you point out the car that you had driven?"

"Yes. It was under a street lamp."

"That was the car that keys for which had been provided by your son, is that correct?"

"Yes."

"Then at some time later, did you provide the keys that you had used to operate the car to Detective Ragulsky?"

"Not that day."

"I see. So, sometime later?"

"Yes. Yes."

"Do you know car models?"

"No, I don't."

"Did you know the kind of car you were in?"

"No, I didn't."

"Did you notice anything about its interior that was significant?"

"There was a cellular phone inside the car."

"Your Honor, those are my questions of Mrs. Meyer."

JUDGE: "All right. Any cross-examination?"

SHAW: "Mrs. Meyer, when you got home with your son Scott at around 7:30 on the 10th, the first thing he does is shower and have a meal, correct?"

"Well, he had his meal first and then he showered, yes."

"OK. And talk with his younger brother some?"

"Yes, he did."

"Were you there with him the whole time that evening before he went to Louisville?"

"No, I wasn't with him physically, no. Not in the same room all the time, no."

"How long a period was it you would say that you were home between the arrival from Boulder and leaving for Louisville?"

"An hour and a half."

"Anyway you can characterize how much of that hour and a half period you were watching your son, your son Scott, or were there with him?"

"I really wasn't watching him. He wanted to spend time with his brother, and they were catching up with each other. And so I really wasn't watching him."

"Do you know…did he make any phone calls while he was home there that night before he left for Louisville?"

"Not that I'm aware of."

"Would it have been possible for him to do that during that hour and a half period, or would you have noticed? Were you always near a phone?"

"It would have been possible. I was in my office working, but I just didn't notice him using the phone."

"Who picked the time to leave for Louisville?"

"It really wasn't a time picked. After Scott had dinner, took a shower and then said 'OK, I'm ready'."

"So it was Scott's desire to go to Louisville?"

"Yes."

"What did he tell you his purpose was in wanting to go to Louisville?"

PICKERING: "Objection, hearsay."

JUDGE: "Objection sustained."

SHAW: "It's to show the defendant's state of mind as intent to…concerning where he was going."

JUDGE: "The objection is sustained."

SHAW: "Judge, the exception to hearsay rule I'm referring to is 803(3), then-existing mental, emotional or physical condition."

PICKERING: "If we can approach the bench?"

JUDGE: "No, the objection is sustained. Go on."

SHAW: "After you reached the convenience store, Mrs. Meyer, what did you see your son do?"

"Outside there was a telephone booth on that convenience store and Scott was on the telephone speaking with someone."

"You watched him do that?"

"Yes, I did."

"Did he take anything with him, any objects, when he got out of the car?"

"No. He didn't even have a jacket."

"Next you heard from your son was around 11 p.m. that night, is that correct?"

"That's correct."

"How long a phone conversation was that?"

"It was very short."

"Can you estimate in terms of minutes or seconds on…"

"He said to me, 'Mom…"

PICKERING: "Objection hearsay."

JUDGE: "Yeah, sustained."

I can't believe it. Why don't they want to hear what happened? Don't they want to hear the truth? Why won't this judge let me tell them what happened that evening? None of this is making sense. Don't they want to decide what happened based on the facts? I kept looking at Scott's attorney, then Scott.

SHAW: "Just the length of the phone call."

EVE: "It was very short. It was maybe a minute."

"Do you want to look at the clock and estimate?"

"Yes."

"See the second hand above the jury?"

"I just want to run through what was said in my mind."

"All right, go ahead."

"Maybe ten seconds. I thought it was longer. Maybe ten seconds, 15 seconds."

"OK. Now, were you in bed when you received that call?"

"Yes, I was."

"And did you stay there, then, until you next heard from your son Scott?"

"Yes, I did."

"What was the next thing you heard from your son, Scott, then?"

PICKERING: "Objection, hearsay."

JUDGE: "Sustained."

SHAW: "When did you next hear from your son Scott?"

EVE: “I was waiting for Scott to come home and I heard a car pull up outside. I heard car doors slam. I heard a car speed away, and then Scott came through the door.”

“OK. When did you see…what did you say after you heard those sounds you described?”

“I turned to my husband and I said, ‘Steve, Scott doesn't have a car. Someone just dropped him off’.”

“What was the next thing you heard after you heard the car sounds that you've described?”

“After the car sped away?”

“Yes, ma'am.”

“There was a pause, and then the front door slammed. I remained in bed. I was waiting for Scott to come in. He came to my bedroom doorway and said, ‘Mom…“

MILLER: “Objection.”

JUDGE: “The objection is sustained.”

Damn it! This idiot won’t let me tell them what happened. Why was this being allowed to happen? Why can’t I get out what happened that night? I looked over at Scott again. He knew I was frustrated. I wanted to tell everyone what really happened that night and the prosecution wasn’t going to let me. Why?

SHAW: “Probably an excited utterance, Judge.”

PICKERING: “We probably would object, Your Honor.”

JUDGE: “Go on.”

SHAW: “The objection is sustained?”

JUDGE: “Yes, go on.”

SHAW: “So you hear him say something and you get out of bed?”

EVE: “Yes.”

“Did he…did you see him then?”

“Yes, I did.”

“What if anything did you see on his arms?”

“All I saw was he was bleeding quite a bit. There was a trail of blood all along my…I have very light blue carpet in my home, and there was blood everywhere.”

"Now, at some point in the course of events there in your home, then you ask Scott for his car keys; is that correct?"

"This is prior to him leaving with the paramedics."

"OK. And what made you think that there…that he had a car there?"

"My husband had told me that there was a car, in fact, outside."

"What made you think that that was Scott's?"

"Because that's why Scott left, to go get a car."

PICKERING: "Objection, Your Honor. Hearsay. Move to strike. Nonresponsive."

JUDGE: "Overruled."

SHAW: "Those are my questions of Mrs. Meyer."

MILLER: "Just a moment please. Mrs. Meyer, where is the…where are the phones…or where is the phone located in your home?"

EVE: "There are two. There are three phones located on the first floor. One is in my office, one is in our bedroom, and one is in the kitchen."

"In the time when your son was home between 7:30 and 9…actually 7:30 and sometime…"

"Eight, right, that's correct."

"Did you see him on the telephone?"

"I did not see him use the phone, no."

"All right, did you ever hear him on the phone?"

"No, I did not. I was back in my office at one point that evening."

"My only other question, Mrs. Meyer, is that concerning the car door slam, are you clear on hearing one door slam?"

"No, I'm just…I am clear, yes, on hearing at least one car door slam. And I'm clear on a car speeding away that night."

"Thank you. I have no further questions."

"You may step down."

As I left the witness stand I approached the table where Scott and his attorney sat. I stopped and looked at Scott's attorney.

"I had more to say!"

Shaw glared at me.

"I said, 'I had more to say.' " He took his eyes away from mine. Scott looked at me and smiled.

MILLER: “Your Honor, the witness has asked if she is excused from her subpoena. The people would certainly do that. I don't know about the defense.”

SHAW: “We can't yet. We have Mrs. Meyer under subpoena. We may need her, so I'll be in touch with her concerning arrangements to testify, but she shouldn’t stay in the courtroom.”

I closed the transcript and wiped away the tears that were flowing down my face. I couldn’t understand then, and I understood less now. Why didn’t they want the whole truth to be told? Why did it have to come down to win or lose with these men? Didn’t they realize they were playing with our lives? I couldn’t imagine men that were so driven by their own self-serving purposes. If they truly felt Scott was guilty, why did they care if the jury heard all of the truth? There were so many questions with no answers.

I looked around at all the families that had gathered on the beach. I watched the mothers and fathers laughing and playing with their children. “Hold tight onto those little ones,” I thought. “You’ll never know when your children will be snatched away…you’ll never know when your lives will suddenly change. Hold on tight to them…keep them close.”

I shuddered, struggling against the anger inside me, and opened the transcript again.

JUDGE: “Ready for your next witness?”

MILLER: “People call Detective Ragulsky. How are you employed?”

RAGULSKY: “I’m a detective for the Louisville Police Department.”

“And how long have you been there?”

“Been with them almost nine years now.”

“So you were employed in that capacity on the…late on the 10th of September and in the early morning hours of the 11th of September, 1991?”

“Yes sir, I was.”

“And do you consider yourself a person that’s on duty 24 hours a day?”

"Yes, sir."

"Did you get a call at a time when you're not normally working your shift on, I think, the 11th of September?"

"Yes, I did."

"Tell us about your first contact or anyone else's first contact with what has been...what we refer to as the Mutchler case or Scharf case?"

"On September 11th at about 3:20 in the morning, I received a staff page, which is a radio transmission to a pager advising me of what was known as a double homicide that occurred on Van Buren Court."

"Is that in Louisville, Colorado?"

"Yes sir, it is."

"Was there any...was any other details in the page?"

"None that I can recall."

"What was your next source of information from any law enforcement officer or dispatcher about that incident?"

"A few minutes later, I got a call at home from Sergeant Don Berg of the Louisville Police Department."

"What did Sergeant Berg add to what had been outlined to you in the page, the staff page?"

"Initially, Sergeant Berg stated that he and other Louisville officers did respond to an address on Van Buren Court in Louisville at the request of Broomfield Police Department to check and see if the owner or the occupant of that home had given his permission for another man to be driving his car. So Sergeant Berg further stated that Broomfield police was in contact with the young man at St. Anthony's North Hospital who was..."

"You said Broomfield, or did you say Louisville or..."

"Broomfield police was in contact with the young man at St. Anthony's North Hospital in Westminster. The young man was suffering from some kind of wounds, and he had been driving that car...or the car that Broomfield was questioning about. Sergeant Berg stated that upon checking the residence, they were unable to get anybody to answer the door. Further checking, they noticed blood on the floor."

"Did Sergeant Berg give you a name? Do you recall him giving you a name of the person that Broomfield was in contact with at the hospital?"

"Yes. That was Scott Mutchler."

"Did that name at that time mean anything to you in terms of any prior knowledge or contact?"

"No, sir."

"What did you do next? What contacts, if any, did you make or what others were made with you following the Berg conversation?"

"Shortly after concluding my conversation with Sergeant Berg, I received a telephone call from Lieutenant Don Glass of Louisville Police Department. Lieutenant Glass verified the information that Sergeant Berg had given me. I was instructed to respond to St. Anthony's North Hospital and conduct follow-up investigation into the matter at that time."

"Did you make your way to the hospital?"

"Yes, I did."

"Do you remember from your reports, or from your memory rather, what time you arrived at the hospital?"

"At about 3:44 in the morning."

"What was your first law enforcement contact at the scene at or near the hospital?"

"Broomfield police officer Scott…I believe his name is LaFleur. He was in the parking lot at St. Anthony's North Hospital. I contacted him and got a basic rundown that he had been dispatched to St. Anthony's North Hospital in reference to a reported assault; that the victim of the assault was in the hospital now and that LaFleur was watching the car that the victim reportedly had driven and that Detectives Hartmann and Schuler of the Broomfield Police Department were at St. Anthony's North Hospital."

"What if anything did you know from any contacts about the presence or absence of Westminster officers at the scene?"

"When I got to the hospital, Westminster police officers were present."

"Did you, perhaps not initially, but…may I approach the witness Your Honor?"

JUDGE: "You may."

MILLER: "I'm jumping ahead here a bit perhaps. Take a look at what's been marked People's Exhibit 4. Read it over first before I ask you the next question. Let me know when you summarized it or reviewed it."

"Do you recognize, notwithstanding, the fact that it's a copy, your own signature on there?"

RAGULSKY: "Yes, I do."

"Where does that appear?"

"It appears on a block that says signature of person receiving."

"OK. And what…is there a time attached or near that signature?"

"Yes. The time is oh-4:48."

"OK. Do you recall what happened at that time as reflected by the report from your own memory?"

"At that time, I advised Westminster police officers that I would be assuming custody of Scott Mutchler and I signed for him."

"Now, I'd like to address your attention to the time between your arrival, let's say inside the hospital as opposed to when you saw Officer LaFleur and the time when you signed the document at 4:48. What period of time were you inside the hospital before you took custody of Mr. Mutchler?"

"Approximately an hour."

"And now, can you review what you learned from other officers in that period of time that added, if anything, to what you already knew or that gave more detail to what you had heard?"

"Initially, I spoke with Detective Hartmann of the Broomfield Police Department. Hartmann explained that he had been sent to St. Anthony's Hospital to assess Broomfield…I'm sorry, to assist Broomfield Detective Schuler."

"Hartmann provided me information saying that Schuler was called out to investigate a reported assault that occurred on 120th, I believe the intersection was at 120th and Perry at a convenience store gas station-type building."

"In investigating or trying to investigate this, Detective Schuler was talking with Scott Mutchler. Schuler told Hartmann who told me that Schuler's feelings were that Mr. Mutchler was less than accurate in describing the location of the attack or any other details of the attack."

"Were you aware…did they relay to you their efforts to discover or detect the crime…assault crime scene?"

"Yes sir. Detective Hartmann said that he had assigned Broomfield officers to transverse the 120th corridor looking for the sight of the attack. Hartmann further said that when they couldn't find the location of the attack, that he had instructed Broomfield officers to expand their search to all areas of Broomfield.

"Was there…did Detective Hartmann relate to you a call that he had with John Gutterman?"

"Yes sir, he did. Detective Hartmann explained to me that he had a telephone call while at St. Anthony's Hospital from a bondsman named Jonathan Gutterman. Gutterman explained to Hartmann that he and…Gutterman had posted bond for Scott Mutchler earlier in the day on September 10th."

"Detective Hartmann said that Mr. Gutterman explained to him that Scott had been recently released from jail. Gutterman had received a call from Mr. Mutchler's mother, Eve Meyer. From what Hartmann told me, Eve Meyer told Jonathan Gutterman that Scott was in possession of a car that did not belong to him and that she felt that Scott was possibly involved in a crime. She further described to Mr. Gutterman, the bondsman, the injuries that Scott Mutchler had received."

"Did you have a conversation with Detective Schuler at the hospital?"

"Yes, I did."

"Before you took custody of the defendant?"

"Yes sir."

"And did he relate to you anything about a phone conversation with Mrs. Eve Meyer, the defendant's mother?"

"Yes. Detective Schuler did say he spoke with Mrs. Meyer on the telephone and learned that again Scott Mutchler had been recently released from Adams County Jail and that Mrs. Meyer had transported Scott Mutchler to Louisville at about 9 and that Scott was given orders by Mrs. Meyer and her husband, Steve Meyer, to be home at 11 that night. Miss…or I'm sorry. Detective Schuler told me that shortly before 11, Mrs. Meyer said she got a telephone call from Scott Mutchler in which Mutchler said that he was three miles from home and would be home in just a couple of minutes."

"Did she detail anything else to Detective Schuler that he passed on to you?"

"She said that Scott Mutchler had gotten home to an address in Westminster in unincorporated Adam County between 11:15 and 11:20. And at that time, he was suffering from stab wounds."

"Again, before 4:48 did you also speak with any hospital personnel, specifically nurse Paula Gutzmer?"

"Yes sir, I did."

"And what, if anything, did she provide to you that you had not learned from any other sources about the case involving Mr. Mutchler?"

"That Mr. Mutchler had wrapped around his arm a cloth pillow case and also a pair of boxer shorts, and that she found this unusual to have boxer shorts on his wound but he wasn't wearing any kind of shorts or underwear at that time."

"Did you learn from anybody at that time the source of those items; that is, the pillowcase and the shorts?"

"Not at that time, sir."

"Then at 4:48 or thereabouts…well, I guess you already testified that you signed the form. Tell us what kind of contact you had with Mr. Mutchler?"

"At about 4:45 in the morning I contacted Mr. Mutchler and asked him if he would accompany me to a private room. In that room was Detective Schuler and Detective Hartmann.

"When Scott went and sat in the room, I made sure that he was attended to for his comfort and wasn't aggravating any of the injuries. Then I went out and signed the custody papers at 4:48. After I signed the custody papers, I returned back to the room. At about 4:49 that morning I advised Scott Mutchler of his rights under Miranda."

"Did he say he understood his rights?"

"Yes sir, he did say he understood his rights. He did say that he knew the rights could be exercised now or at any time during the interview."

"What did he say after you finished the advisal to him that he understood them?"

"He said he didn't want to talk to me at that time."

"Did you press? Did you continue to interview or interrogate him after that?"

"No sir, I didn't."

"In that portion of information you gathered from Detective Schuler in turn from Mrs. Meyer, did she…did you learn exactly what time and date of the release from the hospital…or the jail? Pardon me."

"Yes sir. During this time from the information I received, Mrs. Meyer got a telephone call at about ten minutes until 7 to pick up Scott Mutchler from what I originally believed was the Adam County Jail. She had picked him up and apparently transported him in at that time. I don't know where she took him. Then later on I found out that she took him to the family home in Westminster."

"And in your conversation with Detective Schuler and or Hartmann, did they talk about their observations of the defendant's person or clothing when they first saw him at the hospital?"

"I remember that I was told that the clothing had been picked up before I got there."

"I understand. I'm now talking about if they had described him or the clothing to you before its removal?"

"Sir, not that I can recall."

"What had you understood from any source about his condition when he first came to the hospital, Mr. Mutchler's?"

"He was suffering from stab wounds to an arm and a hand. According to nurse Gutzmer, he was hysterical."

"And?"

"He was complaining an awful lot of the pain."

"Did she detail the hysteria beyond what you said in addition to that about pain?"

"No sir, not really."

"She didn't give you an example of how?"

"No."

"Did the briefing or conversation with Schuler and Hartmann include any information about the car's ownership or its registration?"

"Yes sir, it did. At that time, they, meaning Hartmann and Schuler, advised me that after the statements made by Gutterman that Mrs. Meyer said the car didn't belong to her son, they did do a check on the license plates. They requested that the dispatch officer find out who owned the car. That's when it was learned that it was registered to a Evan Scharf out of Louisville. They then contacted Louisville police and they asked Louisville police to respond to Mr. Scharf's home to find out if Scharf had given permission for Mutchler to have the car."

"Understood. Did they talk...did they give you any information about documentation at that time, documentation in the form of papers in the car?"

"They said that in the car they saw some business cards that said 'Evan Scharf' on them."

"All right. Did you and Detective Hartmann...were you involved in the transport of Mr. Mutchler from the hospital to Louisville Police Department?"

"Yes sir."

"When did that occur? When did that transport start?"

"At approximately 5:15 that morning."

"And how...that is, what kind of vehicle was he transported in?"

"He was in an unmarked white Chevy Caprice four door."

"Your automobile?"

"Yes, it's the car that's assigned to me by the City of Louisville."

"Understood. Who drove the route between the hospital and Louisville?"

"I did."

"Who was in the car with you?"

"Scott Mutchler and Tom Hartmann."

"And who determined the route to be taken?"

"I did."

"Had you traveled that route before in your capacity...well, either way, as a police officer or as a private citizen, from the hospital to your department?"

"Yes sir."

"And what route had you taken on previous occasions?"

"I went from the hospital westbound on 84th to Federal, north on Federal to 120th, west on 120th to 287, north on 287 to Colorado 42, west on Colorado 42, then I continued north to Pine Street in Louisville, west on Pine Street and about half a block west on the intersection of Pine and Main is where I turned north and went to the alley behind the police department."

"That's the route you took that morning?"

"Yes sir, it is."

"Is that the route you had taken on other occasions when you were traveling that distance from the hospital to the police headquarters?"

"Yes sir."

"Did you have occasion to note or record any responses by the defendant?"

"I had watched for responses, but there was none noted."

"Did you have any other purpose for taking that route?"

"That's the way I always take. And also, I thought that it would be… since I'm going that way anyway, I just wanted to make sure that maybe something would happen and Mr. Mutchler would remember and make a comment."

"OK. There was no comment or reaction that you saw?"

"The only comments made from Scott were about his comfort. At one point he did tell Detective Hartmann the route we were going to take."

"He told Detective Hartmann the route you were going to take?"

"Yes. Detective Hartmann asked me to let him know when we were going to turn, and Mr. Mutchler told Detective Hartmann before I turned which way we were going to be turning."

"What part of the trip was that?"

"This was on 287 slightly south of Colorado 42."

"You included this in your report, did you not?"

"Yes, I did."

"Detective, I'm now going to refer your attention to later, after the detention and arrest of Scott Mutchler, when you talked with Eve Meyer yourself, OK?"

"Yes."

"Did you have such a conversation?"

"Yes, I did."

"And when and where was that?"

"I had several. But the…"

"That is on that day, I guess."

"I had one at about late morning on the morning of September 11th, which took place at the Meyer home on Oakwood in unincorporated Adam County."

"Was there another conversation at some later time as well?"

"Yes sir, there was."

"When you first met with her, however, did you take from her information relating to that which you'd already heard but perhaps in more detail about her contact with her son that day?"

"Yes, I did."

"And then did she give you any information about when he was first incarcerated in jail in Adam County and then did she give you information about his release and her contact with him following his release?"

"She told me that he was arrested sometime around the end of June and I believe she said June 23rd."

"Very well."

"He was at the Adams County Jail. She had arranged for bond to be posted on September 10th. Scott Mutchler was released from the Adam County Jail on the evening of September 10th. And he called his mother, Mrs. Meyer, at about 6:50 that evening from the Safeway store in Brighton, Colorado. Mrs. Meyer said she didn't have her clock in her car, nor did she have a watch when she left her home. She thought she picked him up around 7:15. She took him directly home. She felt she got back home about 7:45 that evening."

"And did she transport him anyplace else? Did she tell you that she transported him anyplace else later that evening?"

"Yes, she did. She stated that she and her husband, Steve Meyer, at Scott Mutchler's request transported him to Louisville and dropped him off at the 7-Eleven store on McCaslin Boulevard in Louisville."

"There's been an exhibit previously marked and identified as a portion, or I guess a sketch of the Louisville community and a couple of locations indicated there. Do you recognize that? Would that...what does that apparently depict?"

"Yes, I do."

"Does that exhibit accurately reflect in the fashion that it does that portion of Louisville and Boulder County?"

"To my knowledge it does."

"You see the two red circles?"

"Yes sir."

"You got a pointer there. The one on the lower left, do you know where that location is?"

"The lower left is Centennial Center. And this is the 7-Eleven store that Mrs. Meyer said that Scott was dropped off at that evening."

"Is the other circle…can you see that neighborhood or that part of Louisville?"

"Yes, I did."

"Do you know is there anything significant about that as it relates to this case?"

"This is…the area circled is Van Buren Court and that is where the house that the crime occurred…murders occurred is located."

"Have you had occasion, since this case began, to address the distance between those, driving or walking distance between those two points?"

"Yes sir."

"What can you tell us about it?"

"Tell you the driving."

"And the route that you drove, if indeed you drove?"

"Yes, I did drive."

"All right. Go ahead."

"In driving that, you can drive it in less than five minutes obeying all traffic laws. I had no reason to walk it."

"The distance as reflected…the scale is reflected as one mile per 17 inches. See that in the lower right hand corner?"

"Yes, I do."

"Using that scale on what you see there, can you estimate the walking distance it would be from the 7-Eleven to that neighborhood or that address?"

"Approximately one mile."

"One final question. Detective, I think I asked you whether Detective Schuler or Hartmann talked about the condition of Mr. Mutchler or his clothing when they first saw him. Did they describe to you any detail about his condition or his clothing at any time while they were in contact with him that night?"

"They said he had a lot of blood on him."

"Thank you. I have no other questions."

CROSS EXAMINATION BY SHAW: "You executed some search warrants for medical records in this case didn't you sir?"

RAGULSKY: "Yes sir, I did."

"Judge, I hope the court file has the affidavits and warrants for seizure of medical records in this case. I'd ask the Court to…Detective Ragulsky, you executed the warrants for search and seizure of medical records in three different places, isn't that correct?"

"Yes sir, I did."

"And was Officer Workman with you each time?"

"No sir, he wasn't with me at all."

"Judge, have you looked? Do you have the affidavits and warrants for search and seizure of the medical records?"

JUDGE: "I think so. The one where the affiant was Dave Workman and the warrant signed by Judge Bellipanni on September 18th?"

SHAW: "Does it…

JUDGE: "For search at St. Anthony's North."

SHAW: "I'd ask the Court to recognize that affidavit and warrant for purposes of consideration of the motion to suppress filed by defense in this case."

JUDGE: "All right."

SHAW: "So Officer Ragulsky, at some point you received the affidavit and warrant from…is it Detective Workman?"

RAGULSKY: "Yes sir."

"Detective Workman, which he had signed by a district court judge of this district, correct?"

"Yes."

"It was your assignment to execute the warrant, was it not?"

"Yes, it was."

"OK. And that was for search and seizure of Mr. Mutchler's medical records at St. Anthony's Hospital, correct?"

"Yes sir."

"OK. Did you execute that at St. Anthony's North Hospital?"

"Yes, I did."

"On what day?"

"I'd have to look at the warrant, sir. I don't remember the date."

"You'd have to look at the return?"

"Or the return of service, I'm sorry."

"Officer Ragulsky, I'll hand you a copy of the warrant, affidavit and return and see if that refreshes your memory about when you executed it."

"It was September 19th. I'm sorry."

"OK. Did you make an inventory of what you seized there at St. Anthony's?"

"I just listed it as one packet of medical records."

"That was filed with the district court?"

"I believe so."

"Did you file a return with the district court?"

"I gave it to Detective Workman."

"But you completed the return and gave it to Detective Workman?"

"Yes, I did and also a copy of St. Anthony's."

"Did you execute that warrant for search and seizure of Mr. Mutchler's records anywhere else?"

"Yes, I did."

"Where else?"

"I executed it at the Alpine Plastic Surgery Clinic."

"Let's take that one before you go to the next one, if there are any more. When did you execute the…did you say Alpine Medical Clinic?"

"Alpine Plastic Surgery I believe is the name of the place."

"All right. When did you execute it there?"

"Also on September 19th."

"OK. And did you pick up anything there?"

"I picked up two pages of medical records."

"OK. That's indicated on the return?"

"Yes sir."

"And by what authority did you search and seize records of Mr. Mutchler's at the Plastic Surgery Clinic?"

"Under the warrant, sir."

"The warrant indicates the Plastic Surgery Clinic?"

"The warrant indicates St. Anthony's Hospital."

"Where else did you search and seize with that warrant that indicates that you could seize Mr. Mutchler's medical records from St. Anthony's North Hospital?"

"Also at the Ambulance Service Company in Denver, Colorado."

"What day did you do that?"

"On September 20th."

"What did you seize there?"

"A copy of the ambulance report form, which consisted of one page."

"Did you indicate that on the return?"

"Yes, I did."

"And again, what was your authority for seizing those medical records at the Ambulance…"

"The warrant."

"Same warrant?"

"Yes sir."

"One that said St. Anthony's?"

"Yes sir."

"Doesn't say anything about the ambulance company, does it?"

"No, it doesn't."

"Judge, I'd also ask the Court to the extent my other request didn't cover it, to take judicial notice of the returns filed with the affidavit and warrant."

JUDGE: "All right."

SHAW: "Did you tell me the day you seized the records from the ambulance company Detective?"

RAGULSKY: "I believe so. May I refer back and give you that date?"

"Go ahead."

"That was on September 20, 1991, sir."

"You had no release from Mr. Mutchler to seize those records from either location did you, or any of those locations?"

"No sir, I didn't."

"Nor his verbal consent?"

"No sir."

"And none of the doctors that…well, let me back up. None of the people who gave those records to you at any of those places indicated to you that they had a release or consent from Mr. Mutchler, did they?"

"No sir, they didn't."

"At some point, you'd discussed Mr. Mutchler's injuries with Dr. Schmidt, did you not?"

"Yes, I did."

"That was on September 14th, is that correct?"

"Yes. I don't recall the exact date, sir."

"Does that sound correct?"

"Very close to that time, sir."

"Was there only one occasion when you talked with Dr. Schmidt concerning Mr. Mutchler's injuries?"

"I've spoken with one of the doctors once either Dr. Schmidt or Dr. Squires. I spoke to the other doctor twice."

"OK. You don't know which was which?"

"I'd have to refer back to my report to give you the name. It might take a few minutes, but I do have the report with me."

"If you would please."

"I spoke with Dr. Schmidt on September 13th. As near as…I believe I spoke with both Dr. Schmidt and Dr. Squires on the 19th also."

"So you talked to…would that cover your conversations with physicians concerning Mr. Mutchler's injuries, then, those two conversations; the first with Dr. Schmidt and the second with both Dr. Schmidt and Dr. Squires?"

"Yes sir."

"You had no release of information or consent from Mr. Mutchler for either one of those conversations, did you?"

"No sir."

"And the doctors didn't indicate that they had any release or consent in either conversation, did they?"

"No sir."

"And by what authority did you feel that you could discuss with them Mr. Mutchler's medical condition?"

"The warrant, sir."

"Prior to your conversation with Dr. Schmidt on the 14th, did he review the warrant?"

"No sir, he didn't."

"OK. And on the 19th, did either doctor review the warrant?"

"I don't remember. I know I had the warrant with me at that time."

"Did you put into your report, Officer Ragulsky, the one that you provided the District Attorney's office regarding this case, the substance of both of those conversations?"

"Yes sir, I did."

"You've never personally observed Mr. Mutchler's injuries have you?"

"I didn't see them open, I saw them closed up."

"You saw the stitches?"

"The bandages sir."

"And you've only seen them covered?"

"Yes sir."

"When you got to St. Anthony's North in the early morning hours of the 11th, if I understand it correctly, the second law enforcement officer you met with was Detective Hartmann?"

"Yes sir."

"And at that point Detective Hartmann briefed you on what he knew about the case, is that correct?"

"Yes sir."

"And he told you that Detective Schuler had told him that Mr. Mutchler was giving inconsistent statements when he met with Detective Schuler initially at that time at the hospital, is that correct?"

"Yes sir."

"Subsequent to that, you met separately with Detective Schuler, correct?"

"Yes, I did."

"And he told you also that he felt that Mr. Mutchler's account of how he'd been assaulted was vague?"

"Yes."

"And he couldn't name the store where he was allegedly assaulted?"

"That's correct, he couldn't."

"Nor the brand of gas?"

"No sir."

"After you met Mr. Mutchler at 4:45 in the morning, he took pain medication, did he not?"

"I was informed later that he did."

"And around that time, he also reported to you that he was feeling nauseous, isn't that correct?"

"That's correct."

"When you talked with Eve Meyer later in the morning on the 11th, she reported to you concerning Mr. Mutchler's condition by her observation at the hospital, isn't that correct?"

"I don't know. I don't understand, sir."

"Did she tell you her perception of Scott's condition at the hospital?"

"She said he was in pain, if that's what you mean."

"Did she tell you he was shaking and babbling?"

"She said he was upset. I don't recall her saying shaking and babbling. That doesn't sound familiar at all."

"Was that the conversation with Mrs. Meyer that was tape-recorded and transcribed?"

"No. The conversation with Mrs. Meyer that was tape-recorded and transcribed came several days later."

"In that conversation, do you recall her telling you that he was babbling at the hospital and shaking?"

"She may have said shook-up, but I still…I can't recall her saying babbling."

"Do you have a copy of that transcription with you?"

"Yes, I do."

"Refer to page 31, the second complete paragraph where Mrs. Meyer is speaking. Read through that paragraph and tell me if your memory concerning her statement to you regarding his babbling is refreshed? Just read through it to yourself."

"Yes, it is in there twice where she said babbling."

"One of the reasons you took Mr. Mutchler on the route you took him back to Louisville was to see if he would make any statements about the area where he said he was stabbed, isn't that right?"

"Yes, that's one of them."

"I think you indicated on direct examination that Detective Hartmann asked you at some point about which direction you'd be going?"

"Yes sir."

"Do you know why he was asking you that?"

"Because I asked him to record the way we were going."

"So he was taking notes about where you were going, is that correct?"

"Yes sir. I asked him to."

"OK. And so you got to some junction and he said, which way are we going to go here?"

"Yes sir. His statement was something more of, 'Tell me which way we're going to be going Alex'."

"Were you at some junction at this point?"

"We were approaching an intersection."

"He had been to the Louisville Police Department before?"

"Yes, he had."

"He had been there before on that route, hadn't he?"

"I don't know if he'd been to Louisville Police Department before on that route."

"When you first get to St. Anthony's Hospital in the early morning hours of the 11th, the first police officer you see is Officer LaFleur?"

"Yes sir."

"And he refers to Mr. Mutchler as a victim at that point?"

"Yes sir."

"Detective Ragulsky, do you have in your files on this case, the records that you seized or copies of the records that you seized pursuant to the search warrant for medical records of Mr. Mutchler?"

"I don't have those with me."

"Do you have those back in Louisville?"

"There's a copy of the records in Louisville with the original case files."

"Do you have those separated so that you could tell us which case came from which source?"

"I could identify them. I can tell you which came from where."

"OK. Off the record, Judge. I'm going to ask that he do that so that we can introduce them into evidence at some subsequent hearing so that you know what came from where and in case you want to review them or decide to suppress some and not others. I think this is a significant issue here about seizure of records that wasn't authorized by the warrant. I think you're going to need to know the source of the various packages of records and to that I have no objection. It would be useful for the Court to have."

JUDGE: "You want to be able to introduce all the medical records from St. Anthony's North at this trial?"

SHAW: "That wasn't direct to me was it?"

JUDGE: "No."

SHAW: "I don't have anymore questions."

JUDGE: "That was just a rhetorical question. Any other questions?"

SHAW: "Not from me, Judge."

MILLER: "None Your Honor. May the witness be excused?"

I glanced up at our hotel and wondered what Steve was doing. This wasn't much of a vacation for him. He knew I had to find a way to help get my son's case reopened, and he was letting me have all the room I needed to work on it. I had written to the top attorneys in the country searching for help but they, too, wanted money I just didn't have.

That's the problem...if you have the funds, you can buy yourself a fair trial in this country. If you don't, you get what you get, which in most cases means tragedy of some kind.

There had to be a way to reopen this case for Scott. There just had to be! I pulled out the next volume.

DNA Testing is a Joke

JUDGE: "With regard to the DNA, I still haven't read that because I'm sort of peeved off at both sides for failing to understand what I think was an absolutely clear ruling and that is …maybe I'm wrong. I guess it's one on page three: 'It is inappropriate, at least in the context of novel scientific evidence such as DNA testing.' I don't think it's all that novel, so I'll leave that out.

" 'It's inappropriate for the defendant to oppose DNA testing as unreliable and inadmissible.' I don't care about that either.

"It says it is inappropriate to influence the jury based on the absence of such evidence as part of the People's case.

"This case will…there will be no evidence in this case presented to the jury about the failures of any police investigation, the inappropriate conduct of any police investigation, the opportunity to do other things they did not do in that investigation. That is not an issue in the trial and no one, no one, will ever in any time during the time in front of the jury submit any evidence or make any argument about that."

SHAW: “Is that concerning DNA?”

JUDGE: “Yes. For example there will be no 'Ladies and gentlemen, they could have done DNA and they didn’t. They could have done something else and they didn’t.' That is irrelevant. And what is it about it that no one understands for some reason? Why is it I’m having to tell you that it’s inadmissible, inappropriate and irrelevant evidence, which is not going to be allowed in this trial?”

SHAW: “Judge, I’m only concerned that I think that the suggestion that DNA testing isn’t valid, hasn’t been found valid, and I want to be able to call an expert to refute that. I don’t think it would take very long but I certainly want time to put an expert on to testify so that I can establish that it is relevant when it’s done right.”

JUDGE: “Let the record reflect that the Court has just lost its composure with laughter. You can go on for another hour if you want. I don’t think there’s any necessity that I remain in the courtroom while you do so, but you can stand there and talk to the record for as long as you want about your attempt to introduce some irrelevant matters that I said will not happen.

“What I’m telling…what I’m warning you about is that if I think that you are now or if I think that if you do at the trial make some veiled attempt to sneak it in or to do something, then I’m going to draw the line right now. Having drawn the line, I know you won’t cross it. Any effort to do so will be dealt with severely. I’m just warning you. In this case I don’t think it makes any difference and we don’t have time for it.

“We’re going to proceed…I think more importantly than whatever remote value DNA might have to either side or the scientific validity of it is far outweighed by Mr. Mutchler’s right to get the case tried and the People’s right to get the case over with. “Call your next witness.”

PICKERING: “People would call Scott Pratt.”

JUDGE: “You may be seated. Mr. Pratt, you have been previously sworn in this case. You’re still under oath.”

PICKERING: “Just to refresh the jury’s recollection, Mr. Pratt, how are you employed?”

PRATT: “With the Colorado Bureau of Investigation.”

"And specifically, what's the nature of your work at CBI?"

"My primary duty is in the latent print section, which involves the examination of evidence for latent fingerprints, also shoe and tire impressions and we also do major crime scenes."

"How much of your regular working day is devoted to fingerprint or footprint analysis?"

"Probably about 90 to 95 percent of it."

"How long have you been engaged in the practice of examining fingerprints?"

"Approximately 19 years, 18 or 19 years."

"What's your educational background or professional training that would qualify you to do this kind of work?"

"Well, my initial training in fingerprints was with the Federal Bureau of Investigation in Washington, D.C., where I was employed for two years. I then spent 12-and-a-half years with the State of Utah Crime Laboratory. And I've spent the last four-and-a-half years with the Colorado Bureau of Investigation."

"And all of that examining fingerprints?"

"Most of it was with fingerprints. Probably the last five or seven years has been doing shoe and tire impressions also."

"Have you had occasion during that time to identify people by comparing latent fingerprints with known samples?"

"Yes, I have."

"Approximately, how many times have you done that?"

"Well, I've examined probably thousands of cases."

"Have you ever been qualified as an expert witness in court before?"

"Yes, I have."

"Roughly how many times, and give us a sample of the jurisdictions?"

"Well, to give you rough estimate would be I've testified in excess of over 50 times. That includes having been subpoenaed and stipulated to in the courts. I've testified in federal court in the state of Oregon and the state of Utah. I've also testified in state civil and local courts within the state of Utah. I've also testified in the district courts within Colorado also."

"Your Honor, I would move to qualify Mr. Pratt as an expert witness in the field of fingerprint and footprint analysis."

JUDGE: "He may express his opinions."

PICKERING: "What's a latent fingerprint?"

PRATT: "General definition of a latent fingerprint would be a fingerprint that is left behind when an individual touches an item. It also may be an impression, which is usually referred to as a patent print, which is one in which an impression is left in a substance such as putty. A patent print may also be a print in which a substance is acquired upon the ridge of the fingerprint and then transfer those images to another item."

"What's a known sample or known fingerprint for purposes of your analysis?"

"For our purposes, a known set of fingerprints is one in which a substance, most commonly is what we refer to as ink, which is very similar to printer's ink, is applied to the surface or ridges of the hands or feet. Then this is applied to a cardboard or heavy paper for the purpose of recording the individual's ridge structure."

"What are some of the distinguishing characteristics, if there are any, of a fingerprint? What do you look for?"

"Basically on fingerprints the things that we look for are ridge endings. This is where a ridge may continue from one direction and go another direction and stop. We also look for what are islands. An island is where one ridge proceeds, divides itself and then comes back upon itself thus forming an island.

"We have a dot, which is very similar to a period at the end of a sentence. We have short ridges. That's where one ridge starts, proceeds but a short distance and then ends. And we have bifurcations. That's where a ridge goes, divides into two different ridges and continues on as two different ridges. We have variations of those types of ridge details.

"And what makes fingerprints individualistic is that these types of fingerprints…is the relationship that they have one to another. And in order for two prints to be the same minutia, they must have the same type of ridge configuration and details and they must lie in the same relative position in both prints."

PICKERING: "How do you go about...how is it possible to leave fingerprints?"

PRATT: "There are several different ways of leaving fingerprints. The most common way is that one of the things that happens is we sweat. Within the ridge structure of the fingerprints is sweat pores. As sweat is exited and we touch an item, this sweat is then transferred to the item, which we touch.

"Other methods may be a foreign substance such as grease, blood, even sometimes just fingerprint ink, we can touch...apply that or get it applied by touching things to an item. That again transfers that material to the item, which we touch.

"Another process of leaving fingerprints is kind of a reversal-type system. This is where an item may be dusty. In this case, the dust would adhere to the ridge detail and go with the hand. Rather than the hand leaving a fingerprint, it leaves its impression in the dust. Or when you touch putty, your impression of the fingerprint is left in the soft putty or soft item, whatever it may be."

"What effect does the particular surface have on the ability to leave behind a fingerprint or to get a fingerprint off a surface?"

"That is one factor of leaving fingerprints. A very loose item such as a screen in a window, the screen itself is so wide and has so much open space that it would be virtually impossible to get an identifiable print on such a wide surface.

"Cloth is the same way depending on the weave, as there are different weaves in cloth. Some are very tight. And identifiable fingerprints have been found on real tight weave. On very loose weave it has not. On glass, painted surfaces, varnished surfaces, aluminum cans ... the smoother the surface, the better it is for receptability of fingerprints."

PICKERING: "What if anything, does the presence of any kind of liquid or any kind of substance over that smooth surface...how does that effect, if it does, your ability to get a print?"

PRATT: "It does have a great ability. If you have a real oily surface, chances are you will not leave behind identifiable fingerprints. An example of this would be like the knobs on a radio of a car where people routinely constantly hit that and leave behind the oils of their hand.

Very seldom do we find identifiable fingerprints because of that buildup of moisture and substance."

"What about climate? Does humidity affect your ability to leave prints?"

"Yes, it does."

"How?"

"Well, the sweat of a fingerprint is basically about 99 percent water. And in a dry climate, that water dissipates rather quickly. Also, in a very hot climate, people have a tendency to sweat more to leave fingerprints behind. Whereas when it's a very cold-like temperature, we get around here down in the zeros or teens or high 20s, people don't sweat as much when it's cold outside, so they do not leave fingerprints very often."

"Are fingerprints specific to an individual?"

"Yes, they are."

"Can two people have the same fingerprints?"

"No two people have ever been able to have the same fingerprints."

"Did you make some fingerprint comparisons in this case?"

"Yes, I did."

"Did you dust…or I don't know if that's the right word. Did you examine or process the entire crime scene for fingerprints?"

"Yes, I did."

"Would you tell the jury where you looked for fingerprints and how you did it."

"Initially responding to the scene was to look for points of entries, points of exit and work it in a…try to work it in a systematic-type method so that we could enter into the house. We began by fingerprinting the front door of the house and then working kind of in a counterclockwise direction in through the living room, kitchen, and then going up the stairs to the upstairs area and process the upstairs area.

"We did this and then we did the basement level. After doing the main floor, the top floor and the bottom floor, the process that we used was basically using the flashlight and looking for visible fingerprints that were seen on the scene and also used dusting powders to dust the walls, the doors, and the items within the house at the scene for the detection of fingerprints."

PICKERING: "Were you able to…well, let me back up. Did you test a knife? In this case a knife that you found for fingerprints?"

PRATT: "Yes, I did."

"Did you find any prints on the knife?"

"I found no identifiable prints on the knife."

"OK. Does that mean you didn't see any on there? Or is there a reason why you couldn't identify any fingerprints?"

"When one processes knives with wood handles, it tends to be difficult anyway because wooden handled knives normally have an oil or substance applied to them to help preserve the wood. Another reason is that they get washed an awful lot and that doesn't seem to be a very receptive surface for fingerprints.

"In this particular case, the knife happened to be covered with an extreme amount…in my opinion, an extreme amount of blood both on the handle as well as the blade of the knife. There was; however, certain ridge structures that I did notice in the blood, but it was insufficient for comparison purposes."

"Did you examine a fireplace poker that was taken from the scene?"

"Yes, I did."

"Were you able to find any prints on it?"

"No, I was not."

"Could you explain why, if you can?"

"Again, we use certain methods of process to try and enhance any fingerprints we found; however, the size of the poker handle being a small size and plus the surface area did not really lend itself to finding fingerprints that well."

"When you examined the fingerprints that you found in the house, were you able to find any identifiable fingerprints that did not belong to the Scharfs?"

"Yes, I did."

"If I may approach the witness, Your Honor?"

JUDGE: "You may."

PICKERING: "I'm going to hand you what's been marked for identification as People's Exhibit 11. Do you recognize that Mr. Pratt?"

PRATT: "Yes, I do."

"How do you recognize that?"

"Up in the corner of this particular piece I have my case number and my initials."

"OK. What did you do with that particular piece of evidence?"

"This was a standard that I received which bears the name of Mr. Mutchler for the purpose of comparing with any latent fingerprints that I would find."

"Your Honor, for purposes of this trial Mr. Shaw has agreed that, in fact, that is the fingerprint card obtained at the Boulder County Jail belonging to Mr. Mutchler."

SHAW: "That's correct, Judge."

PICKERING: "Move to admit People's Exhibit 11. I've handed you what's been marked as People's Exhibit 56. Would you examine that for me and can you tell me what it is?"

PRATT: "People's Exhibit 56 is an A&W restaurant coupon."

"Did you examine this for fingerprints?"

"Yes, I did."

PICKERING: "Your Honor, I may have not heard. Did the Court admit People's Exhibit 11, the fingerprint card?"

JUDGE: "Yes, it's admitted."

PICKERING: "Did you compare the fingerprints that you found on the A&W ticket, which is People's Exhibit 56, with the known fingerprint samples from Scott Mutchler?"

PRATT: "Yes, I did."

"If I can show you what's been marked for identification as people's exhibit…Mr. Pratt, it might be easier for you to come out here, wherever you're comfortable. We can put this…would you prefer to do it at your chair?"

"If it's all right with the Court."

JUDGE: "That's fine."

MILLER: "Do you have a pointer?"

PICKERING: "Would you identify what we're looking at here that's marked People's Exhibit 119?"

PRATT: "People's Exhibit 119 is a chart that is made for demonstration purposes and explaining how an identification is made. The impression which is shown in the photograph on your left side, which is labeled as the latent print, is a fingerprint which was found on the A&W coupon brochure which was located in this region right here, which was found in a reddish substance on the coupon.

"The impression found on the right side of the chart is labeled as the index fingerprint. It is a photographic reputation of the right index finger as found on the card bearing the name Scott Mutchler, which is People's Exhibit 11.

"Mr. Pratt, is this the thing you actually used to make the comparison, or is this just for demonstrative purposes?"

"This is just for demonstrative purposes. I'd already made the identification prior to this."

"Would you show the jury specifically what you were looking for and I guess explain the term 'points of comparison'?"

"Be happy to. As previously explained, we look for any ridges, dots, bifurcations, which is where one ridge combines into two. And for the purposes of this demonstration, we started with a point, which we have labeled as point number one. Now, what we're looking for again is we have to find the same types of fingerprint minutia on both fingerprints. They have to be the same type. They have to be in the same relative position on both hands.

"Now, one thing to remember in identifications is that the skin is pliable. There is some flexing that can happen and so there may be a little bit of explainable difference. We also have a substance, a reddish substance in which this print is applied to which may or may not make the ridges wider or thinner at given points.

"So, we can begin at a point that is labeled point number one, which is a ridge ending that comes from the top, as I understand, at this point right here. And then dropping down from the point, which we have labeled number one, which is an ending ridge, we may drop down one, two ridges. At this point, we have a ridge, which comes down from the top, divides into two different ridges. And as it proceeds down, it again comes into itself forming one ridge. Again, this is a giant island is basically what it is. And coming from point number two going down one, two, three, four ridges, we have just a small little dot down here, which we have labeled point number three. From point number three moving in one, two, three and then going down we come to another ending ridge.

"Now, if those two prints are the same, we should be able to come from the latent print and then come over to the fingerprint and find that same minutia in the same relative position on both prints. They should be the same.

"Starting at point number one, we do have a ridge coming from the top, going down and ending by labeled point number one. Coming in one, two ridges, we have a ridge coming from the top, going down, which divides or bifurcates in two ridges. And as it proceeds down, it does come down to a point where they both come back together again to form one ridge causing that big island. From point number two, we can come in one, two, three, four ridges. And here we have a small dot located at this point marked point number three. Moving in one, two, three ridges going down, we come to an ending ridge that is marked point number four.

"Now, the remaining points on here are marked the same with the same type. The print minutia is that they are in corresponding areas of the fingerprint. So this...in my opinion, the latent fingerprint as found on the A&W brochure located in this area right here, was made by the same individual who made the right index fingerprint as found on the People's Exhibit 11, bearing the name of Scott Mutchler.

PICKERING: "Mr. Pratt, now we see here eight, I guess we'll call them points of comparison. Is this for illustrative purposes, or did you find more than eight points of comparison? Could you explain that?"

PRATT: "There are more points on here than what is marked. I only marked eight points just for the demonstration purposes of the jury and of the Court so that they can see how, indeed, identification is made. There are several other points which have not been marked on here."

"Do you have any doubt that these two prints are made by the same person?

"They were made by the same individual."

"If I could hand you what's been marked for identification as People's Exhibit 49. If you would open it and examine it for me. People move to admit 119."

JUDGE: "Any objection to this?"

COOKE: "No objection."

JUDGE: "It is admitted."

PICKERING: "Would you identify that?"

PRATT: "Yes. This is State's Exhibit 49 which is CBI No. 28, which is the phone from the kitchen wall."

"Did you examine that phone for fingerprints?"

"Yes, I did."

"I'd refer your attention to what's been marked for identification as People's Exhibit 120. Would you identify that for the record please."

"Yes. Again, this is a chart which I've made for the purposes of explaining how an identification is effected and the purpose of fingerprints."

"Would you identify what's on…I guess it would be the jury's right and the jury's left please."

"On the left is a photograph of the latent print which was found on People's Exhibit 49. That is a latent fingerprint found on the phone in this vicinity right here on the handset. And that was found in a reddish substance on the phone also.

"The photograph on the right listed as the index fingerprint is represented in a photograph of the right index finger as found on the card bearing the name of Scott Mutchler, People's Exhibit 11."

"Would you describe what, if any, similarities you found between the two where you did your comparison and what your conclusion as to…"

"OK. In coming with fingerprints…and again, looking for the fingerprint minutia that we have in the…and the ridges, dots, bifurcations. In this particular case, the fingerprint was somewhat smeared on the top. And so what we had to do was go down to the second joint of the print, which also has ridge minutia that was identifiable and individualistic to each individual.

"By going down here, we came to a ridge, which comes to your left…from your left to the right and ends, which is marked point number one. From point number one, we can drop down to a point right below It which again, is another ridge coming from the right…or left to the right and ending. That is point number two. From point number two, we can drop down one, two, three, four, five, six, seven ridges. And at this point, we have a ridge coming from the left upwards in an upward direction and ending, which is point number three.

"Now, if these two prints were indeed the same, we would have those same types of points on the fingerprint as the latent fingerprint. We have some kind of a ridge coming from the left to the right and ending. We have marked that point number one. Dropping down one, we have ridge coming from the left to the right and ending, which has been marked point number two. Dropping from point number two one, two, three, four, five, six, seven ridges, we have a ridge coming from the left upward in an upward direction, which is ending, which is marked point number three.

"Again, we have the same types of minutia on three…or on four through eight, ending, ridges, and bifurcations. And they are in the same relative position. They are the same types of minutia on this, the latent print, as found on the ink fingerprint."

PICKERING: "Mr. Pratt, does…and again, I notice you can explain this to some degree, the point of comparison in this one are on a different part of the fingerprint. Does that affect the reliability of your identification?"

PRATT: "No it does not."

"And again, I see on here eight points of comparison. Is that for illustrative purposes? In fact, did you find more than eight points of comparison?"

"Again, I just marked eight for the demonstration purposes for the jury and for the Court. There are in fact several more minutiae on that which are in the same relative position and the same types that were not marked by red numbers."

"Do you have an opinion as to the relationship between the latent print found on the telephone, People's Exhibit 49, and the inked fingerprint belonging to Scott Mutchler?"

"My opinion is the latent fingerprint, which was found in the reddish substance on the phone, on the handle of the phone, is the same and it was indeed made by the same individual who made the right index fingerprint on the card bearing the name Scott Mutchler, which is People's Exhibit 11, which is demonstrated by the ink fingerprint on the right side of the chart."

"Do you have any doubt whatsoever as to that conclusion?"

"No sir."

"If I can...Your Honor, I don't think I moved to admit People Exhibit 120."

COOKE: "No objection."

JUDGE: "It's admitted."

PICKERING: "If I can direct your attention to People's Exhibit 51. You may be just as comfortable sitting down I think, Mr. Pratt. Would you identify what's been marked for identification there?"

PRATT: "People's Exhibit 51 is a portion of the kitchen flooring which was taken near the stove as is indicated in the writing down here. It was removed by myself because it does have an impression, what appears to be a footwear type impression in reddish substance.

"Mr. Pratt, did you do a comparison to try to identify the source of that footprint?"

"Yes, I did."

"If I can approach the witness Your Honor."

JUDGE: "You may."

PICKERING: "I've handed you what's been marked for identification and previously admitted as People's Exhibits 5 and 6. Could you have a look at them and see if you would recognize them."

PRATT: "Yes, I recognize these."

"Did you in fact use these in your identification of People's Exhibit 51?"

"Yes, I did."

"Which one of those did you use?"

"Well, I used both shoes in order to make a comparison and to determine whether there was a right or left shoe impression here. So I did use both of them."

"Would you tell the Court and the jury how you go about making a footprint comparison, and specifically, how you went about it in this case."

"Well, initially what we do is examine the bottom of the shoes for any foreign substances which may prove to benefit further on in the case. In this particular case, there was some reddish substance on the bottom of these shoes, so we preserved some of that. The next thing we do is we try to record the bottom of the shoe. In this particular case, we dusted it with fingerprint powder and then we make a lift, which gives us a basic representation of the bottom of the shoes. Then we make a photograph onto acetate film of that copy that we made with print powder, thus making an overlay that we can use."

"Did you in fact do that? Did you bring it with you?"

"Yes, I do have one."

"Would you show the jury what you brought."

"This would…this clear acetate would represent what we end up with the photographic copy of the bottom of the shoes."

"How did you go about doing that?"

"Again, through the use of photography, we photographed the dust lift that we made off the bottom of the shoe and photographed it onto a clear acetate. And the purpose of this is that initially when we do take a lift of a bottom of a shoe, it's in the reverse or opposite direction that we need in order to compare it with an item on here. So by putting it on clear acetate, we can reverse it over and put it in correct order for comparison purposes."

"What's the other part of what you're holding?"

"What the other photograph is, is a copy of…is a photograph of the impression as found on the People's Exhibit 51, which is the floor in the kitchen."

"When you're comparing them, how exactly do you do it?"

"Well, we examine this first off to virtually determine which direction that this foot…or somehow that this may have been made. In this particular case, we can see a circular motion here, which is similar to a design that would be found in the ball of a shoe. Also, underneath it, we can see some bar designs coming from what would be the jury's right to the left. This indication would lead us to believe that this would not be made by a right shoe because it has an opposite direction from that. So we can eliminate the right shoe from having made this particular design; however, observing the left shoe, we do have a ball design or circle design in the ball of the shoe followed by bar designs coming from the right to the left, which very easily could have made this type of…"

"Do you look for points of comparison similar to fingerprints?"

"Yes, we do."

"Are the points of comparison as unique as they are in fingerprints?"

"There are various things that we look at. One of the things that may come into play is right from a…right from a manufacturer of a shoe. Some shoes can be positively identified without having ever been worn just due to the manufacturing process that they go through makes them individual.

"Other things that contribute to individuality of shoes is the wear. Example of this would be as the shoe has been worn, this shoe is becoming more and more smooth in the ball area, so we can eliminate a shoe which would have the designs here because the wear would not be there as opposed to a new shoe.

"Other things we looked for in this particular case on this shoe at this point right there, which may be a little hard to see from that distance, but there is individual wear. This is caused by cuts by maybe glass chipping out pieces, rocks cutting into the shoe or rocks even being found in the shoe or like maybe seen here in the material getting caught in the creases of the shoe."

PICKERING: "Did you compare the acetate of the shoe with the foot print you found on the floor?"

PRATT: "Yes I did."

"What points of comparison or level of similarity did you find?"

"In our report, we reported out that they could have…the impression as found on People's Exhibit…in this vicinity, which contains the ball design and the bar designs going in the proper direction is that the left shoe, which is People's Exhibit 5, could have made that particular impression."

"When reaching your conclusion, what…what part did the size of the shoe, for example fit into…"

"The size is part of it. We looked at design, size. If it's a different size, then that shoe can be eliminated even though it does have a similar tread design. And then we tried to look, again, for the individual or wear designs that are present or lack of wear. As it gets worn down, then we again try to look for some of the individual characteristics."

"So the similarities would be the size and the shoe tread?"

"Right."

"Yes."

"Then we also do look for indications that may exclude that particular shoe."

"Is there something there that would exclude that shoe having made that? Did you find any of those?"

"No sir, I did not."

"If I can approach the witness again, I'm going to mark…do you mind if I mark this?"

JUDGE: "No, please do."

PICKERING: "I'm going to mark this as People's Exhibit 121. And we'll say that is a copy of an acetate and copy of a photograph of the impression testified to by Mr. Pratt. We move to admit 121."

COOKE: "Is that the photograph of the overlay?"

PICKERING: "Yes."

COOKE: "No objection."

JUDGE: "It's admitted."

PICKERING: "I'm going to hand you what's been marked for identification as People's Exhibit 52. If you could open that and have a look at it for me, Mr. Pratt. Would you identify what's been marked as People's Exhibit 52."

PRATT: "Yes, People's Exhibit 52 is a portion, again, of the kitchen flooring that was located over towards the kitchen table and towards the phone area in the kitchen. And it contained…again, the reason it was collected was there was some impressions available on there that were similar to a footprint impression."

"Did you again compare that print with either one of the shoes that are marked Exhibits 5 and 6?"

"Yes, I did."

"And what, if any, conclusions did you draw from that comparison?"

"Again, we were able to basically eliminate the right shoe from having made any of these impressions and that it was consistent or could have been made by the left shoe of which is People's Exhibit 5."

"Did you perform the same method of analysis as you did on the other one?"

"Yes, we looked at size, design, wear, individual characteristics. We also looked for any particular individual minutia or points of comparison that would exclude these shoes. And we could find none."

"Was the size the same?"

"Correct, yes."

"Was the wear the same?"

"Yes."

"Was the shoe pattern the same?"

"Yes, from what could be determined there."

"Mr. Pratt, I'm going to just show you what's earlier been marked for identification as People's Exhibit 98. Did you have prepared prior to testimony, at your direction, a summary of the results that you were to talk about today?"

"Yes."

"OK. Is this such a summary and does it contain your conclusions?"

"Yes, it does."

"We'll move for the admission of 98."

COOKE: "No objection."

JUDGE: "It's admitted."

PICKERING: "Did you use the same acetate for the second one as you did for the first one, or did you remake another acetate?"

PRATT: "We make different acetates when we are doing our comparisons."

"So I don't' think I asked the question very artfully. When you analyze the first shoe and the first print and you used that acetate, did you use that acetate to analyze the second print or did you make another acetate?"

"Usually, we make another acetate of the left shoe."

"Did you do that in this case?"

"I didn't bring it with me, no."

"But did you do it?"

"Yes."

"Thank you. I have no further questions."

JUDGE: "Cross examine."

COOKE: "Mr. Pratt, let's talk first about your fingerprint analysis if we may. Would you mind stepping down here. We're going to give you your exercise this morning. In addition to the fingerprints that you testified to you received, any item that you testified to…you received a number of items for comparison; is that right?"

PRATT: "That is correct."

"And in fact, the total number of items…I'm not talking about the number of fingerprints, but the total number of items that you received for comparison was 25?"

"That would have been probably the item numbers. There was numerous items within those items also."

"OK. But in terms of CBI numbers, there were 25 different item numbers?"

"Approximately that, yes."

"And of the…of those 25 item numbers, it's correct, isn't it, that there were 13 of those items that had no prints that were suitable for comparison?"

"That sounds approximately right."

"Would you like to check your report?"

"I can do that. Thirteen would be the correct number. Again, there may have been numerous items within those items."

"But there were 13 CBI item numbers?"

"Correct."

"OK. And I think you explained this on direct examination. But when you say there's no prints suitable for comparison, that doesn't mean the absence of prints. It could mean the absence of prints, but it could also mean the presence of prints that could not be compared for one reason or another?"

"That is correct."

"And I have listed on that chart, I believe, the 13 CBI item numbers that did not contain prints suitable for comparison. Is that accurate?"

"Yes, that's what I have. I show as 13 CBI numbers."

"For instance, when you're talking about there may have been more than one item, you're talking…maybe you can give us an example from that list just out of the ones that had no prints suitable for comparison or one that…"

"Well, just out of those, yes."

"If you can."

"Probably the prime example would be Exhibit 163, which was a sack in which the knife was found with, oh, hundreds of items of various types, papers, school papers, and items like that. Some of those did not contain any identifiable prints, either."

"So we're talking about one exhibit number. But there were a number of things that were in that?"

"Correct. Another example would be a wallet. There were numerous items found within the wallet."

"And the number of items with prints that were suitable for comparison was 12, is that right?"

"Actually, there should have been 13. May I take a look at your report? Maybe I can ask you to change these numbers, then, so that they accurately reflect your report. And I think you'd have to change the top number as well."

"That may be correct. Let me just…OK. Does that chart now accurately reflect the items there?"

"Yes, ma'am."

"Judge, I'd at this time move for admission of Defendant's Exhibit F."

PICKERING: "No objection."

JUDGE: "It's admitted."

COOKE: "Mr. Pratt, I'm now going to show you what's been marked Defendant's Exhibit G, which concerns the items that were suitable for comparison. And on the items that you received where you found prints that were suitable for comparison, is it accurate that there were 127 different latent fingerprints that were…latent or otherwise, fingerprints that were suitable for comparison?"

PRATT: "That would be correct."

"And is it also correct that the number of fingerprints that could be identified as Scott Mutchler is two?"

"That is correct."

"That's the wall phone and the A&W coupon or flyer that you discussed earlier?"

"Yes, that is correct."

"Is it also correct that the number of items that contained fingerprints that matched with Mr. Scharf is 14?"

"Yes, ma'am."

"And is it also correct that the number of fingerprints containing…or number of fingerprints that could be matched with Robbie Scharf is 87?"

"That's approximately close. I think I came up with 86, just rough quick count."

"OK."

"I think I did it by the subtraction method. But if you want me to change that to 86, I'm comfortable with that."

"Finally, isn't it also true that the number of prints that were suitable for comparison but for which you couldn't make an identification was 24?"

"That is correct."

"Those prints came from five different items, did they not, those 24 prints?"

"That is correct, five CBI numbers."

"And are those five items the five items that are depicted on that exhibit?"

"That is correct."

"Judge, I'd move at this time for Defendant's Exhibit G."

PICKERING: "No objection."

JUDGE: "It's admitted."

COOKE: "Mr. Pratt you may go ahead and resume your seat. Let's turn now to the footprints. The number of questioned items that you received for comparison that were footprints is nine; is that right?"

PRATT: "I don't recall if there was nine or not."

"Well, maybe we can break it down in another way. There were several items that you were given for comparison, for footprints comparison analysis, that contained no footprints or no footprints that could be analyzed, is that right?"

"Those were the floor mats, the clutch pedal and the brake pedal of the car."

"Right, and also there were two floor mats, correct?"

"That is correct."

"So there were four items total?"

"From the car, yes."

"And no footwear impressions were found on any of those items, is that right?"

"That is correct."

"Then you also received two…the two footprints that were on the kitchen floor that you have already testified to that were consistent with the exhibits…with Exhibit 5 received from Scott Mutchler."

"That is correct."

"And then in addition, you received two additional items for footprint comparison that were in the form of plaster casts, is that right?"

"OK. Yes. Those are plaster casts that I made outside. I didn't count those."

"Can you tell me where you obtained those specifically?"

"Well, outside the residence of the main level by the garage. If I may use the chart I could…"

"Sure."

"On the main floor of the house to this direction here is the garage, which is not indicated here. But to the side of the house is what I would consider a monkey bars-type thing where kids would play. And in the dirt in this location were found several footwear impressions in the dirt."

"And you took plaster casts of those as you already indicated?"

"Yes. I photographed them and took plaster casts."

"And during the course of your analysis, you attempted to analyze them to see if they were consistent with exhibit number…or what's been…you've already identified as People's Exhibits 5 and 6. Those may not be the CBI numbers."

"Right."

"Can you tell the jury what your results of your analysis of the casts, the plaster casts and the photographs of the footprints on the outside of the house."

"The plaster casts or photographs, I use both to make the comparisons. But I found them to be different tread design than the shoe impressions as found on People's Exhibit 5 and 6. So it was my conclusion that these shoes, People's Exhibits 5 and 6, did not make any of the footwear impressions as found on the outside of the house by the playground equipment."

"Is it fair to say, Mr. Pratt, that the reason that you took the impressions of the footwear prints that were found outside the house, is because they appeared to be consistent at least in size, with those that you'd observed inside?"

"I did no size comparisons of the shoes inside or outside. My process at that time is that there were footwear impressions and that they may or may not be of importance to this particular case being around playground equipment like that. They could be neighbor kids or anything. But I did not differentiate that at the time, so I made an effort to record those for future comparisons."

"But in fact in your examination of the plaster casts, those were not created by small children's-size shoes, were they?"

"They were of a smaller shoe than what these shoes were. They were of a different size."

"They were a different size, but we're not talking about a small child's shoe?"

"Define for me what you're saying, small child's shoes. I've been a scoutmaster. I've had scouts with size 13 feet."

"Well, I guess I'm just looking…I understand that kids shoe sizes all vary. But in general they are...they're not…we're not talking about a toddler for instance."

"No, we're not talking toddler."

"We're probably not talking the next category up from toddler either are we?"

"Again, it would depend on the individual. One of the things when you look at the size of the shoe impression found at the scene is different manufacturers. If I may use these again; for example, these shoes actually have a very small tread design as opposed to somebody who might make a running shoe or something that would have footwear that sticks out considerably farther than the shoe itself. And different size is actually depending, again, on the manufacturer. They use the same size bottom footwear for several different sizes of shoes. So, it's many times difficult to say that that impression is a size 8½ because it may fit a size 7½, 8½ and size 9 shoe."

"OK. So I think what I hear you saying is that one size of footwear bottom may be used on several different sizes of shoes."

"That is correct, ma'am."

"And also, the size of the bottom of the shoe, the sole, would depend on the type of shoe it is. And for instance, some shoes have inordinately large soles for their size."

"That is correct."

"Or the converse?"

"Or the reverse may happen."

"So really, we can't tell a lot about the size of the person's foot from the size of the footwear impression?"

"Not always."

"Thank you."

JUDGE: "Any redirect?"

PICKERING: "Yes, Your Honor.

"What size are those shoes there that you've been looking at, People's Exhibits 5 and 6?"

PRATT: "It is a size 10½."

"Now, I think Ms. Cooke asked you about a two-by-four. What, if anything, is there about the surface of a piece of...People's Exhibit 48, which is the two-by-four, that would make it difficult to lift fingerprints off of?"

"Wood is a very porous type of surface. And many times, especially unfinished wood, which I consider this, absorbs fingerprints and makes it very difficult to ever get identifiable-type prints off of."

"With respect to People's Exhibit 32, what is there about the surface...what, if anything, is there about the surface of this exhibit that would affect your ability to lift fingerprints?"

"Well, part of the problem is that the size is of...if somebody were to grab it they wouldn't necessarily even leave their prints. They might leave a portion of the palm. But again, movement would have a factor on it also. This is a harder surface. Other factors would be the individual themselves, whether they would be sweating enough or be the type of person that would leave fingerprints on the surface."

"Would you identify People Exhibit 69 please."

"This is the knife which I found in the paper bag in the basement bedroom."

"What, if anything, is there about the surface of that knife that would affect the ability to leave prints?"

COOKE: "Judge, objection. This question was asked and answered. I realize I discussed it by way of my chart, but I think we're getting redundant at this point."

JUDGE: "Overruled."

PRATT: "Again, there is on the surface of the knife there…the handle, there's an extreme amount of reddish substance. And also on the blade of the knife was an excessive amount of reddish substance, which would preclude or make it very difficult to get identifiable prints."

PICKERING: "Thank you Mr. Pratt."

JUDGE: "Anything further?"

PICKERING: "No, Your Honor. Thank you very much."

JUDGE: "You may step down. Call your next witness."

I couldn't believe the testimony I'd just read. They cut blood-soaked carpet out of our home for evidence against Scott, but barely acknowledged evidence that can't be linked to Scott or the Scharfs. They have fingerprints on a knife, but don't know whose they are so they assume they're Scott's. They have footprints everywhere that they can't identify. And the car…they checked the car, and there was nothing there. Scott was bleeding profusely. If he had been in that car, wouldn't there be some evidence? How could these people not have searched for solid answers?

I shook my head. The prosecution presented Scott as a knife-wielding maniac running through this house intent on killing these people. They have him running up and down the stairs, all through this house like a mad man, but he only left two fingerprints in the whole house?

My mind drifted to the day Sam's assistant told me there was a lot of evidence the prosecution didn't have answers for. Some beer cans, or something of that nature, in the window wells were never examined for prints. She said she had discovered evidence that the prosecution had been hiding, a bag filled with money and some other objects, which had never been accounted for. What were they trying to hide?

I returned to the transcript.

MILLER: "The People call Mool Verma. Sir, how are you employed?"

VERMA: "I'm a forensic anthropologist and an agent of the Colorado Bureau of Investigation in Denver."

"And how long have you worked for CBI?"

"19 years."

"What is the nature of your work at CBI?"

"Forensic anthropologist essentially is a specialist who can assess skeletal remains and study man in relation to his origins, physical characteristics and classification. There are specialized areas within the larger field of forensic anthropology. One of them is called forensic tricology and that deals with the examination of hairs. I specialize in that area."

"What characteristics can distinguish one person's hair from another person's hair or hairs?"

"A hair essentially is, to put in layman's terminology, can be compared to an ordinary pencil. The hairs have layers of scales on them just like scales on a fish. The wooden portion of the pencil corresponds to what we refer to as the cortex. The cortex of the hair is where the pigment is distributed in many different ways. And the lead portion of the pencil would correspond to what is referred to as the medulla of the hair. And this medulla is, again, of many different types. I do have a chart with me if I may be permitted to use that."

"Yes, I'll put that up on the easel. Sir, your report would indicate that you also looked at several other items recovered from the crime scene and elsewhere to determine the presence or absence of any hairs that were similar to one another, is that correct?"

"Yes sir."

"And indeed, you list some 15 or 20 items that you looked at for the presence or absence of hairs."

"Yes. Of all of the 23 items which were submitted to me for examination, nine of those are control samples and the remaining 14 items are questioned samples taken from the victims."

"Did the articles submitted to you for possible hair analysis or comparison include a black T-shirt?"

"Yes sir. The black T-shirt, which is CBI Exhibit 1, contained one hair of animal origin."

"How about No. 2, or the jeans. Were they submitted to you?"

"Yes sir. Once again, that particular item contained no human hairs. It contained only animal hair."

"Wood-handled knife?"

"That contained a dark brown Caucasian head hair which was not similar to the suspect's control sample."

"Your report indicates that there were some hairs from the kitchen floor of the Scharfs home that were submitted to you. Did you examine them?"

"Yes. The hair recovered from the kitchen floor was found to be a Caucasian pubic hair. And that hair, once again, was not similar to the suspect's control sample."

"Your report indicates a hair from outside the basement window was submitted to you?"

"Yeah. That is referred to as CBI Exhibit 164. And that particular hair, again, is an animal hair."

"Did you examine hairs and fibers or were hairs and fibers submitted to you from the hands of the Scharfs?"

"Yes. Neither one of these exhibits contained any hairs or fibers. That is, there was no hairs or fibers recovered from the hands of Robbie Scharf."

"Those are my questions for you."

COOKE: "Mr. Verma, let me ask you just a few questions to see if I can sort of summarize and correctly understand your testimony."

VERMA: "Of course ma'am."

"You indicated that you collected…that a number of other items were submitted to you for purposes of conducting comparisons?"

"Yes ma'am."

"Other than the hair that you've identified as being consistent with having originated from Scott Mutchler?"

"That is correct."

"And as to most of those other items that were submitted to you, you were able to perform comparisons?"

"Yes. That was…I made an attempt to do that, yes."

"And as to the ones that you were able to perform comparison on, you compared them to each of the control samples you received? In other words, you compared them to Scott Mutchler, and the Scharfs."

"That is correct."

"And some of those that you examined were human hair that were consistent with Mr. Scharf."

"Yes."

"And I believe that there were two items that you testified that were human hair that did not originate from either the Scharfs or Scott Mutchler?"

"Is that a particular exhibit that you're referring to?"

"Well, let me take it one by one. For instance, CBI 59, was hairs from the kitchen floor correct?"

"That is correct, yes."

"And you determined that those hairs were not…did not originate from any of the people who you were given control samples from. In other words, they did not originate from the Scharfs or Scott Mutchler."

"No, those…that particular hair was compared only to the pubic hair control sample from Mr. Mutchler. It was not compared to the pubic hair control sample from Mr. Scharf. And I believe that the younger victim did not have any pubic hairs."

"OK. And the color of that pubic hair was what?

"Dark brown."

"And the wood handled knife, you also obtained a hair comparison, a hair that you were able to compare from that, did you not?"

"Yes. That was a segment of a dark brown…"

"I'm just asking you if you were…you did a comparison?"

"I did, yes."

"And that hair also was not…did not originate from Mr. Mutchler?"

"That is correct."

"Thank you. I have no further questions."

JUDGE: "Redirect?"

MILLER: "Mr. Verma, let's just return to those two exhibits again; No. 59, the kitchen floor. What did you determine that to be?"

VERMA: "That was found to be dissimilar to the pubic hair control sample taken from the suspect in this case. It was not compared to the pubic hair control sample from the victim. And there's a reason for that. In any given house at any given time, there are many different types of hairs that are found on the floor material or in the vacuum, etc., and unless control samples are provided from all the parties involved, it becomes very difficult to make an assessment in terms of evidentiary value to do a comparison.

"The most important element here was at that particular time, that evidence was given to me to see whether or not that hair came from the defendant in this case. And that was done."

"You determined that that particular pubic hair in the kitchen did not originate from the defendant?"

"That is correct."

"And No. 33, the knife or knife handle. What was it you found at or near on the handle of the knife?"

"Once again, that particular hair was compared to the hair control samples from Mr.…the suspect in this case. And that hair was not from the suspect."

"Who was the…can you describe that hair in any more detail?"

"It's a very small segment of a Caucasian dark brown head hair."

"Did the size or length of the hair contribute to any part of your inability to match or compare it?"

"There was an insufficient length. It was of insufficient length to compare it to the control samples from the suspect."

"Thank you, Mr. Verma."

JUDGE: "All right, you are excused."

Pubic hairs? What the hell was all that about? Why are they talking about pubic hairs? What is the connection here? I was becoming more confused by the testimony of the witnesses that the district attorney presented. As hard as I tried to make sense of it all, it was becoming more of a blur. What made it worse was the letter Scott had forwarded to me that he had received from Sam Shaw about a year after Scott had been convicted. I searched for that letter in my bag. Slowly I reread that letter.

"Dear Scott: A few weeks ago I was made aware of information concerning Evan Scharf, which I was not aware of while your case was pending. Linda Cooke learned from another Public Defender in a different office that John Pickering had information related to unusual sexual practices by Evan Scharf. I contacted Pickering and he told me that last spring, he visited his urologist and the urologist advised him that Evan Scharf had been a patient of the doctor's before his death. The doctor told Pickering that sometime not too long before Scharf's death, he had treated Scarf for the removal of a small metal object, which had been lodged in Scharf's bladder. The doctor told Pickering that Scharf had told him that the metal object had ended up where it did through some sort of sex act. That is the extent of what I know. The doctor has refused to talk to us about it so far." Oh my God.

MILLER: "The next witness is Byron Silvus. We would ask that this witness be questioned outside the presence of the jury."

JUDGE: "Dismiss the jury."

SHAW: "For the record, we are out of the presence of the jury and we're asking Mr. Silvus questions concerning alleged threats that he's reported. Mr. Silvus, you've indicated I believe to law enforcement and to investigators from my office that over the last couple of days, you received one or two threatening phone calls, is that right?"

SILVUS: "Yes sir."

"Tell us please. Take each one and say where you received it and what the caller said. Start with the first one if you would."

"OK. The first one."

"When did you receive it?"

"The first one was late Sunday night, actually after midnight. I was at home and I received the call. I answered the phone and he said that I would advise you not to go to court tomorrow. I said, 'Excuse me?' and they said, 'Just don't show up in court tomorrow.' After that period I received two more phone calls where no one said anything and I took my phone off the hook after that night."

"Are you still on…those are both Sunday night?"

"Yes."

"Actually, it was a total of three Sunday night, two where no one responded."

"And then, yesterday, when I got back home from court yesterday I received a phone call that said, 'If you go to court again, I'll take my shirt and choke you like we did the boy'."

"Now, did that seem to be the same voice that you heard Sunday night, early morning hours of Monday morning?"

"Yes sir."

"OK. Anything else that's happened to you that you consider suspicious or threatening in the last couple days?"

"I feel that yesterday I was followed back from Boulder on my way home."

"Did you...were you able to make any identification about the car or..."

"Just that it was..."

"Driver? Passengers in the car that was following you?"

"I don't know what it was. It was just a white car that looked like either a Honda Prelude or Honda Accord, a newer one."

"And to what law enforcement agency did you report this?"

"I reported the last threat on yesterday to my law enforcement agency in Thornton. They came out and took a report. I spoke with Mr. Ragulsky yesterday also."

"Going back to the second phone call, were you able to speak to the caller and ask any questions?"

"No, they just said that and hung up."

"How sure are you that was the same voice that you heard on your phone in the early morning hours of Monday?"

"I'd be positive."

"That's the testimony Judge. I don't know if Mr. Miller has any questions."

MILLER: "Just a few. The call Sunday night was essentially a statement of advice to you?"

SILVUS: "Right."

"I advise you. We advise you."

"He said, 'I advise you'."

"Not to go to court tomorrow?"

"Right."

"And that was about all that you heard this person say?"

"They said, 'Just don't show up in court tomorrow'."

"And what I missed is the second call, what time that was, time of day?"

"I would say between 6 and 6:30. It was after I arrived home from here yesterday."

"These are both phone calls you received at your home number?"

"Yes sir."

"Was that a single person on the phone as opposed to more than one person?"

"I only heard one person talking."

"I have no other questions of Mr. Silvus on that point, Your Honor."

SHAW: "I don't have any more questions Judge."

JUDGE: "OK you may step down. When you're called again, I'll probably swear you again because of the jury being present ,OK?"

SHAW: "The…"

JUDGE: "The reason for the asking this question or cross?"

SHAW: "Judge, it fits right in with the defense theory in this case that other people were present at the Scharf residence when they were killed and account for the actual killing. And now…"

JUDGE: "It's pure, unadulterated, perfect first-class definition of hearsay. Offered for the truth of the matter asserted."

SHAW: "Well nonetheless judge…"

JUDGE: "It's worse."

SHAW: "It's worse? What do you mean?"

JUDGE: "It's just…it's just…you know, sometimes I do what you've asked me to do on other occasions, that's tell the jury what the law is and why without giving them an eight-hour lecture on evidence, one of the hardest courses in law school. But this is one that would be easy. This is pure hearsay. And the reason we don't admit hearsay is it can't be cross-examined. We permit something that somebody said because it shows us why we did something else.

"But in this case, the only possible reason to offer that kind of testimony would be for the truth of the matter asserted and we don't know anything about it."

SHAW: "Well…"

JUDGE: "It didn't cause him to do anything."

SHAW: "Well, that's not entirely true. But as far as what the Court's talking about here in terms of whether it developed…he used it to develop any evidence, you're right. But we're offering it not to show that that person was involved in killing Robbie Scharf, but to show that these unsolved portions of the case extend for that reason on that theory.

"It's not being offered for the truth of the matter asserted but that only to show there's someone out there saying these things, which corroborates our claim that the prosecution hasn't turned over every stone in this case and mysteries exist which would lead the jury to believe that other people were present in the home and killed the Scharfs."

JUDGE: "Well, you will not be permitted to ask that question. And, any attempt to do so will be dealt with swiftly, as you might imagine. Are we ready for the next witness?"

I jumped to my feet and threw the transcript down on the cabana. Damn them! Damn this whole system! How could this judge not allow the jury to hear this testimony? How could they not, at the very least, investigate what this person had said?

I walked to the edge of the water and kicked at the waves rolling in, watched the water trickle away from my toes. There had to be a way to let the world know what this judge had done, what Alex Hunter's office had done. There had to be a way to let the world know what the Boulder County Judicial System was all about.

There had to be a way to right the wrong and stop this insanity.

I turned and walked back to my chair and stared at the transcript on the cabana. With a sigh, I sat down and opened the pages again.

The Neighbors Tell a Different Story

JUDGE: “Your next witness Mr. Shaw.”
SHAW: “Call Oscar Salgado. Mr. Salgado, where did you live?”
SALGADO: “I live on Van Buren Court in Louisville.”
“How long have you lived there, sir?”
“Approximately a year and a half.”
“Were you…do you own your own home there?”
“Yes, I do.”
“Were you residing there in your home on September 10th and 11th?”
“Yes, I was.”
“Did you know Evan and Robbie Scharf?”
“Never met them, no.”
“Were they neighbors then?”
“No.”
“The Scharfs?”
“The Scharfs, yes, I’m sorry.”

"They were your neighbors in the days preceding the 10th of September?"

"Yes."

"OK. Directing your attention to the late evening hours of September 10th, I ask you if you had occasion to be awakened from your sleep?"

"Yeah, I was."

"What happened?"

"Well, we were in bed. My little girl woke up screaming. She was describing…"

"Who lives in your house besides your little girl and you?"

"My son, who is 8 years old, and my wife."

"OK. I didn't mean to interrupt you. You heard your little girl screaming, you woke up and what?"

"She was crying."

"What time of day was it? Do you know?"

"It was roughly around 11:15, around there."

"OK, and what did she do after she woke up and cried?"

"She ran into our room. She was screaming that she…"

MILLER: "Objection, hearsay."

SHAW: "Judge, this is an excited utterance."

JUDGE: "I'll permit it. Go ahead."

SALGADO: "That she had heard noises outside that woke her up. People were screaming and there was a lot of noise outside and she woke up. She was scared."

SHAW: "Where is her bedroom located in your house?"

"It faces towards the west, towards the Scharf's house."

"Were windows open that night?"

"That night, yes, slightly opened, about half open."

"Did you get up with her then?"

"Yes. Me and my wife both got up. My wife grabbed her in her arms and calmed her down."

"Right after that did you hear or see anything unusual out in the cul-de-sac?"

"At that time I…my wife had control of my little girl to put her back to sleep. I myself went to the restroom. At that time a car went by or leaving the cul-de-sac. It was around 11:30, about 15 or 10 minutes after she had woken up crying."

"Those are my questions of Mr. Salgado."

MILLER: "No questions."

JUDGE: "OK, you may step down. Call your next witness."

I leaned my head back and looked at the beautiful blue sky. It was funny how the prosecution didn't have any questions for this witness. I guess they didn't want to bring any more attention to this man's testimony. There is no way Scott could have been in the house during that time; he was in the emergency room. Someone else was in that house!

SHAW: "The defense calls Carol Hampf. Ms. Hampf, where do you reside?"

HAMPF: "Van Buren Court, Louisville, Colorado."

"How long have you lived there?"

"About a year as of now."

"So you were living there on September 10th? Directing your attention to the evening hours of that day, I ask you if you heard voices at some time that sounded loud and argumentative?"

"Yes I did, between 10:30 and 11 at night."

"Let me ask you about your recollection concerning the time. Is that your present recollection or is that refreshed by a document that you created soon after the deaths of the Scharfs?"

"That recollection is referred by a statement I gave the Louisville police. The Louisville police knocked on our door about 3 in the morning. Shortly thereafter they knocked to see if we knew anything about our neighbors' whereabouts. I gave the statement probably at 4 or 4:30 in the morning."

"When you gave the statement, how confident were you about those times?"

"I was plus or minus a half an hour at the time I gave that."

"Did they sound to you like they were coming from the Scharf residence?"

"No. At the time I heard the voices, they sounded like they were coming from across the cul-de-sac, whereas the Scharfs are next...like next...side by side with my house. It sounded like the voices came from across the street."

"Well, on the day you gave your statement it was your conclusion they could have come from next door at the Scharf's house?"

"Yes, it was. And in the morning and having found out at that point what had happened, I decided it was possible that they had come from next door. Basically, there are no windows on the side of the houses where they face each other. So any sound comes in from across the cul-de-sac, if that makes sense."

"Is it fair to characterize what you heard as sounding like a domestic fight?"

"That's what I put in my statement to the police. The reason why I said that is that struck me that way at the time. It sounded like two people who knew each other were yelling at each other. It was very short. I didn't hear any specific words. I didn't hear what was being said. I...it just sounded like somebody came home from work and yelled at whoever they were living with. It was very short. It just...for some reason it sounded like two people who knew each other."

"Thank you. Those are my questions of Ms. Hampf, Judge."

MILLER: "Good morning. When you say it sounded like a domestic dispute, to me that triggers up an image of a man and a woman. Is that what you recall about these voices or did you distinguish sex of the voices?"

HAMPF: "What I can tell is that one voice was definitely male. The second voice was either male or female and I can't tell you which."

"You said that upon reflection and after learning what had apparently occurred at the Scharf's residence the next day you determined that the voices may have come from that house?"

"It's speculation. I'm not sure if determined is the..."

"All right. Thank you. I think I understand. And indeed, your first reaction was that whatever voices you may have heard between apparently now as early as 10 and as late as 11:30. I've added 30 minutes to the time you've given us."

"Actually, why don't I clarify that. When I said it would vary a half an hour and I gave a range, it would not have occurred between 10 and 11:30. My recollection at the time was based on the fact that I was working at my desk. My husband came home and went to bed. When I got up a few hours later, I was still aware of what time my husband came home.

"So more specifically I would say I heard the voices sometime between 10:15 and maybe 11 or a little later. I was thinking that it was half an hour from the start time that I was uncertain about, which was 10:30. It's been a while."

"In any event, the first impression, indeed the part that you wrote in your statement, was you thought that this sounded like a short domestic dispute, which may have involved two male voices or a male and a female voice, and emanated or came from the two houses across the street?"

"Everything you said is accurate."

"And the houses across the street do not include the house of Evan Scharf?"

"No, they do not."

"Thank you, no other questions."

JUDGE: "You may step down. Court is in recess."

JUDGE: We are outside the presence of the jury panel. There is apparently one more witness for the prosecution. That witness, I'm told, is very short. Rather than take the witness who is anticipated to testify for maybe less than five minutes, what I would like to do is give Mr. Mutchler the Curtis advisement, let Mr. Shaw make a motion and then we can make a further and more detailed record on his motion at the next recess. So that following the Curtis advisement and following the motion, we'll hear the witness and then the defense will present its case and then make a further record on the motion, anticipated to be judgment of acquittal motion to the Court. I'm trying to save bringing in the jury for five minutes and then sending them back out.

SHAW: Judge, while you're pausing this, just so the record reflects that back in chambers, I objected to that procedure and I asked that we do the witness and then the Curtis advisement and then my motion for judgment of acquittal."

JUDGE: "Mr. Mutchler, I'm required by the case called People versus Curtis to give the following advice. Do you understand that you have a right to testify in this case? Do you understand that, sir?"

SCOTT: "Yes sir."

"Do you understand that if you want to testify, no one, including your lawyer, can prevent you from doing so. It is your right to testify."

"Yes sir."

"Do you understand that if you testify, the district attorney will be allowed to cross examine you the same as any other witness? Do you understand that?"

"Yes."

"Do you understand that if you have a felony conviction record the district attorney would be allowed to ask you about it, but not about any juvenile adjudications? Do you understand that?"

"Yes."

"Do you understand that if you have a felony record and it *is* disclosed to the jury, the jury will be instructed to consider your record only as it bears upon your credibility and for no other purpose? Do you understand that?"

"Yes."

"Do you also understand that you have a right not to testify in this case, as this jury has been prepared throughout the trial? Do you understand you do not have to testify; you do not have to prove anything?"

"Yes, Your Honor."

"Do you understand that if you decide not to testify, the jury can be instructed that your decision may not be used as evidence of your guilt and should not in any way prejudice you in the eyes of the jury?"

"Yes."

"Do you understand that? Have you discussed your decision with your attorney?"

"Yes, Your Honor."

"And is the decision you have made...you don't need to tell me at this time what your decision is. But is the decision you have made entirely your own?"

"Yes."

"Having observed the demeanor of the defendant, I find...and his answers to the questions I've just asked, I find that his decision to or not to testify is voluntary, made knowingly and intentionally. Mr. Shaw, do you want to briefly make a motion just prior to the next witness?"

SHAW: "Judge, my motion is a motion for acquittal on all counts. We can cite the Bennett case for the proposition that the prosecution's case, even when considered in the light most favorable to the People, has not convinced a reasonable juror beyond a reasonable doubt that they prevail on each and every element of each count. I ask the Court to dismiss all counts."

JUDGE: "I'll permit you, if you want, to make further argument on that motion. It is now denied. Let me tender to you, Mr. Shaw, a copy of the deposition. The Court has an original and the district attorney has the original...I mean a copy.

"All right, we're ready for the jury. Bring them in. Your next witness."

SHAW: "Michelle Ferguson. Ms. Ferguson, what is your occupation?"

FERGUSON: "I'm a police officer with the City of Louisville."

"How long have you been employed in that capacity?"

"Approximately five and a half years."

"Were you employed in that capacity in early September?"

"Yes, I was."

"Did you have the occasion in your job as a police officer to become involved in the investigation of the deaths of Robbie and Evan Scharf?"

"Yes."

"In the course of that investigation did you interview a gentleman by the name of Joseph Graham?"

"Yes, I did."

"Have you had the opportunity to review your notes or your report of that interview with him recently?"

"Yes."

"I'd like to ask you a couple of questions about that. Did you talk with Mr. ...I know you talked with him about a number of things. But specifically, did you have the occasion to talk with him about when he had last been at the Scharf home?"

"Yes, I did."

"What did he tell you?"

"He told me that he had been..."

MILLER: "Your Honor, I object to the hearsay nature of this testimony. There's been...if we may approach the bench."

JUDGE: "Objection overruled."

SHAW: "Did he tell you what his purpose was in being at the Scharf home?"

FERGUSON: "Yes. He often used the Scharf's computer."

"He used the computer. Did he indicate to you whether or not he used that computer on September 10th?"

"Yes. He said that he had."

"And where is that computer located?"

"It's in the downstairs room of the house."

"Did you ask him about the window, the basement window that is adjacent to the computer desk?"

"Yes."

"And did he tell you something about the window in relation to his use of the computer?"

"He advised me that he often opens the window due to the fact that the computers generate a lot of heat. To let the heat out he opens the windows."

"Did you ask him if he recalled whether he had opened the window when he was working there on September 10th?"

"He had advised me that he was fairly certain that he had opened the window on that date."

"Did you also ask him if he had closed the window prior to leaving that day?"

"Yes I did."

"And what was his answer?"

"He could not recall if he had closed it or not."

"Thank you Ms. Ferguson."

MILLER: "No questions."
JUDGE: "OK, you may step down."

With a heavy sigh, I rubbed my forehead. My God. I remembered the day Scott had called to tell me that his attorney said he was not to testify. I didn't understand that reasoning, but I didn't understand much of anything that had gone on.

From Officer Ferguson's testimony, there seemed to be more than reasonable doubt that the Scharf's house had been broken into. But the prosecutors still led the jury and everyone else to believe that Scott had broken in through the basement window. They knew from the start that someone else had opened the window. No wonder the prosecution tried to object to this testimony. No wonder the prosecution had no questions of this police officer.

Next were the closing arguments. I'll never forget what I heard in the courtroom that day.

Part 4

Closing Statements

Prosecution

MILLER: "May it please the Court, counsel, ladies and gentlemen, last week during the voir dire selection process each of you that was questioned by counsel agreed that there was a burden of proof on the prosecution. Mr. Pickering and I have acknowledged that to you during the jury process and would remind you that in any criminal case, the burden of proof lies with the prosecution. The agency that brings the charges has the burden of proving them.

"It was also said last week during the process of selecting a jury that we give you a hard job, but we don't give you an impossible job.

"You now have heard all of the evidence that will govern your deliberations in this case. Just now you heard all the Colorado law that applies to this case. You all indicated at one time or another that you would follow that law, not your own, but to apply that which is given to you to the facts of this case.

"Indeed, everything you need to decide this case has been given to you.

"But the law does permit both sides to give a summation or closing argument about the evidence in this case. Following our arguments you'll retire to decide and make this important decision.

"You've learned now that the People, if you didn't know before, charged four counts of murder in the first-degree. There are only two victims, but the instructions of law tell you that the prosecution has charged Mr. Mutchler with the killing of the two, Evan Scharf and Robbie Scharf, after deliberation with the intent to do so.

"And we've also charged him with a felony murder on each victim; that is to say, we have charged that during the commission of a burglary, a serious felony, the death of those two people were caused. So, we have the four counts, one each as for after deliberation on each victim, and one each on the felony murder doctrine count.

"Let's look a minute at the first-degree murder counts, after deliberation. I submit to you that you have evidence before you that suggests deliberation in several areas. You have the deliberation that is shown by the defendant's conversations with his young acquaintances that you heard testify yesterday. You have deliberation that shows up in both the list that he prepares,
which you'll have a chance to see. No one has read it to you, but
it lists things to do, equipment, things to do before leaving.

"And the letter to Zac Page. Zac Page, where he writes to a friend in Florida, talks about his plans. Significant part he talks about breaking into this house. 'The only people that live there are this man and his kid. Anyway, I'm going to put chloroform on his mouth and nose, then tie him up so he can't move ever. Then same for the kid. Well, then his money, checks, credit cards and car with cell phone are mine since he'll be all tied up.'

"You'll have a chance to see these exhibits, get an idea of what was going on in the mind of Scott Mutchler before these events ever occurred.

"You'll also have a chance to consider, pondering the deliberation, that you may draw from what you learn about what Mr. Scott Mutchler did once inside the home.

"The evidence before you and the inferences you can draw from that evidence are that he entered that home with the two-by-four. Later, he armed himself...he gave up the two-by-four and armed himself with a poker in the living room. And from the kitchen he obtained the knife, the butcher knife.

"I submit to you Ms. Cooke argued that the evidence showed that the defendant did not intend to harm. Well, we have other evidence. The young people who testified said they formed an impression that he didn't mean to harm anybody. But take a look at that letter. Take a look at the plan that went into it, what the defendant said he was going to do. He did say he was going to tie up the man and his son with ropes and apply chloroform to them. That sounds like harm. He told in the letter to Zac Page about what his plans were concerning the man and his son.

"Ms. Cooke said in her opening statement it made no sense to hit the head of a sleeping man. I agree if the evidence shows that the defendant was attacking the sleeping form of Evan Scharf with first the poker. I submit to you the evidence is consistent with him striking the back. You have the photograph of...Dr. Meyer took of the brand, the impression on the back. You have the sketch of the blows to the top of the head consistent with a blunt instrument. It makes no sense to hit a man who is sleeping with a blunt instrument unless you intend to harm him.

"But the harm didn't stop there because after being hit by the poker, Evan Scharf didn't roll over. He didn't become unconscious. He didn't yield. He fought back and he fought for his life, ladies and gentlemen. He fought for his life.

"And you saw the wounds that were inflicted on his hands and his fingers and his arms as he fought to live. But he was hit several times. He had stabbing wounds that went into his body, slashing wounds that cut parts of his body. You saw the deadly, vicious blows that were rendered on Evan Scharf that cost him his life. Dr. Meyer says that that knife is consistent with all of the wounds that were inflicted on Evan Scharf.

"We now have from the evidence that the trail of blood led from the bedroom bathroom of Evan Scharf down the hall to the bedroom where Scott Mutchler, because he knew this house, he knew this family, he'd been there before, he baby-sat before. He knew the bed that Robbie Scharf slept in. But Robbie Scharf wasn't there.

"The evidence also would suggest and show the blood…trail of blood would show that he went looking for Robbie. Trail of blood led downstairs to the main level and then down again to the lower level. Bleeding from wounds that he had suffered in the struggle, the trail was left. And Scott Mutchler found Robbie Scharf hiding in the bathtub or in the bathroom. What was the defendant's intent? What did he mean to do when he confronted Robbie? You can only find from the evidence that supports how he was killed that he intended to kill him; that it was after deliberation that he knew what he was doing.

"We have deliberation if we didn't have deliberation beforehand. And I submit to you that we do…you do through the statement that he made to friends, the writings that you may certainly find that there was deliberation that was intent on his part inside the home to do what he did.

"But apart from killing someone after deliberation, the law in Colorado, we learn, also says that you can find the person guilty of first-degree murder if they're committing a serious offense like burglary and they kill someone.

"That's what happened here too, ladies and gentlemen. You need only find that the defendant entered and remained unlawfully in a building or occupied structure, the Scharf home, and that during the time he was there, he was either armed when he came in, or during the time he was there he became armed with deadly weapons. 'The intent to cause theft or to steal something and that death results.' It resulted twice.

"Had Scott Mutchler gone to the Scharf home and just taken the car and not done anything else he might be on trial for car theft. Had he gone to the Scharf home and entered the window without any weapon and didn't get a weapon after he'd gotten in but had the intent to go there and steal something, he might be on trial for second-degree burglary. Had he gone to the Scharf home and entered with a weapon or, after gaining entry, armed himself with a weapon with the intent to steal something, he might be on trial for first-degree burglary. Indeed, had he armed himself, entered the home, armed himself, and gone upstairs with his weapons, killed Evan Scharf and then later Robbie Scharf, he might only be guilty of felony murder; that is to say, a murder that occurred during the course of a burglary. But he did all of that. He did all of that."

SHAW: "I'm going to object to counsel suggesting that there's some different graduation of felony murder and the other charges of murder, anything, by saying he might just have been charged with felony murder."

JUDGE: "Overruled."

SHAW: "I understand. But that's a misstatement of the law."

JUDGE: "Well, you may argue that."

MILLER: "Ladies and gentlemen, I was saying that yes, there are two ways to commit first-degree murder in relation to this case, and the defendant committed murder on both theories, during the course of a burglary in progress and also after deliberation.

"Count five is first-degree burglary. Said burglary is indicated by entering a building or occupied structure with the intent to commit the crime of theft, and while in the building or occupied structure the defendant is armed with a deadly weapon, in this case, a knife.

"Second-degree burglary is unlawfully entering and remaining in a building or…dwelling or building or occupied structure with the intent to commit the crime of theft.

"Aggravated motor vehicle theft is knowingly obtaining or exercising control over a motor vehicle belonging to another person without authorization.

"Those are the seven counts. Those are the seven definitions that you'll be given here, and you'll have a chance to have copies of these instructions with you. And you can take them and you can apply them to all of the evidence that you have heard in this case.

"What about the evidence in this case? You have heard about the plans to break into a house where a man and his kid lived, people he knew and that he had worked for and baby-sat for. He talked about his plans. He wrote about his plans.

"The evidence would suggest that after being in jail for six weeks on September 10, 1991, the defendant moved fast within two hours of his release. He had his mother and stepfather dropping him at the Louisville 7-Eleven store. You heard how he dressed, his clothing: black shirt, black pants, black shoes. And when he was at the hospital he had no identification on him.

"You heard how the evidence supports how the entry was made; that Evan, a friend, had been in the home earlier on the day of the 10th; how he had left the window, by his recollection, ajar, unlocked and ajar because it was hot that day.

"We know and can reconstruct how entry was made in that house by the exhibits and testimony you've heard. Scott Mutchler entered that house and took those weapons from within the house and went upstairs. He was ready for anything. Could it be that he thought a blow in the back of the head would knock out Evan Scharf and that he could do what he wanted, or that it would incapacitate his victim in someway? We can only conclude that these blows did not render Evan Scharf unconscious and that he fought, as I've described.

"You've heard that he used the knife, stabbing the victim and eventually killing him. You've learned that Robbie Scharf died quickly but no less violently than his father."

SHAW: "Objection Your Honor. Appealing to the passion of the jury."

JUDGE: "Overruled."

MILLER: "Killed savagely by this defendant. He took no chances. Dr. Meyer described the blows, the killing blows and the post-killing blows.

"There's evidence that the defendant used the telephone and touched the telephone at the Scharf home. His fingerprint is there in blood. It's consistent with his own. He'd handled the phone sometime after his own blood had begun to flow.

"The evidence also shows that Eve Meyer, the defendant's mother, received a phone call after or near 11 o'clock, the time that they had agreed he would be home. She said he sounded normal, that he would be home, he had to get some gas and he would be home. He came home.

"And you heard the testimony that he came home with these same black clothes he had on when he left, but this time they were covered with blood. Ted Davelis told us about the blood on those clothes, they had blood consistent with the defendant, yes, but also blood consistent with that of Evan Scharf and Robbie Scharf. Silent evidence of his deadly crime was on his own clothing when he came home and ten minutes later went to the hospital.

"The evidence before you has included the testimony of the officers, the emergency technicians, the nurse, and the police officers who responded to the hospital and acted upon the information the defendant gave them about his being assailed by three people and being injured.

"EMT Yusko, Officer McNair, Detective Hartmann, Detective Schuler, Nurse Gutzmer all talked with him. All heard what he said about his injuries.

"They tried to find the location but they could not find the place. They couldn't get any more details, enough detail to find out what had happened.

"And then the turning point in the case, I suggest to you, was the attention drawn to the car, the car that Mrs. Eve Meyer pointed out to the police as the one that her son had left at home, the one that he had given her the keys to, the reference to his car, when it was checked by the police they found out it was not his car. It was listed to Evan Scharf. And it was that piece of information and how it was acted upon by the police at the scene and the Louisville officers.

"If you recall Sergeant Berg testified very graphically in great detail about what he found when he went to the home, about what the police found.

"You will see in pictures and sketches what this trial is all about, the deaths of Evan and Robbie Scharf.

"Consider the police work in this case: that after they determined there were two bodies at the home no one could answer why this man had Evan Scharf's car. The owner certainly couldn't answer. But he was detained. And they detained his clothing and they sealed the car and later they sealed the home and they obtained exhibits from that home that you'll see. They have a lot of exhibits from that home that help you determine Scott Mutchler was there and that he was the killer. Ladies and gentlemen, in its entirety I submit to you that the evidence has shown, beyond any reasonable doubt, that on September 10, 1991, within four or five hours of his release from jail where he had been for six weeks, the defendant carried out a plan, a plan that he had developed prior to going to the jail, according to the statements to the young people, and the writings.

"And he went back to the old neighborhood, back to the place where he talked about, place he talked about to Scott Seppers, Eric Peterson, Lee Schafer, Andrea Tyson and Jeff Upton, back to the place he wrote Zac Page about in his letter, back to the place where he had done yard work, back to the place where he had been a baby-sitter and, apparently, friends with the family at some point, but this time not as a neighbor, but as a thief, a burglar, and as a murderer.

"And I submit to you, ladies and gentleman, that when you review the evidence and you review it carefully, we invite you to do that, and the testimony that's been presented, and you take these instructions of law as they guide you through the definitions of murder after deliberation, after planning, after intending to kill somebody, killing them, murder during the commission of a burglary, and indeed the offenses that are defined also; first- degree burglary, second-degree burglary, and car theft, that you'll find that the evidence presented will meet the burden that you must reach, the level that you must find to show that the People have proven their case beyond a reasonable doubt.

"And the prosecution charges you with having reviewed that evidence, having applied the applicable Colorado law to this case, we charge you to come back with the appropriate verdicts in this case and that is guilty on all seven counts made against the defendant."

Defense

JUDGE: "Mr. Shaw."

SHAW: "Thank you, Judge. Mr. Miller's comments pretty much pattern their case and his opening statements. His argument and what you've heard over the last few days is heavy, heavy on the side of Mr. Mutchler planned to burglarize the Scharf residence, and Mr. Mutchler was there. And we've conceded that from day one, that he planned to burglarize the Scharf residence and he was there at or near the time of the deaths of the victims in this case.

"And then he tries to encourage you with some appeals to prejudice and sympathy to take a leap from there because a young boy and his father died; to take a leap from there and imagine a lot of things. And you can't do that.

"The jury instructions will remind you that you can't do that; that you have to try to figure out what happened in that house from the evidence presented and reasonable inference. And if you can't, you can't. And no matter how sad or how mad you are about what happened there, you can't take it out on Mr. Mutchler and abandon the jury instructions in this case.

"After three days of testimony, three-and-a-half, you know from at least six different witnesses that Scott Mutchler planned at some point prior to September 10, 1991, to burglarize the Scharf residence. And you're pretty well satisfied from the testimony of Mr. Pratt and Mr. Davelis, if not from the testimony from much of Mr. Mutchler's former friends, that he was there.

"But what do you know about these crimes, particularly the really serious crimes we're talking about here, the homicides? What do you know about what the prosecution wants you to believe happened in there? You can't guess. You can't speculate. It has to have come from what you heard from the witness stand and evidence presented.

"Mr. Mutchler's in a deep hole because of his talk about burglarizing the Scharf residence and because he was apparently there the evening hours of September 10, 1991. And that's his own fault. That's his own making to discuss it and then to go there.

"But I ask you not to take the blame that he has for that and stretch it to a conviction for first-degree murder.

"This is a case that you've known from the beginning was an emotional case. And what I ask you to do is take the jury instructions and shelter yourself from misguided verdicts in this case. Clutch those instructions and follow them and adhere to them and do what they tell you you've got to do so that you don't make a serious mistake in Mr. Mutchler's case. Because when you do that, when you look at just what was presented in this case, you'll be satisfied that all you know is that the Scharfs died, that Mr. Mutchler talked about burglarizing their residence, and that he was there.

"And you know no more now than you did on the day one about what happened in that residence. If you were to be satisfied beyond a reasonable doubt in this case that Mr. Mutchler had caused the death of the Scharfs, I submit to you that you would know what happened there. I submit to you that if you don't have a reasonable doubt, you're not plagued by inconsistencies and questions about the evidence that you heard over the last three days. But that's not the case.

"In reviewing what I heard over the last few days, I've come up with some things that I think conflict with the prosecution's theory and they're inconsistent and don't hold true to what they would have you speculate about what happened there. And all of those are sort of in the context of them wanting you to believe that an 18-and-a-half-year-old kid with a plan for a shortcut to a better life would find himself in the residence of some people that he knew, and from everything we know, had a friendly relationship with them, smashing this man over the back with this, and then killing the people in the house with this.

"All of that…all of this…all of this evidence has to fit with that wild scenario, and there's nothing you heard about Mr. Mutchler's plan or Mr. Mutchler himself that would support that stretch.

"Mr. Silvus talked to you about Defendant's Exhibit J, which he found in his truck, which he got out of the Scharf residence."

MILLER: "I think there was a misstatement, the Meyer residence."

SHAW: "The Meyer residence, right. Got out of the Meyer residence. And you'll see it. You'll take it back into the jury room with you. But you heard what he said was on it, and it's clearly directions to the Scharf home. But it's not in Mr. Mutchler's handwriting, and arguably, wasn't written even when he was available to write it. But it was on a piece of paper that was in the Meyer residence and conceivably could have been written by Mr. Mutchler, if it was his handwriting, at some earlier date.

"Mr. Silvus told you he thought that it came from the mobile home that Mr. Mutchler was living in for a while before he went to jail in Adam County, a home where you heard him say it appeared that other people were living.

"At the house of the Scharfs, we have unidentified shoe prints in the backyard. We have underwear that's unidentified that doesn't seem to fit anybody in this case.

"We've got Ms. Justice coming home at 8:45 and not noticing whether or not Mr. Scharf's car was there. And we have Ms. Justice hearing voices, which I think she described as some sort of elevated discussion. And I can't remember her exact words, but they were voices that she thought she heard coming from the Scharf residence. And for a while, she thought they were from a talk radio show and it seemed to her that it wasn't a friendly exchange that was going on, as I recall.

"Then we have the keys that are found in the window well. These keys, Defendant's A, you'll get to take them back there with you. You didn't hear any testimony from Detective Workman about how those keys were covered with dust or cobwebs all over them. It's pretty clear that law enforcement didn't think that those keys were something that they could brush off.

"You heard about the extent to which Detective Ragulsky went to try to find a door that those keys would fit, a door that they would unlock. Nothing at the Scharf residence. Nothing at the Meyer residence. No friends or former friends of Mr. Mutchler's. Not Mr. Silvus' residence. Not Mr. Pollard's residence or anyplace he ever lived before. He did that because those keys didn't belong there. Those keys were in the window well they say Mr. Mutchler went in and out, and they don't jive with their theory of the case. But the harder they looked, the less they found, and the bigger the doubt got.

"When you go back to the jury room, look at People's Exhibit 71B. It shows a picture of the desk with the computer and the papers on it and the open window where they claim Mr. Mutchler entered. Nothing is out of place. There are no markings on it. There's no blood. There's no dirt. There's no grass. There's nothing that would seem to support that someone entered or left through that doorway.

"Think about the prosecution's claim that Mr. Mutchler starts out his burglary by whacking a sleeping person across the back with a poker. That doesn't make sense if you believe Mr. Seppers, Mr. Schafer, Miss Gonzales, Miss Tyson and Mr. Upton. That's not the plan that they want you to rely on so heavily for their felony murder count. That was never discussed.

"The only thing that would have incapacitated the people in that house was the fairly immature fantasy of use of the chloroform to knock them out. I mean, how well thought out was that? But something like this was never part of the plan.

"Even if you have…if you had an experienced and vicious burglar, you wouldn't start out by smashing someone that's asleep across the back with a fireplace poker. I mean, there goes your plan to commit a burglary and get away.

"Whoever did that, whoever hit Mr. Scharf across the back while he was sleeping had a different plan than the plan that Scott Mutchler had talked about so much; had a different plan from Mr. Mutchler's plan of getting some money, getting some credit cards, getting some checks and getting down to Florida to live with his grandparents and Irene Gonzales. Whoever did that had a different agenda.

"And whether or not it was the person that Mr. Mutchler was looking for to help do the burglary that you've heard about consistently or someone else, or whether or not it was the person that he got to help him and the person decided to do things differently, when you get in there, you don't know what you have but you do know that it doesn't make sense and it doesn't fit with the evidence you've heard about what Mr. Mutchler was out to do or if he was ever going to do a burglary at the Scharf residence..“They don't give you any evidence to support a theory on how Mr. Mutchler suffered his injuries. These aren't little tiny scratches. These are serious stab wounds, and they're stab wounds that are described by the paramedic and I believe Officer LaFleur, as defensive wounds.

"How did they happen? If you're going to know what happened there, if you're going to decide that Mr. Mutchler's guilty of four counts of first-degree murder, you've got to know what happened. And I don't care whose fault it is; you've got to know. And if you don't know, you know what your verdict has got to be and should be.

"They've offered you no evidence to support this rather extreme, obvious circumstance that we know Mr. Mutchler suffered sometime between 9 and 11 that night. Why would someone who planned to subdue people living in the residence and do a simple burglary with no violence intended to the victims walk upstairs armed like this? It makes no sense. And it has to make sense if you're going to be convinced beyond a reasonable doubt.

"This doesn't fit with the plan. This was someone else's plan. Who stabbed Mr. Mutchler? If it was Mr. Scharf, how did it happen? If it was one of Mr. Mutchler's confederates, why did it happen? If Mr. Mutchler wasn't trying to derail a train or plan to hurt Mr. Scharf and his son, then they would have given a better theory. But they got to tell you something. This is major, and they're just saying 'I don't know. It doesn't matter.'

"Mr. Miller talked to you about the blood on Mr. Scharf's foot. What about the blood on his hand? It's unidentifiable. And I believe Mr. Davelis said in response to one of Ms. Cooke's questions about that, 'I can't say that that's the only place in the house where whose ever blood that is on Mr. Scharf bled in the house.'

"You know from the pictures and you know from the slides that there's blood all over that house. And you know from Mr. Davelis' testimony that he picked and chose where he picked blood in that house.

"We're not saying Mr. Mutchler wasn't there, but what we are saying is that they can't come close to showing you this was just Mr. Mutchler and Evan Scharf and his son in the house that night.

"How come the only blood of Mr. Mutchler's near Robbie Scharf is the blood on the T-shirt on his neck? The prosecution's theory would have you believe that at that point, Mr. Mutchler was seriously stabbed himself. But none of his blood was anywhere but on that T-shirt that's found on Robbie Scharf or near him.

"How come Mr. Scharf's injuries are primarily to the right side of his face, and how come Robbie Scharf is cut…I've got to make sure I get this right…right to left like a left-handed person would? Why do they have these postmortem wounds? And they describe for you someone so bent on killing Mr. Scharf and his son that after they were dead, they continue to try to kill people that were already dead. Is this part of the plan that you heard about from Mr. Mutchler's friends? Is this part of the person that you've been led to believe that Mr. Mutchler was?

"It doesn't fit. It fits with someone else's plan and somebody else's agenda, not Mr. Mutchler's. And you know that from what he told the six young people who testified here today and yesterday.

"When you retire and you take the evidence back with you, look at People's Exhibits 33A, 30A, and 114. They say that Mr. Mutchler was the only person that came out of that house alive that night. But these pictures show adult male blue jeans, presumably those of Evan Scharf, laying on the bed with no blood on them, the pockets turned inside out with no blood on them, items from the pockets laid out on the bed with no blood on them. And you know how badly Mr. Mutchler was stabbed at that point, according to the prosecution's theory.

"Who was turning the pockets inside out? Who was putting the blue jeans on the bed? Who was filing through the items that laid on the bed? Not somebody that was bleeding like Mr. Mutchler was supposedly bleeding.

"And look at People's 91. This is the drawer where Mr. Scharf kept his underwear, the drawer where they would have you believe Mr. Mutchler pulled some boxer shorts to wrap around his bleeding arm. He had to do it because according to their theory, he was the only other person in the house. Not a drop of blood. Not a drop of blood in the drawer. Not a drop of blood across the top of the dresser. Somebody else pulled that underwear out of that drawer.

"The poker is supposed to be one of the weapons that Mr. Mutchler picked up as he came upstairs. There are no prints of Mr. Mutchler's. There's no blood of Mr. Mutchler. There's no hair of Mr. Mutchler on that poker. And Mr. Pratt said, 'Well, some people just don't leave fingerprints.' But we know that's not Mr. Mutchler because he left a couple of fingerprints there.

"And how about the knife that Mr. Mutchler supposedly had in his hand while he stabbed Evan Scharf numerous times and while he stabbed Robbie Scharf? They want you to believe that he had that in his hand for a good while as he did those initial deeds. They want you to believe that, even though they can't give you any evidence that he ever held it; his blood is not on it; his hair is not on it; and his fingerprints are not on it. So they will tell you 'It's just got to be that way because he planned to burglarize the Scharf residence because we have a lot of evidence that he was there and we don't know who else did it so convict Mr. Mutchler of four counts of first-degree murder.'

"Please understand, we're not saying that Mr. Mutchler wasn't at the Scharf resident that night. But these exhibits of the prosecution, I think, are misleading when they give you long columns like this and they say pants, Mutchler; tennis shoes, Mutchler. Understand that, while that might lead you to believe that that is a positive certain comparison like a fingerprint, what Mr. Davelis is really saying is that that's consistent with Mr. Mutchler's blood and another 7 percent of the population.

"But remember, Mr. Davelis also said, 'We have unidentified blood here, we have blood we didn't seize, and we have blood that is mixed or masked. And I can tell you this, that it could be Mr. Mutchler's blood and Evan Scharf's blood or Robbie Scharf's blood, but it also could be some other person's blood and their blood.' They want for you to go a long way on Mr. Davelis' testimony.

"And we don't deny that it gets you far enough to say that Scott was there, but it doesn't by a long shot exclude the possibility that someone else was there.

"The fingerprint evidence. Remember Defendant's G and Defendant's F. We have 26 items, question items, received. We have 13 suitable for comparison. We have 13 items with no comparison, and we have these where they couldn't get positive prints. Twenty-four prints where Mr. Pratt couldn't make an identification.

"My recollection of Detective Ragulsky's testimony was that at the autopsy, he took hair and fiber from Robbie Scharf's hands. And then I heard Ms. Verma from CBI say 'We got no fiber from Robbie Scharf's hands.' I don't know what that's about. I don't know if Detective Ragulsky didn't know that he didn't have hair and fiber in his hands or Mool Verma didn't know that he did have hair and fiber from Robbie Scharf's hands, or if it got lost somewhere in between. But I think you deserve to know what happened with it, where it is, and whose it was.

"What about the dead bolt on the front door of the Scharf residence? The prosecution has essentially presented to you that while that dead bolt was secure, we think that Sergeant Berg broke it trying to get out in his haste. Well, if that's the case, if we accept that that dead bolt was there when the police arrived and it was set and it was locked when Detective Berg…excuse me, Sergeant Berg came down and tried to go out, where did Mr. Mutchler leave the residence? Did he leave the residence through this window? It was left open without moving any of these papers around and without bleeding on any of them, without leaving a footprint, fingerprint, or footprint anywhere there.

"Look at that and tell me if you think that a man who had been stabbed to the extent that…the doctor said it was a serious bodily injury and was bleeding to the extent that you know he was bleeding from the testimony of Mr. Davelis, could that person negotiate that exit without leaving any evidence of departing?

"So if he didn't go out the window, where did he go out? And if he did go out the front door, how did the dead bolt get thrown after he went out if that's where he went out?

"And how come somebody that was supposedly bleeding as much as Mr. Mutchler was, they can't find any blood, not to mention Mr. Mutchler's blood, between the Scharf residence and where the Scharf vehicle was supposedly parked?

"And how come Mrs. Meyer and her husband about the time they're expecting Scott to drive up hear a car drive up and a car door slam and a car drive off? And how come later when they see the Honda automobile out there and that location is pointed out to Detective Ragulsky, there's no blood around it?

"I think he said the nearest blood was either 50 feet from the curb or 50 feet from the door of the Meyer residence. I can't remember which. But I do think that he said that there wasn't any blood in the area where, at the point where it was pointed out to him the Honda automobile had been parked.

"And how come there was nothing taken from Mr. Scharf's wallet if in fact that's what Mr. Mutchler's plan was, or if there was nothing that would have apparently been taken from his wallet found on Mr. Mutchler?

"The prosecution's theory would certainly have you believe that Mr. Mutchler ran in terror and pain from the Scharf residence directly home. But he has none of the Scharf's property, none of Evan Scharf's property or money or checks on him at all.

"And what about the noises that the Salgados hear in the late evening hours of September 10th? What woke up Vanessa and caused her to run in terror to her father? And who did her father hear driving off out of the cul-de-sac?

"Some of those things are just big questions, and some of those are major inconsistencies. You all can get together and you can decide 'This doesn't bother me or that doesn't bother me.' But last time I counted them, there were about 25 of those. And some of them are very bothersome and some of them greatly conflict with what the prosecution wants you to believe in this case. And some of them aren't circumstances, they're just facts, and they're facts they can't get around.

"They're going to ask you to just push them aside and bulldoze on through like doing a crossword puzzle. You put a word in that doesn't match just go ahead and keep going. Have a few words in there that don't fit and say it's done.

"The prosecution tells you well, if you don't believe murder after deliberation, if you don't believe that Scott Mutchler for some reason outside of the burglary…because they say, 'If you believe the burglary, you can convict on the felony murder theory. If you don't believe that, believe that he went over there just wanting to kill those people and these 25 inconsistencies and problems you'll just have to disregard. And the fact that he never mentioned to anyone any plan to ever cause that kind of harm to those people, you'll just have to disregard.

" 'Because whatever happened in there, we know that whoever did it thought about it. And it had to be Mr. Mutchler because he's the only one that we have any tangible evidence of having been in there and come out alive.' But they say if you don't believe that, if you don't like this one, try this. Try felony murder.

"Well, the judge read to you the affirmative defense of felony murder. And it indicates to you that if you're not satisfied beyond a reasonable doubt of these seven conditions, then you should acquit Mr. Mutchler of felony murder.

"And how about the statement of Mr. Mutchler on the way to the 7-Eleven to his mom? I'm going to call somebody up. I got to get together with somebody to get some money and a car. And they see him go immediately to the phone.

"And how about the evidence from the Salgados and Ms. Justice and Ms. Hampf that they thought they had heard other people over there at different times? And in the case of Ms. Justice and Mr. Salgados, at times when we know that Mr. Mutchler couldn't have been there. Ms. Justice said she heard voices over there before 9. When they get to the 7-Eleven, Mrs. Meyer tells you it is 9. Mr. Salgados hears fighting and arguing over there…excuse me, his daughter did, about midnight, I think he said, when you know Mr. Mutchler's in the emergency room at St. Anthony's.

"How about that there's no blood leading to or from the Honda automobile or no blood or no property of the victims on Mr. Mutchler? And how about the unidentified shoe prints and underwear in the yard? What about how Mr. Mutchler got in and out of that residence? Those are solid reasons to doubt that Mr. Mutchler was not the only participant in what went on at the Scharf residence in the evening hours of September 10th.

"Number two, that Mr. Mutchler didn't kill or in any way solicit or aid in the deaths of or the killing of the Scharfs. Look to the plan that he told his friends he was going to be involved in. It never included anything like that. They were all quite sure about that. They were all quick to say 'He never gave us the impression that he meant any significant long-lasting harm to these people', nothing like that is represented here.

"He had a notion that he could use chloroform like in the movies, and they'd be unconscious for about ten minutes, they come…they come back, and he'd be down the road with their property.

"How about what appears to be assault on Evan Scharf by a left-handed person? And how about some sort of motive for Mr. Mutchler to ever want to cause that kind of mayhem at the Scharf residence?

"Number three, he was not armed with a deadly weapon. He had no weapon when he left. There's no evidence that he touched either the poker or the knife. And the statement of his friends that he never meant to use a deadly weapon in the course of the burglary or cause any harm.

"And number four, there's no reason to believe that any other participant would be armed with weapons like that or deadly weapons. The weapons, according to the prosecution, came from inside the house. And again, there's no evidence that Mr. Mutchler ever held them. So how could they say he knew that they were going to be involved?

"And again, they definitely weren't part of his plan at that time the prosecution wants to rely on so heavily for felony murder.

"And the defendant didn't engage in or didn't think that his confederates would engage in conduct to cause the victim's serious bodily injury or death.

"Again, the plan as he represented to his friends, the strange blood on Evan Scharf, or the way those people died, or the way they were assaulted after they had apparently died being so inconsistent with anything you've ever heard about Mr. Mutchler's relationship with the Scharfs or his plan to burglarize them.

"Number five, is that as soon as things went awry from the plan of the burglary that he disengaged. And for that I ask you to consider the testimony of Ms. Hampf and the Salgados because that lends credibility to the argument that things were going on in the Scharf residence after Mr. Mutchler left and Mr. Mutchler beat a fast track to his home.

"And how about the dead-bolted door and no other apparent exit for Mr. Mutchler?

"I expect that when I finish the prosecution is going to get up and say that these are little things. But it's our position that therefore, the little things…that these 25 or so inconsistencies range from so-significant-you-can't-get-around-them to so-problematical-to-their-theory-that-you-can't-get-through-it. They wouldn't be there if their theory were right. And they're there, and there's nothing they can do about it.

"Take a hold of those instructions and hold on for dear life. Because if you don't you will…you'll go that extra yard and Mr. Mutchler will suffer a serious injustice because you want to do something when you see a crime like this done to anybody. You want to get somebody, and you want to turn them over to the judge and say, 'Have on'.

"But they haven't given you the kind of proof you need to do that to Mr. Mutchler in this case. When they say to you 'Our case is proven', ask them when and how did Mr. Mutchler get into that residence, and then when and how did he get those wounds and who did it?

"Ask them what went on in that house for two hours if Mr. Mutchler was there for two hours, or what was Mr. Mutchler doing for those two hours? Ask him how long he was there if he was there?

"Ask them how and why Evan Scharf died and died the way he did.

"Ask them how and why Robbie Scharf died and died the way he did. Ask them really how did Robbie Scharf get down to that basement?

" 'Show us some evidence to believe your theory. Show us what happened with evidence. Don't ask us to stretch it out because we're so angry.'

"If you do that and you hold on to the instructions, you'll see that their own evidence presents too many problems for you to believe what they want you to believe.

"And the testimony of Miss Tyson and Mr. Seppers and those people describes for you the kind of guy that was going over there to burglarize the Scharfs. And there's nothing that you got at all to make you think that he's the kind of guy that would have done the acts that were involved here. And he's not the kind of guy that ever had the plan to do that. That was someone else's plan.

"And I ask you to find that that's what the evidence shows, and acquit Mr. Mutchler of all of the charges brought against him today. Thank you."

Rebuttal

PICKERING: "I think what we need, folks, is a good taste of plan and some common sense and reality. Mr. Shaw has made an attempt to…or attempted to make real headway with all these little things. Let's go through them.

"Footprints in the sand. Ms. Cooke went to great length to talk about the footprints in the sand. Where were the footprints in the sand outside? They were beside a swing set where kids play, where adults walk around in a backyard. That doesn't necessarily mean there's anything diabolical about footprints in the sand by a swing in the backyard of the child's house.

"Unexplained fingerprints? Again, they went to great lengths to explain to you, whatever it was, 24 fingerprints that were unaccounted for in that house. That house is a home, folks. People live there, they eat there, they play there, they laugh there, they cry there and, in this case, they died there. But they also have friends that come over. Robbie Scharf doesn't live in a vacuum. He has friends that come to play. I think that's a reasonable assumption. Evan Scharf has friends; some lady friends, some male friends that come to visit; mail men that come to the front door; Joseph Graham comes to his house to use his computer in the basement. Is it so unusual to think that there's going to be unaccounted fingerprints in a house? Would you have to live in and wear little booties and a hat and a mask not to leave anything in a home? So there's 24 fingerprints they can't account for. Do you think any one of you folks could account for every fingerprint in your house? No, of course not. Does it matter? No. It's ridiculous.

"Hairs. He made a big deal about a hair on a screen. They had the same reports we did. He still made a big deal about, what did you…"

SHAW: "Judge, this is rebuttal. I didn't say anything about a hair on my closing."

JUDGE: "Overruled."

SHAW: "I didn't talk about that evidence. I didn't bring it up in my closing."

JUDGE: "This is argument. The objection is overruled."

SHAW: "I understand. But he can't talk about what I didn't address the jury about even though it is argument. He can only…

JUDGE: "I have ruled."

SHAW: "…only argue about what I have said."

JUDGE: "The jury is the fact finders. I have ruled."

PICKERING: "The bleeding phantom. Who is this phantom? Mr. Shaw says, 'Well, there could have been someone else there. There must have been because there better have been, I guess. And if there was and he bled, then he did it.'

"Listen and think back to what Ted Davelis said on the stand. He didn't say he didn't know whose the blood was, that it was strange blood or unaccounted for blood on the hand of Evan Scharf. What Ted Davelis said from that witness stand was that it was consistent with the mixture of Evan Scharf and Scott Mutchler.

"Ms. Cooke is the one that said, 'Well, it could be someone else's and maybe it was masked.' And after we went through all of that rigamarole at the end it was Ted Davelis saying from the stand, 'By my conclusions the blood on Evan Scharf's hands was consistent with a mixture of Evan Scharf and Scott Mutchler.'

"Mr. Shaw wants to say that all I got just puts him in the house. We gave you that, you know. We'll admit he was in the house. I would submit to you they didn't give a whole lot to us. They didn't have a choice because the evidence is overwhelming that he was in the house. So this isn't some gift that they're giving you by saying 'OK, he was in the house.' You bet he was in the house. They didn't have a choice about that. But he wasn't just in the house.

"Mr. Shaw said there isn't any fingerprints on the knife. Scott Pratt said there was a large amount of blood on this knife, or a great amount of blood on this knife. There's no way that fingerprints could adhere to it. Does that mean that Mr. Mutchler didn't handle it? No. We can put blood consistent with Scott Mutchler within…you look at the photographs. And I'll be generous. Six foot of this thing we can put Scott Mutchler leaning over the body of Evan Scharf after he was down. Does that sound like we can just put him in the house? Huh-uh.

"The car door slamming. Look folks, we know Mutchler drove the car back to his house. How do we know that? Blood consistent with his blood was found on the gearshift and found on the steering wheel.

"According to Ms. Cooke's charts 42.9 percent of the population probably could have shifted the gears but only 7 percent could have steered it. Who took the car back if anybody did? Scott Mutchler drove the car back.

"Now let's say…let's follow Mr. Shaw's logic for a minute with that. Where is he going with that? If the idea is the phantom, because Mr. Mutchler got hurt, had to take him back to his house, we know that didn't happen because Mutchler drove the car. OK. Then why would the phantom sit in the passenger seat? Does that make any sense? I mean let's get this straight. Somebody, the phantom I guess, has just killed an adult and a 10-year-old child. They got out of the house, and he goes with Mr. Mutchler. And he doesn't have to, he's just going to for the hell of going, to make sure that Scott gets home. Does that make sense to you? No.

"But lets continue with that for a minute and say, OK, the phantom is in the passenger side of the car. What do we know about that? Well, Detective Schuler testified that at St. Anthony North when he looked into the car, the only car door that was unlocked was the driver's side. That means the passenger side was locked. What does that tell you? Think about that for a minute.

"Again, the scenario with the phantom and Mr. Mutchler runs this through your mind. They just killed...the phantom has just killed somebody or two people in the Scharf house and he rides back with Mutchler. They drive up on the front lawn, the phantom gets out of the passenger side of the car. Does that make sense to anybody? No. There was no phantom. There was no phantom in that car. The passenger door was locked.

"Did Mrs. Meyer hear a car door slam? Did she hear a car drive away? I don't know. But I can tell you that there wasn't anybody in the passenger side of that car. The only person in the driver's side was Scott Mutchler.

"The keys, the phantom's keys, I guess. If you're going to burglarize a house, if you're the phantom, are you going to carry something like this with you? Listen to it. Is it something a burglar is going to carry with him? Huh-uh.

"It's a whistle. I can't tell you exactly whose keys these are. But those of you who have children, ask yourself, do your children ever have keys to play with for no other reason than to have them that ...to play with them. Can I tell you that's in fact what they are? No, I can't. But ask yourself, is the phantom going to take this when he goes in the window or the front door or the chimney?

"Mr. Shaw says 'Hey, I'm going to admit my guy was in there, but they can't tell you how he got in there so he's not guilty.' I don't care if he came in the chimney for that matter or whether he came in the basement window and he left through the front door. How do we know he left through the front door? Because blood consistent with Mutchler was not only in the entranceway. We checked it over there. We checked the pictures. And you should have a picture to match every one of those over there. Blood spots on the carpet directly in front of the front door, and blood consistent with Mutchler on the light switch directly in the entryway. What does that tell you? Does that tell you he cut himself before he came in? No, it tells you that's the way he went out. I don't know.

"My recollection of Mr. Salgados' testimony is that he said his daughter woke up and heard some disturbances and he heard a car drive away about 11:15. Well, what does that mean? We can probably…no, we can put Mr. Mutchler in that house at 11, two minutes to 11. Could somebody's watch have been off by 15 minutes and would have thought it was 11:15 if it was 11? Is that so inconsistent?

"How do we know Mutchler is in the house at 11? We have got a fingerprint in blood, his blood, blood consistent with him on the telephone. And what's he doing on the phone? He calls up his mom and says 'Hi Mom, I'm going to be a few minutes late. I'm about three miles away but I'll be home in just a few minutes. Thank you.' And he hung up. What his mother couldn't see through the telephone lines is he's standing soaking in his own blood through to his socks when he said that. But the idea that something happened after he left doesn't fly, folks.

"Mr. Shaw says "Any doubt you got, you know, this is reasonable doubt stuff here folks. We've created a reasonable doubt.' Well, for the last week or so you all have been asked to look into the jaws of the abyss; that is the human mind. It is unique and capable of unfathomable violence. And yet, at the same time, as jurors, you must deny yourself the luxury of your own humanity. This is not the time to look at things emotionally. Pull back from that, and use reason and common sense. And that will show you the way.

"The defense on the one hand says "Hey, can't use emotion.' But on the other hand they will tell you 'Hey, you know, you're going to make a decision about an 18-year-old kid that's going to affect him tremendously for the rest of his life.' Well, don't give me emotion. Don't give Scott Mutchler emotion. You look at the evidence in this case, cold, hard evidence. Rely on your own collective wisdom and common sense."

That was it. Steve's mother had agreed to attend the closing statements with me. I looked at her. We couldn't believe it. How did they not look for who else was in that home?

The murder weapon: We just heard Scott's prints weren't on the murder weapon. And their own witness testified that the blows that killed the Scharfs probably were made with the attacker's left hand. Scott was right handed.

I sat in the courtroom numb. A three-day trial. I had never heard of a three-day murder trial.

The haunting words were coming back to me, 'This is election year for Alex Hunter…this is going to hurt us'.

Two young women came up and knelt beside me.

"Mrs. Meyer, you don't know us, but we're law students. Your son is not guilty. We've heard everything that's been said."

The speaker pointed to a pretty blonde nearby. "That girl is a clerk in the DA's office. She's told us of horrible things John Pickering is doing to get your son convicted, but we know he's innocent."

I didn't know these girls, but it was comforting to hear that someone on the "outside" world believed in Scott.

The courtroom had almost emptied. Scott was at the defense table with his attorney. Guards were everywhere. I stood up and approached the bar behind Scott. I looked at one of the guards and asked him if I could give my son a hug.

"Yeah, go ahead," he said after glancing around. My son and I held each other tight, tears pouring down both of our faces.

I tried to do the comforting this time. "It'll be OK, Honey, it'll be OK."

Scott called again that night. "Mom, please do not come here when they read the verdict."

"Scott, please, I honored your wishes during the trial, but let me be there for you."

"Mom, if things go wrong, the media will swarm you. I can't help you; no one will be able to help you. You can't do anything anyway. Please, stay home."

"If that's what you want, I'll stay home."

Rebuttal

"Mom, never forget how much I love you."
"I love you, too. "

The Instructions

Morning Session

JUDGE: “The people of the State of Colorado versus Scott Mutchler. It is 8:20 a.m. and the jury is scheduled to begin its deliberations at 8:30 a.m. The record should reflect that the case was submitted to the jury. The evidence, instructions of the Court and closing arguments were completed sometime in the neighborhood of 4:30 yesterday afternoon. The jury had been in recess for more than two hours when the jury was advised that the bailiffs would be bringing the evidence into the jury room and the instructions at a later time.

“Before the instructions were copied and delivered to the jury, the Court received a note that the jury wanted to go home and come back and start deliberations this morning at 8:30.

As a result, the jury has not at this time ever seen any of the instructions that were read to them.

"There was some colloquy between the Court and counsel after the jury had taken its recess and gone into the jury room with regard to the instructions and 20A, which was not read to the jury. That's the Court's recollection during the three or four hours before the case was submitted to the jury with regard to the instructions. During that period of time, there was an off-the-record discussion with regard to the various instructions that the Court was going to give.

"In light of the fact that the Court was given an affirmative defense to felony murder with regard to the statute on the crime, the Court had agreed that it would, at the request of the prosecution, give 20A, which is the complicity instruction. It was that instruction which was apparently inadvertently omitted from the instructions read to the jury, and the Court didn't notice it until during rebuttal closing arguments by the prosecution when Mr. Pickering made a statement with regard to…with reference to complicity.

"The Court notes say I didn't give all the complicity statute. In reading it, it says, 'Note: after jury had retired. The Court's recollection is there was some colloquy with regard to whether I should bring the jury back to read the complicity instruction. The Court said it would not do that but that it would insert the complicity instruction as No. 20A.' The jury, again, was never permitted and has not yet seen any of the instructions of the last evening.

"The Court's analysis is that it would be prejudicial error to the defendant if the Court were to give the complicity instruction, because the instruction reads in pertinent part that all of the elements, including Element No. 2, must be established beyond a reasonable doubt. Element No. 2 is that another person must have committed all or part of the crime.

"There is no evidence presented by the prosecution or in the record that another person…that anybody could find beyond a reasonable doubt that another person must have committed all or part of the crime. The Court is partly relying on its own analysis to support that analysis. In the case of People vs. Gonzales, 728 p.2d.384, that was a 1986 Court of Appeals opinion, which held that a related complicity instruction was not appropriate for aggravated motor vehicle theft was not supported by any evidence that a person other than the defendant committed all or part of the alleged offense.

"There are other reasons why that instruction should not be given to the jury, among which is the fact that the record is made with regard to instructions by counsel for both parties and the instruction was not in the packet and was not read. It is the burden of the prosecution to introduce evidence by which a jury could find beyond a reasonable doubt that another person must have committed all or part of the crime. There was no such evidence. The prosecution didn't try their case in any way on the complicity theory and only argued from the complicity instruction because the Court was giving the instruction on the affirmative defense to a felony murder submitted by defense counsel.

"The defense counsel's burden, of course, is totally different than the prosecution's. As the jury was instructed, the defense doesn't have to prove anything and need only raise evidence that a jury could find a reasonable doubt.

The record should reflect that this record is being made outside the presence of the defendant. His counsel has indicated to me, and will do so on the record in a few moments, that his presence is not waived. Let me state for the record the reasons why Mr. Mutchler is not present. I didn't think it was necessary for him to be here. Yesterday there was a request by counsel for Mr. Mutchler that he not be required to be at the courthouse until sometime probably 20 minutes away, because he didn't want to sit down in the holding cell awaiting a verdict. I initially said that wasn't possible, that I wanted him to be within ten minutes of the courthouse and in the courtroom. But later, I felt that the jury would probably not reach a real quick verdict and if they did, we would have to bring him over and take a half an hour to get him here. I indicated it would be OK if he remained at the jail until 11:30. Then, I wanted him to be within ten minutes of the courthouse.

"I think it is important that this record be made. There certainly would be no prejudice to anyone or anything if I were to change my mind and instruct on the complicity or if I were not to instruct. But, in any event, it would be in the defendant's favor, I'm convinced, in an appeal of this case, if there were to be a conviction, and we don't know if it would be on the complicity theory or not would be reversible error. There is no evidence in the record to support the instruction. Counsel may make any record that you think is appropriate. First of all, enter your appearances."

MILLER: "Phil Miller and John Pickering are present and have been present and here since 8 a.m. this morning.

"Just a word or two on the record to reflect that during the discussion off the record about the theory of the defense giving the affirmative defense under 18-3-102(s). The prosecution on this part theory was that if the defense tells the Court it was to be given and the defendant was entitled to it, then the prosecution would seek to have a similar or companion, if you will, in that section of the instructions, the complicity instruction.

"This was not objected to prior to the reading of the instructions by counsel and there was no recent objection on the record about that the instruction was not to be given if there was objections on the record during Mr. Pickering's comments on complicity.

"What I'm trying to establish is the good faith efforts of the prosecution. It was a fair comment certainly in light of the contemplated instructions. Indeed, the closing remarks of Mr. Shaw, which discussed or attempted to interject in the case of the people.

"This instruction has never been read to the jury and putting that caution aside, the Court has expressed and indicated, we think, that since the Court may yet give the instruction to the jury on the fact they were determining this case based on evidence and instructions that were given that that will take care of any possible error that may have been introduced by reference to this theory which was a good faith reference by the prosecution.

"One other thing, Your Honor, Mr. Pickering who represented our office when Mr. Shaw made comments to the effect that his affirmative defense instruction was his theory of the defense and that prosecution was wanting to deny him the opportunity to have that theory of defense in this regard, in this trial, execute, I guess implied in his comments essentially it's been offered and since they were given a chance last time that there would be a little saving of time if the Court were to read instruction No. 23 to them, which would a fair remedy, that they're to govern their deliberations by the instructions they are given and nothing else."

JUDGE: "Mr. Shaw?"

SHAW: "Judge, it's my request first off that the Court grant a mistrial in this case. As I have said before we got on the record, the jury heard one of the prosecutors in this case and someone that they would consider to be an authority figure talk to them about complicity. It's anybody's guess what they think complicity is, but certainly, they think it's something they can consider at this point, whatever it is. And that's extremely dangerous because as the Court has pointed out, it goes to the appropriate law in this case and it's not something they should be able to consider.

"That instruction on complicity was not in the packet that the Court gave to each side to read and make objections before we commenced giving instructions and closing arguments. And they were on notice that it wasn't there when they commenced their arguments.

"Yet they made reference to the statement that the only way to protect Mr. Mutchler from some of these jurors convicting on the complicity theory is grant him a mistrial. It's particularly dangerous in this case because they don't have any instructions about complicity.

"If the Court isn't going to do that, it's my request that you read the instruction advising them that there is no complicity law applicable to this case so they don't try to apply some notion that they have of what complicity is to the facts in this case and make it a factor in their determination as to whether or not Mr. Mutchler is guilty. Those are my two requests.

"I guess I have one more, which goes to the prosecution's request if you are not going to do one of those two things. You heard Mr. Miller say in instruction No. 23 advising they're to decide guilt on that law that is appropriate in this case, and arguments of counsel are not law. Those are in the order of what I consider to be appropriate priority.

"Concerning Mr. Mutchler's presence, I think this is significant enough so that he should be here. I think the Court wants to get the jury the instructions so they can decide those and what it wants to do…what it should do is stop this hearing. You are going to do what you are going to do and we can, on making the record, and could hear…Mr. Mutchler can hear the Court's position at a hearing later this morning when he gets over to the courthouse.

"I don't see where anything would be slowed down by getting Mr. Mutchler so he would have an opportunity to hear what's happening if we were to do it that way. That's all I have to say on the record about this.

"I have some news articles from yesterday's Times Call and this morning's Daily Camera and I'd like them to be part of the record. I would like the Court to inquire if any of them have been exposed to any publicity or anything outside the courtroom that could affect their verdict."

"MILLER: "Your Honor, one other item. Contrary to being on notice that…that we should be on notice that the instructions were to be given was the exact opposite to the one contemplated and I understood that this was to be…that there was agreement and no objection that it would be given. The only thing I am not…that while we were given a chance to look at the instructions, there was no longer an opportunity to do so and neither side was provided with their own copies of the instructions before they were actually presented to the jury.

"I think given the time constraints that we placed on ourselves at that time, that should not happen and the parties did not agree that the complicity was to be included."

"But, the record is, there was no objection to that being in the instructions read. It is now 25 minutes until 9. The jury does have the instructions. They are probably now deliberating and I think it would totally be inappropriate to emphasize any of the instructions.

"The instructions that they do have contain all of the appropriate law to be applied in this case including the fact, again, that their verdict must be based on the evidence and what counsel -- or the Court -- and what counsel said about the law is not the law, and that what the Court said is the appropriate law.

JUDGE: "The motion for a mistrial is denied. Motion to now instruct during deliberation is denied.

"If you desire at some later time, we can have Mr. Mutchler read the transcript of this hearing and then he can say anything he wants on the record with regard to it."

MILLER: "Your Honor, since the record may not reflect this, I think my comments are, that is there is another instruction that is being given to the jury that was not read. Instead, it was discovered by the defense after the reading that a right not to testify was also contemplated, and is not lost or misplaced and that error was corrected. So, in the context of our case, it is obvious that perhaps two instructions got lost in the shuffle. Instructions that were considered by the Court were admitted in favor of the defendant that includes one in the light of the prosecution's request to consider another. We understand the Court's ruling and are in agreement with it."

SHAW: "Judge, I object to them putting it in on us, and that's what they are trying to do."

JUDGE: "That's moot. It doesn't make any difference with regard to the presentation of the instructions.

"In this case, there were four days of jury selection; less than probably…probably less than three full days of testimony. There was at least three hours, if not more, of discussion about preparing all of the appropriate instructions to be given. The record on the instruction probably took a half an hour.

"This Court practiced law for more than 15 years and has been on the bench almost ten. It seems to me that the reason all the courts are moving toward more control and responsibility in the trial court giving the appropriate instructions is because there's too much waste of time. It appears to me, and I'm going to suggest to the bench in this district that in any serious cases, there be a full day's recess between closing of the evidence and instructions of the law.

"Because then, each side will have an opportunity to make the absolute fullest, longest, most complete record that they desire about what a judge should do in deciding which instructions are appropriate. It might be appropriate to do what we did on the record, although one would have to worry that no appellant court would be able to make sense out of the informal discussions that go on with regard to arguments and discussions about which instructions should be given, which grammatical structure should be used, which words and phrases would be appropriate, whether or not the jury could probably understand the English language, and on and on.

"This would also give the court and counsel an opportunity to proofread every single instruction, to correct every single typographical, which even in this case there were some. But in all cases, there are some. It would give counsel an opportunity to spend the entire evening before the record is made to go through the instructions very carefully, which is their responsibility. And to make appropriate objections and call to the court's attention those that were missed.

"I think, for example, we are starting to lose the focus of a criminal trial and the focus is, 'Did the defendant do what the charges alleged in the evidence or showed beyond a reasonable doubt?'

"With that, Court is in recess."

I closed the transcript. How could something like this happen in our country? How could our government allow a judge like this to sit on the bench and make life-changing decisions for people? If anyone should be prosecuted, I felt this judge should be. How dare he allow this to happen!

This judge not only showed a flagrant disregard for the life of my son but also, in my opinion, did everything in his power to make sure Scott would be convicted.

I packed away the transcript I had just read. I reached in the beach bag and brought out the next one; the transcript that included the verdict. The one that recorded our family's fate. I opened the transcript slowly.

Part 5

The Verdict

The Verdict

JUDGE: "I understand we have a verdict?

CLERK: "That's correct."

JUDGE: "Bring in the jury. I understand the jury has arrived at a verdict?"

FOREPERSON: "We have, Your Honor."

JUDGE: "Would you please hand the verdicts to the bailiff?"

BAILIFF: "Count one, first-degree murder after deliberation. Victim, Evan Scharf. We, the jury, find the defendant, Scott Mutchler, guilty of murder in the first-degree after deliberation."

Scott lowered his head and tears began to fall from his eyes.

BAILIFF: "Count two, first-degree murder during the course of burglary. Victim, Evan Scharf. We, the jury, find the defendant, Michael Mutchler, guilty of count two, murder in the first-degree during the course of burglary.

"Count three, first-degree murder after deliberation. Victim, Robbie Scharf. We, the jury, find the defendant, Michael Mutchler, guilty of murder in the first-degree after deliberation.

"Count four, murder in the first-degree during the course of burglary. Victim Robbie Scharf. We, the jury, find the defendant, Michael Mutchler, guilty of count four, murder in the first-degree during the course of burglary.

"Count five. We, the jury, find the defendant, Michael Mutchler, guilty of count five, first-degree burglary.

"Count six. We, the jury, find the defendant, Michael Mutchler, guilty of count six, second-degree burglary.

"Count seven, aggravated motor vehicle theft in the second-degree. We, the jury, find the defendant, Michael Mutchler, guilty of count seven, aggravated motor vehicle theft in the second-degree. All of these verdicts were signed by the foreman, Jefrey Archibald."

JUDGE: "Was this and are these the verdicts of the entire jury?"

ARCHIBALD: "They are. "

JUDGE: "So say you all?"

JURY PANEL: "Yes."

JUDGE: "Does anyone desire the jury be polled?"

SHAW: "We do, Judge."

JUDGE: "All right. With regard to the seven counts of verdict that I just read of guilty on all counts, Mr. Blackburn, was this and is this your verdict on all seven counts?"

BLACKBURN: "That is correct."

JUDGE: "Robert Arvidson, with regard to the seven counts in which the defendant was found guilty on all seven counts charged that I just read, was this and are these your verdicts?"

ARVIDSON: "Yes, they are."

The litany continued, a monotonous repetition of the judge's question and the jurors' affirmations:

JUDGE: "Eric Frenette, with regard to the seven charges or verdicts that I just read with regard to the guilty findings by the jury, was this and is this your verdict…are these your verdicts?"

FRENETTE: "Yes, Your Honor."

Debra Willis?

"Yes, they are."

Ruth Hupp?

"Yes, they are."

Elaine Breslin?

"Yes, they are."

Dennis Teusch?

"Yes, they are."

"Jeffrey Archibald?

"Yes, they are."

"Heather O'Lear?

"Yes, they are."

Luci Kagoshima?

"Yes."

Wilma Trees?

"Yes, Your Honor."

Marcus Sweet?

"Yes, they are."

JUDGE: "Judgement will enter. The rules…follow the rules with regard to any pretrial…post-trial motions. Sentencing will be May 5th at 10:30. Anything further?"

I was sobbing, again, just like the day I received word of the verdict from the courthouse. I buried my face in my hands. What were those jurors thinking? What did I miss that they thought they heard? How could anyone with any intelligence have convicted anyone on the testimony presented? I thought back to that day. I was in my home, pacing…waiting for someone to call me with the verdict.

Finally, the phone rang.

"Eve, it's Byron."

"Do they have a verdict already? It's only been three and a half hours."

"Eve, they found him guilty on everything."

"Oh my God! No! No!" My mind was racing.

"What about Scott? Byron what's going on with Scott?"

"When they read the verdict, he dropped his head and started to cry."

I hung up the phone and looked around, there was no one there. Steve wasn't home. No one was there. Scott, my God, what was he going through, being all alone? No one was there for him either. Why God, why?

The phone again.

"Eve, it's Toni." I could barely talk…all I could do was cry.

"I'm on my way to your house, I know you're alone. The press will be trying to get to you, too. Don't answer the phone, don't open the door."

"OK." I was numb. I didn't know what to do.

The only sound was the dial tone.

When Toni got there, all we could do was sit and cry. There was nothing to say. She had been a rock for me through this time. She was one of the few people I trusted to be around me.

Later that night, Steve came home with a pained expression.

"Have you heard the verdict?"

"I heard." He was too quiet.

"Steve, what's wrong?"

"They fired me from my coaching job."

"What do you mean?"

"They fired me."

How could they do that to him? He had been there 12 years. They fired him because of Scott. My heart ached for him. He had never done a thing except marry me, and now he was paying with the thing that meant most to him…his coaching. My whole family was falling apart and I didn't know how to stop it or even get control of it.

Part 6

The Sentencing

The Sentencing

JUDGE: "Enter your appearances."

MILLER: "Your Honor, Phil Miller, John Pickering and Bill Nagel for the People."

COOKE: "Linda Cooke and Steve Jacobson on behalf of Michael Mutchler."

JUDGE: "This matter is before the Court on sentencing. There are a couple of matters. The Court has received requests by the Daily Camera for pooled still camera and by Channel 7 for pooled videotaping. Any objection?"

MILLER: "People have no objection Your Honor."

COOKE: "Judge, I would object for the same reasons that we've objected to the media coverage of this case through its course."

JUDGE: "The canon requires that I make a ruling on the record. I'm unable to make the findings required to be made by case law and the Constitution. Therefore, the motion is granted. A still photographer may be present as may a video photographer.

"Apparently, I thought I had ruled on the defense motion to determine applicable penalty. I'm prepared to do that. Any arguments?"

MILLER: "Your Honor, we submitted a memorandum on the applicable penalty and would ask the Court to consider that in making its ruling."

COOKE: "Judge, I've submitted authority, a copy of the district court order from Judge Marroney in Pueblo County. Judge Marroney found that the statute imposing life without parole for somebody who commits an offense between the dates of July 1, 1988 and September 20th 1991, which would encompass the date of the offense in this case, found that it was violation of constitutional prohibition against ex post facto clauses. There is some precedent there for the Court to make such a finding in this case.

"I've also submitted to the Court a portion of the brief in that case in the Supreme…in the Colorado Supreme Court where that case…that matter is currently at issue. I would ask the Court to…based on that authority, to find that the applicable penalty in this case is life with the possibility of parole for 40 calendar years rather than life without parole."

JUDGE: "For all the reasons set forth in the People's motion, I believe the statute to be absolutely clear that the current law in Colorado is that a mandatory life sentence on a charge of first-degree murder is without any opportunity for parole. Anything further? Any statements you want to make with regard to sentencing?"

MILLER: "Your Honor, we'd like to respond to whatever defense statement is made concerning the appropriate sentence."

COOKE: "Judge, if I may approach the bench, I have a copy of a couple cases to tender to the Court that I believe I will be mentioning during the course of my argument.

"First of all, Judge, there is one correction to the pre-sentence investigation report that I'd like to bring to the Court's attention. That indicates on the cover page and on page 1 that Mr. Mutchler was convicted of first-degree aggravated motor vehicle theft, a class four felony. And it discusses the appropriate sentence for that charge, which is a sentence to the Department of Corrections for two to eight years in the…assuming the presumptive range.

"Before trial, the District Attorney moved to amend that count and that motion was granted. And the actual charge that was submitted to the jury was second-degree motor vehicle theft, a class two misdemeanor.

"I think that Mr. Miller would concur that that was the charge that Mr. Mutchler was convicted of and also that the maximum penalty for that offense is a year in the county jail."

MILLER: "That's correct Your Honor. I would agree with that statement."

COOKE: "As to any other information contained in the pre-sentence investigation report, I don't intend to comment on that and the reason for that is twofold.

"Number one. The pre-sentence investigation report alludes to psychological evaluations that were prepared and that we objected to being disclosed to the probation department for purposes of preparing this report.

"Secondly. We withdrew our request for a pre-sentence investigation report upon the Court's ruling that the probation department would have access to those psychological evaluations. Therefore, this report is not prepared at our behest, but rather at the Court's insistence. So I don't intend to comment on any of the information contained therein.

"Judge, in determining what sentence to impose in this case, I think you first need to address the issue of merger. The law provides that when a person is convicted of two offenses that are supported by identical evidence and more specifically, as applies to some of the charges in this case, was thus convicted of a charge as well as a lesser included offense of that charge, the law requires that the two offenses merge and that one sentence be imposed.

"In this case that applies to a couple of …a couple of the charges that Mr. Mutchler was convicted of. The first-degree burglary and the second-degree burglary charges are supported by identical evidence. Therefore, it's our position that those two convictions should merge into one conviction for first-degree burglary and that sentence should enter accordingly. There should not be a separate conviction of each of those charges nor should there be a separate sentence for each of those charges. "

JUDGE: "For the first-degree and the second-degree burglary?"

COOKE: "That's correct.

"Secondly, there's other issues as to merger. And it's our position that, as to the charge of felony murder as to each of the victims in this case as well as to the charge of first-degree burglary, assuming that the second-degree burglary has been merged into the first-degree burglary, again, there must be a merger.

"And the reason for that is because felony murder where the victim's death is caused during the course of or in furtherance of the underlying felony in this case, the burglary, requires proof of the same elements that it takes to prove the burglary. So in essence, by proving the felony murder, the burglary has also been proved because the burglary is an element of the felony murder charge.

"Therefore, the burglary charge is a lesser included offense of the felony murder charge and Mr. Mutchler's conviction of that offense, the greater offense of felony murder, precludes conviction of a lesser included offense of burglary.

"The authority that I'd cite for that proposition…there's two cases. One is People versus Bartowsheski, 661, p2d 235. Also, People versus Raymer, 626 p2d 705.

"The underlying felony in each of those cases is robbery; however, the analysis is identical to the situation in this case. Based on that, I would ask the Court to enter convictions only as to the felony murder count as to each victim and not as to the first- degree burglary count as well.

"There's another issue, which is not technically a merger issue, that has to do with the convictions of Mr. Mutchler as to both victims for both felony murder and first-degree murder after deliberation. The case of People versus Lowe, found at 660 p2d 1261, prohibits the entry of dual convictions and sentences for felony murder and murder after deliberation when the convictions are predicated upon the killing of a single victim."

JUDGE: "Well, you know, it occurs to me though you may be right. But the facts of this case would support convictions on both. You think the case stands for if there's one victim that there can only be one sentence?"

COOKE: "That's right. I think that's pretty clear from Lowe. And I think based on the analysis in Lowe, what the Court should do is enter an entry of conviction to felony murder as to each of the victims in this case, but not for the conviction of murder after deliberation. I think further that because the convictions will enter for felony murder, that there should not be an entry of conviction for first-degree or second-degree burglary. Again, because the second-degree burglary would merge into the first-degree burglary, and because the first-degree burglary would merge in the felony murder conviction.

"So in summary, what I'm suggesting to the Court is appropriate that they enter convictions for first-degree murder, felony murder as to the victim Evan Scharf; for first-degree murder, felony murder as to the victim Robbie Scharf; and for the second-degree motor vehicle theft charge.

"Judge, as to the length of the sentence as to the convictions for first-degree murder, the Court has no discretion. I expect the Court to impose sentence according to the legislative mandate. The court has ruled today that the Court considers that sentence to be life without parole. And I expect the Court to enter conviction accordingly.

"The Court does have discretion; however, as to the count of motor vehicle theft. The maximum penalty for that is one year in the county jail. There is no aggravation because it is not a felony. And the mandatory aggravator of the fact that Mr. Mutchler was on bond at the time of commission of the offense does not apply to enhance that at all. I'd ask the Court to sentence Mr. Mutchler on the motor vehicle theft in accordance with that statute.

"With respect to the burglary, if the Court were to find that the burglary conviction did not merge and were to impose a separate sentence for that conviction because Mr. Mutchler was on bond at the time of the commission of the offense, I would agree with the probation officer's conclusion that there must be an aggravated range sentence, which means he would need to be sentenced between the midpoint of the presumptive range up to the maximum aggravated range.

"If the Court determines, contrary to my suggestion, that a sentence on the burglary charge must be imposed, I would suggest to the Court that there's nothing about the burglary; the facts of the burglary taken alone independent of the deaths of the victims, that warrants a maximum aggravated sentence. And that to rely on the resulting deaths, which are also the subject of murder convictions and will result in appropriate sentences, would result in double jeopardy; because to rely on the resulting deaths to impose a maximum aggravated sentence on the burglary would…would be to sentence him twice for that conduct.

"Based on that, I'd ask the Court to impose…again, assuming that the Court disagrees with my contention that there need not be a separate sentence on the burglary, I would ask the Court to impose a sentence at the midpoint of the presumptive range.

"Perhaps the most important issue for the Court to decide is whether or not to impose consecutive or concurrent sentences in this case. Again, I've already argued that the burglary conviction merges into…the two burglary convictions merge into one, and that that remaining burglary conviction merges into the felony murder conviction because it's a lesser included offense. So what you're left with is sentencing basically on the two murder convictions as well as the motor vehicle theft conviction.

"There is nothing about this case that mandates that this Court impose a consecutive…or make the two life sentences run consecutively.

"The charging document did originally charge Mr. Mutchler with a crime of violence. And the crime of violence statute requires a Court, where two victims are involved and are the victims of a crime of violence, to sentence consecutively; however, the jury was not submitted an interrogatory on the crime of violence and made no finding as to that issue.

"Therefore, under the mandates of the case of People versus VanPatrick, which I've tendered to the Court, located at 789 p.2d 199, the Court cannot, based on the crime of violence statute, impose consecutive sentences. That case holds that unless the procedural safeguards contained in subsections 4 and 5 of the crime of violence statute are satisfied and a specific finding by the trier of fact as to that crime of violence charge is made; then the enhanced sentence required under the crime of violence, meaning the consecutive sentence, cannot be imposed.

"The Court does or may; however, still have the option to impose consecutive sentences; however, it's not required under that statute. It's simply discretionary with the Court. It's not mandatory.

"I would suggest that because of the statute that the Court has ruled applies in this case and that because the penalty as to each murder conviction is life without parole, that it would be of little meaning for the Court to make the sentences consecutive. I think the Court understands that. I think the Court articulated that itself at the last hearing that we had in this case.

"I think there's also…in deciding whether or not to make the two murder convictions that will be entered run consecutively or concurrently, there's also the issue of whether or not it's legal for the Court to impose consecutive sentences. That issue was addressed in a different factual context in the case of People versus Montgomery. That case, at the appellate court level, determined that imposition of consecutive life sentences for incidents arising out of this conduct was illegal and that the life sentences that were imposed were not life without parole, but rather, life sentences under which a person would be eligible for parole in 20 years.

"The Supreme Court took up that issue in that same case. Cert was granted and the Supreme Court reversed the Court of Appeals.

"I think that the Supreme Court's decision in that case is not binding on the Court in this case. And the reason is because of the difference in sentences. In that case, the…as I said, there was a possibility of parole after servicing a minim of 20 calendar years. In this case, 20 calendar years, there is no such possibility. And the basis for the Supreme Court's conclusion was that there was nothing improper about a Court considering a parole eligibility date for purposes of sentencing a person in deciding whether or not the sentence should be served consecutive or concurrently.

"I think this case, this situation with the Court having ruled that the applicable penalty is life without parole, is distinguishable. And I think given that, it would be illegal for the Court to impose the sentences consecutively.

"One of the...one of the comments made in the Court of Appeals decision that is not I think, vitiated by the Supreme Court's decision is that a person basically only has one life to give; has only one life sentence that they can give to serve. And I think that that's even more compelling and truer in a case where the penalty is life without parole. It's obvious.

"Judge, based on all the authority that I've provided to the Court and the arguments that I've previously made, I would ask the Court to enter two convictions for felony murder and to enter conviction for second-degree motor vehicle theft.

"I would ask the Court to impose the life sentence that the Court has determined applies to this case, and I would...as to each of the felony murder counts, and I would ask that those sentences be ordered to be served concurrently.

"I would also ask that the Court impose a reasonable sentence in the motor vehicle theft case, again, looking at it without regard to the deaths that resulted. The Court should look at it simply in terms of a motor vehicle theft, because otherwise, the Court runs the risk of violating constitutional prohibitions against double jeopardy.

"Again, for the reasons that I've argued that the two life sentences should be ordered to run concurrently, I would also ask the Court to order that the sentence imposed on the motor vehicle theft count be ordered to run concurrently as well."

MILLER: "Your Honor, may it please the Court. Some of what has been offered to you by Ms. Cooke, we're in agreement with and some of it we're not. Specifically, in the Lowe case, the case, which I understand was tendered to Your Honor and counsel, we are in agreement about it seems to hold for the proposition that indeed only one sentence, one life sentence in this case, can be imposed per victim.

"And so the fact that the prosecution can and did in this case, advance separate theories of first-degree murder that a jury can appropriately hear and decide upon them, that at the time of the imposition of sentence, the Court is confined to limit itself to one sentence per victim. I agree with Ms. Cooke when she says that you're limited to the imposition of two life sentences here."

JUDGE: "I'm going to ask you a hard question because this case doesn't seem to tell me what I need to do. The…if you look at footnote 14, it says an appropriate form of special verdict in which the jury would only be permitted to make a guilty finding either…well, the law says that there's four ways to commit first-degree murder and the prosecution is permitted to charge all four. But it seems to indicate, though, the jury should only make a finding with regard to one and can't make it with regard to two.

"In this case, it seems to me the facts would support findings, as the jury found, of both methods that were charged. Well, that's still…that's still…probably the next leap is to only one conviction can enter and only one sentence can be imposed."

MILLER: "Per victim."

JUDGE: "Per victim. But what happens…so for example, do I get to choose whether or not…for example, Mr. Mutchler is guilty of either premeditated murder in the first-degree on the victims. What happens…let's assume I do that. I pick one. My inclination would be to say that the facts would support a conviction and sentence for felony murder on conviction of Mr. Mutchler for felony murder in the first-degree in which the victim was Evan Scharf and that the facts would support a first-degree murder conviction by premeditation for Mr. Mutchler…"

MILLER: "After deliberation."

JUDGE: "After deliberation, that's right. After deliberation on the victim Robbie Scharf. But what happens to premed…after deliberation with regard to the charge in which Evan Scharf was the victim and what happens to the felony murder in which Robbie Scharf was the victim? Can we just sort of…"

MILLER: "There's nothing in the opinion that suggests that they are, for example, dismissed, that they are non-happenings. I think the Court…and one of the things that I disagree with Ms. Cooke is, she doesn't get…well, she can request anything she wants about where you should impose sentences, whether or not on the felony murder or after deliberation.

"It is the People's intent to request that the Court impose sentences on the first-degree murder after deliberation theories on each of the cases. But I think the Court has discretion to make a finding and impose sentences on the theory that it chooses. The other ones just are not dealt with at this time. I don't think that any further action is taken on them.

"If for any reason this case is returned on appeal on these sentences that are imposed by this Court, then those matters that were not sentenced upon would be available for a sentencing at a later time, I suggest.

"At any rate, Your Honor, I don't believe that Ms. Cooke, by her argument, can preclude this Court from sentencing on the burglary. I agree that the first-degree burglary is a lesser-included offense of the first-degree burglary. There are different elements; namely, in the first-degree burglary, the presence of a weapon while Mr. Mutchler entered or after he remained in the premises.

In any event, it's available for the Court to impose sentences on two of the murder theories and also on the first-degree burglary. "It's also agreed that earlier remarks about the fact that the motor vehicle theft, second-degree aggravated motor vehicle theft, is a misdemeanor and it's only a county jail sentence and has little impact on the totality of what occurs here today."

JUDGE: "So you disagree that first-degree and second-degree burglary merge. And did you say your position on whether or not burglary in the first-degree or second-degree merge in felony murder?"

MILLER: "I think that was in some of our pretrial motions we determined, and the Court found that either the first- or second-degree burglary would support the felony murder."

"Right, because they merge for the purposes of sentencing, meaning, I think, I can impose...here are the possibilities. It seems to me that the law permits me to sentence for both first-degree burglary and second-degree burglary, but any sentence I impose, must be concurrent with a felony murder sentence. I can't stack those."

"I think you can. I mean, I don't think there's anything that's been suggested by the case law or statutes that says you cannot or you may not impose a consecutive sentence on the burglary.

"Your Honor, I'd like to speak the merits of that portion that both counsel agree is within the discretion of the Court. And that is the imposition of consecutive or concurrent sentences. I'd like to be permitted a little latitude in addressing the Court on this because I think there's several things I'd like to recall to the Court's attention.

"It was only five or six weeks ago that the jury heard this case and returned in relatively short order, guilty verdicts on all the counts that were brought against Mr. Mutchler. They concluded that he killed the victims. The jury members concluded that the evidence before them supported guilty verdicts on all four theories of murder in the first-degree.

"And we've already discussed in People versus Lowe that the Supreme Court recognized that, while we may advance those theories and seek verdicts and obtain verdicts, that the Court in Lowe concluded that the first-degree murder statute must be construed in a way that a defendant can be convicted of only one murder for one victim or one killing.

"And accordingly, the prosecution is asking the Court to sentence the defendant on the verdicts of first-degree murder after deliberation; that is, counts one and three.

"I ask the Court in determining the matter of consecutive versus concurrent to recall the testimony that was presented at the trial, the testimony of Dr. Meyer and agents from the Colorado Bureau of Investigation and Louisville police. I don't need to remind the Court since the Court sat through it.

"The People ask that the Court order the two life sentences be required to be served consecutively. The position on this by the People is that the two murders stand separate and apart. Each a horrible crime in its own right and that he should not stand to benefit in any way simply because the murders occurred within minutes of one another at the same location.

"The evidence about the actions of Mr. Mutchler revealed him to be ruthless, uncaring and a killer who has demonstrated no remorse for the deaths. This makes him, to my mind, even more frightening and dangerous than a killer who admits his crimes.

"The essence of the legislative change to the life sentence without the possibility of parole as punishment for Class 1 felonies was to insure the offender is punished in a fashion that he would not ever be released from prison. This is the degree of protection that society requires. He should never be permitted out of prison.

"To the extent that it is possible that an appellate court may in the future hold that because of the vagueness of statutory construction that a life…that a life sentence without parole might mean some finite period of time, which would permit him to be released from prison, this Court today has the power to protect the public by imposing two consecutive life sentences. The public interest and the legislative intent both support consecutive sentences.

"The Court ought to do this because it is the right thing to do. The defendant has shown himself to be an outlaw in our community and a person who has forfeited his right to ever live free in society again.

"Your Honor, as far as impact, let me say this. The community lives with symptoms after criminal acts. Society has a right to ask that Mr. Mutchler be punished for that with the only appropriate sentence, which in this case, is a life sentence for each victim to be consecutive to one another.

"The probation department has reviewed this case and makes that same recommendation. Each family member and friend of the victims who was contacted by myself or co-counsel has the same recommendation over and over again. Sentence the defendant in such a way that he can never be free again.

"The Colorado Supreme Court has consistently upheld consecutive sentences imposed by trial judges in cases involving multiple victims and indeed, in multiple crimes involving a single victim.

"People versus Montgomery has been cited to you. In that case, the Supreme Court reversed the Court of Appeals and found that there was not an unconstitutional interference with the judiciary…with the functioning of the parole board in that case.

"Ms. Cooke suggests that because of the sentence that has changed, that that should be distinguishable. I think not.

"In People versus King, the defendant sought to overturn consecutive life sentences for the killings of his wife and her sister on the grounds that, in that case, the judge was under the belief that the sentences…consecutive sentences were mandatory. The Supreme Court found the trial Court had properly considered the statutory sentencing factors and concluded that the defendant had committed two murders for which he should be punished separately.

"In my final area of discussion Your Honor, to the extent that the Court has previously expressed concern that the imposition of consecutive sentences might be meaningless, I respectfully suggest otherwise. First, the clear legislative purpose for life sentences without parole is to insure to the public that this class of offender would never be released from confinement.

"For the witnesses who testified in this case and the public, which followed this case, let the sentence insure to the best of the Court's ability that the defendant will never again live in a free society. I submit that the Court should take care that the legislative intent is carried out and society is afforded the maximum degree of protection available by imposing the two life sentences consecutively.

"As mentioned earlier, there is Colorado case law addressing the issue of imposing consecutive sentences in cases involving multiple victims. This case clearly falls into that category. Should subsequent decision or case law result in the possibility of the defendant's release from confinement in the future, a court parole board or governor should have the fullest appreciation of the gravity of the defendant's crimes.

"Finally, I ask for this sentence to truly serve as a deterrence to others in the community. Let us speak to that community and say that you have…of the two options open to this Court today, it chose the one that said the defendant would be held accountable to the fullest extent possible under the law by two consecutive life sentences.

"I submit that counts five and six, the first-degree and second-degree burglary, are not merged by the defense argument. Certainly, based on evidence, similar evidence, the Court should impose sentences on count five, the first-degree burglary, and no sentence on second-degree burglary, or if any, a concurrent sentence.

"Finally, the aggravated motor vehicle theft, a misdemeanor punishable by jail time. The People ask that if a sentence is imposed, that it be for one year concurrent with the other sentences.

"And then in sum, Your Honor, through the sentences you're about to impose, let the defendant and all others who are aware of his crimes know and understand that people who commit deliberate and senseless acts of violence, which result in death, should be held accountable for those acts. The sentences that we recommend by our remarks today seek that accountability and seek that justice in this case."

JUDGE: "Mr. Mutchler, do you desire to exercise your right of allocution? Do you have anything you want to say before sentencing?"

SCOTT: "No."

Scott was numb. He had shaven all his hair off. The look on his face was disbelief and shock. All he did was stare into space.

JUDGE: "The sentence I'm about to impose is a record for me. The last time I imposed a record sentence was only a few short months ago when I said that it deserved that sentence because it was the worst conduct. And I must say that the sentence I'm about to impose sets a record in that regard also.

"It will be the judgment and sentence of this court that on count…I think its seven, the second-degree motor vehicle theft, you be committed to the county jail for a period of one year.

"With regard to the second-degree burglary charge and with regard to the first-degree burglary charge, because you were on bond at the time, and a sentence, aggravated sentence is mandatory by the statutes of the state of Colorado; because of your past record; and because of your history, in particular victimizing these people, they deserve none of your conduct, it will be the judgment and sentence of this court that on each of these Class 3 felonies you be committed to the Department of Corrections for a period of 32 years on each charge.

"With regard to count one and two, although it's clear that the jury found in the evidence, and the evidence supports findings of guilty on both count one and count two in which the victim alleged was Evan Scharf, I'm going to impose the maximum sentence of…the mandatory sentence required by law on count two, the felony murder, because I think the facts even more are supported by that charge. It will be the judgment and sentence that you be committed to the Department of Corrections for the rest of your life without opportunity of parole.

"The sentences...all those sentences imposed are now to run concurrent. With regard to counts three and four, that's the first-degree murder charges in which the victim was Robbie Scharf, with regard to the after deliberation charge, it seems to me that that charge is...is completely supportable by the evidence. And it will be the judgment and sentence of this Court that on that charge you be committed to the Department of Corrections for the rest of your life; a life sentence without the possibility of or opportunity for parole.

"Because I have heard no remorse of any kind from any source, I think this is a case...and my guess, my thoughts about it...I mean, I read in the case of Montgomery even the Court of Appeals said it is not possible to serve more than one lifetime in the penitentiary. And I have consistently argued and thought the law ought to make sense sometimes. It's impossible to serve more than one lifetime and that it will be improper to impose consecutive lifetime sentences because that's not possible.

"However; from a theological concept that I can't quite clearly articulate, and maybe I'll speak of it in terms of...I mean, it came to me through a theological concept. But maybe even in terms of the United States flag or other kind of symbols, I've come to believe that symbols contain some part of the concept of the act, which they symbolize. And I think there's a strong symbol to be sent to the public as a result of this sentence.

"And for that reason, the sentence just imposed on count three will run consecutive to that imposed on count two. Court is in recess."

I closed the transcript and put it back in the bag. I wiped away the tears that were flowing down my face. Where do I go from here? God gave me two children, the only happiness that I had ever found, and now one of them has been taken away. The other crippled emotionally for the rest of his life. "God, why have you abandoned us? Help me, dear Lord, help me."

I kept trying to imagine what life was like for Scott. I kept trying to imagine what everyone's life would be like if he at least had received a fair trial. I couldn't concentrate on anything except finding a way to get Scott's case reopened.

Soon it would be time for Steve to meet me here on the beach. I had to shake the mood I was in. I glanced up to our hotel and could see Steve walking towards me, carrying a blanket and the cassette player. I needed to give him the personal time he needed.

The sun was setting. God, it was gorgeous. This was my favorite time on the beach.

I smiled as Steve approached. I walked to the edge of the water where it was breaking on the sand. Steve was spreading the blanket out. He put a tape in and it started to play.

He walked over and took me in his arms. "Eve, there's a song I want you to listen to. It reminds me so much of us."

I gazed into his eyes and listened to the music. He was playing "Island" by Gerry Rafferty.

He took me in his arms and we began to dance slowly. Steve was singing the words to me. When the lyrics reached the part, "but from now on, we won't worry about a thing, yes, the past is gone," he took my face into his hands and gazed into my eyes.

"Eve, we'll make it. You'll see. We'll find a way to help Scott." Tears welled in my eyes. He pulled me closer.

"Come on, let's go back up to the room." I nodded through my tears. We gathered our stuff and trudged through the sand up the beach to our room. As I reached the door, I turned and gazed back at the sea.

"We'll find a way," I thought. "We'll find a way."

On our last day at the beach, and I was very sad at the thought of going back to Colorado. Steve and I had breakfast, then I headed back to the beach for my last walk. I needed a good talk with God.

It was a beautiful clear day. The air smelled so clean. I walked to my favorite spot and sat down. With my head buried in my hands I prayed harder than I ever have.

"God, I need your help. You've given me too much to deal with. The pain is just too much. Please, help me Dear Lord. Please help me."

I felt like I was going to burst. It seemed every emotion I had was coming out. Something made me look up. Right in front of me three dolphins were swimming and breaking the surface of the water. I looked to the heavens and knew God was sending me a message that he was there and he was listening. God knew that dolphins were one of my greatest joys.

I stood up and watched them. As they swam I walked quickly to keep up with them…then jogged. I kept thinking, "Don't leave me; stay with me." But they were gone before I knew it.

I looked back and realized that I had come a good distance from the hotel. Slowly I turned and walked back to the hotel to get ready for my trip home.

Thank you God. Thank you for letting me know you're near.

Part 7

The Life After

They Did What?

I remember the day I was just sitting at home not really doing anything, but something was eating away at me. Something was wrong.

My thoughts were interrupted by the phone.

“Mrs. Mutchler?”

"Yes.”

"You don’t know me, but get help for your son. They almost killed him today.”

"What do you mean? Who is this?" I knew something was wrong. I just knew it.

"I'm a friend of Scott’s. The guards, they almost killed him. Meat is hanging off his face.” I could hear a very faint voice in the background. It was Scott’s.

"He said to tell you that he loves you and get him help.”

“What happened to him?"

"The guards rushed him and beat him nearly to death. Meat is hanging off his face. He's not good."

"What?" I could hear a faint voice talking. The tears were pouring down my face. I couldn't think.

"Scott said to tell you he's OK, just get him some help in here."

"Tell him I will. Tell him I love him very much and I'm sorry this happened to him."

My God, what is happening in there? How could this happen? He is in isolation 24 hours a day, how could the guards beat him? What was I going to do? How could I help him? Toni, call Toni, she would help. She would know what to do.

"Toni?" I was sobbing.

"Eve, what's wrong?"

"I just got a call from one of the inmates at the prison. He said the guards almost killed Scott tonight. He said that he has meat hanging off his face!" I was losing control. I couldn't get myself under any semblance of composure.

"Listen to me, Eve. I will get down there and see Scott. I'll try to take a camera in to get pictures. Hang in there. I will call you when I get back."

That night was long and sleepless. All I could do was lay there imagining guards rushing Scott and beating him.

The next day I called the physician at the prison. I introduced myself and told him that I would like a status report on Scott.

"Look, he got what he deserved."

"What did you say?" I couldn't believe my ears. What had happened to the oath that physicians took? What kind of world was this?

"I said he got what he deserved." I hung the phone up.

I tried to keep busy the next couple of days waiting for Toni's report. Finally she called.

"Eve, it's Toni. I just got back from the prison."

"Toni, how is Scott?"

"Well, they beat him pretty bad. First I want to say I do not want you to go to the prison and visit him until he has healed. Scott and I don't feel you need to see him the way he is."

`"Did you get pictures?"

"No, they wouldn't allow me to bring the camera in."

"Tell me, what did they do to him."

"Well, they beat him very severely about the head. All of the vessels in his eyes have been broken; there is no white. He has stitches three places on his face. Otherwise, he's doing OK."

"Why did they do this to him?"

"Well, he got into a confrontation with a guard. Eve, they're let out an hour a day. During that hour, they can take a shower. While Scott was in the shower, one of the guards thought it would be funny to keep turning the water on and off on him while he was in there."

"What are you talking about? Are they allowed to do those kind of things to them in there?"

"They can do anything they want to in there. Well, you know Scott. He retaliated by throwing human waste on the guard when he walked by him. They told him to cuff up and he wouldn't. They warned him if he didn't, they were coming in for him. He knew it was coming, Eve, but what he didn't know is once they had him handcuffed they would beat him unmercifully."

"Oh my God, how can they get away with doing this?"

"I don't know; I just don't know."

"What happens now? Isn't there something we can do?"

"We can try." I hung up and sat there in a daze.

As time passed, Steve and I developed into people I didn't know anymore. We were so hateful to one another. The walls I had created were so thick I wasn't sure anyone would ever penetrate them again. He was as unhappy as I was. Dave was so miserable living around us. As hard as he tried, he just couldn't take the life we were all left with. He couldn't handle the hate that dwelled within our own home. Life had become total chaos for us all. The fighting at home had become too much to bear for Dave. He had pretty much decided he didn't want to finish school and he couldn't take the life that he had at home. He was giving up and wanted out.

"Mom, I can't stand it anymore. I'm leaving. I can't stand it here with Steve and his family anymore. Mom, I'm so sad here. I miss my brother and there's nothing here anymore. I've talked with Aunt Sherry and she said I can come there and live with her."

I couldn't believe what I had just heard. I begged Dave not to go. I was on the edge of cracking. Dave looked me in the eye. Tears were streaming down his face.

"I'm leaving, Mom."

He turned away from me and headed to his room. I watched him pack his car. He came in the door the last time. My God, Dave was all I had left. I

"Mom, I'm going now." I couldn't stop crying.

"Dave, please don't leave, please. I will find a way to make things better. Please don't go."

I was pleading with him. This pain was just too much. Not only had I lost my eldest son, now I was losing my youngest.

"Mom, I have to leave. I hate it here." He came up and hugged me. I didn't want to let go. I stood and watched him get in his car. He closed the door and drove away. He never looked back.

I walked back in the house and sat on the couch. My head was spinning. How much more would I have to go through? How much more pain would I have to live with? I heard Steve coming down the stairs. He was dressed and ready to head to a football game. He had heard every word and never even tried to talk to Dave. He didn't even take the time to say goodbye to him.

"Are you going or not?"

"What?"

"I said are you going to the game or not?" His voice was angry. How could he not understand what I was going through?"

"Steve, my son just left! Don't you have any compassion in you at all?"

"Are you going to the damn game or not?"

"No, I'm not going."

"That figures."

The front door slammed. I was starting to hate him. I was alone again. I looked around the empty house, at Scott and Dave's pictures on the walls. They were both gone now. I had no one. I didn't want any more of this. I walked slowly through my house taking in everything around me. I pulled out every photo album I had and sat in the middle of the living room floor. I looked through all the pictures of the boys. We had so much happiness, so many dreams, so much love. It was all gone. I looked at my wedding album. I thought I had finally found someone who loved me. Why couldn't Steve and his family reach out to Dave and help him through this, let him know that he was important and loved, too? But no, not one of them would do it.

I closed the photo albums and walked to my favorite picture of Scott and Dave. I touched the picture in a caressing way thinking somehow my two boys could feel my presence. I turned away and walked upstairs to my bedroom. No more. No more of this. I collected all my bottles of Valium and set them on the bed. I began to pray and asked God to understand why I had to end my life. That He had lied; He said He would never give us more than we could handle. He lied. He had given me more than I could handle. I prayed that He would forgive me, but if not, I told myself that wherever I was going could not be worse than the hell that I had been left to live here on earth. The silence was overwhelming.

I looked at the phone next to the bed. Was there anyone I wanted to call? No there was no one; no one cared. I felt Steve and his family would be glad I was gone. I felt if my own family had cared, they would have been by my side through this trial. My sister would take care of Dave. They loved him with all their hearts. He was on his way to them and would know love every day there.

The guilt was so overwhelming. "If I could only go back and have a second chance", I thought, "If only I had known." The pain was killing me. This whole thing had destroyed so many lives. I lay down and thought of all the misery and heartbreak that everyone was living in.

"God, it's not supposed to be this way!" I screamed. "My boys were all I had and now both of them are gone! Why? Why?" I screamed so loud I was becoming hoarse, but I continued my loud conversation with God.

"Why couldn't you protect us? It's the only happiness I ever had. Why, damn it, why? There's no one here for me. Everyone has abandoned me, even you!"

I opened the bottle of Valium. I took the first pill and then the second and then the third. I closed my eyes and laid still. “Just keep taking the pills,” I thought. “Soon it will all be over.” My mind went back to the days when it was just me and the boys. Our happiest times were at the ocean. We all loved it there. I pictured the waves crashing on the beach. All the happy times we had. All the happiness I would never feel again.

I tried to open my eyes, but couldn’t. Suddenly, calm engulfed me. A feeling of safety. My weeping had almost ceased. It felt like I was being held by someone, someone who cared; someone who understood my pain. Why didn’t I feel the pain anymore? There was no talking, just a calmness; a feeling that everything would be OK.

The ringing phone woke me.

I opened my eyes. It was dark outside.

"Mom…" It was Dave. Oh God, it was Dave. He was sobbing on the other end of the telephone.

“Mom, I don’t want to leave you. I am just so sad. I don’t know what to do."

"Dave, I know, and I love you so very much.”

“You know, Mom, the whole time I was driving I couldn’t get a radio station on and there was a lot of time to just think. It was like God was telling me what I was doing was wrong. I don’t want to leave home, Mom. I love you, but this thing with Scott -- I love him so much and I miss him.”

"I know, honey, I know.”

“Mom, how about if I just take a break and go visit Aunt Sherry?"

"OK, honey, if that’s what you need to do.”

“Mom, I want to come back but I will never live in that house again.”

“I understand. You go visit Aunt Sherry and her kids and have a great time. I’ll take care of things on this end and you’ll have your own place to live when you return.”

"OK, Mom. I love you, and I’m sorry that I hurt you.”

"Dave, it’s OK, everything is going to be OK. Go have fun with your family. Call me when you stop for the night. I love you with all my heart.”

This was amazing. What had happened to Dave and I at the same time? Maybe, just maybe, God was trying to watch out for us. Maybe God saw that things were too much for us. I was so very groggy from the pills. I closed my eyes and went to sleep.

Visitor's Day

The trips to the prison to see Scott were draining. I dreaded the long drive. What I had to endure before even getting in to see Scott was more than a human being could bear. Each time I entered, I was frisked and searched before going in to see my son. Depending on the person checking you in, they could determine if your clothes were appropriate. I had come to fill my car with changes of clothes to avoid being turned away. Then there was the bus ride over to the maximum-security prison. It was a cold setting, barbed wire everywhere. Once in the maximum-security prison, I then had to go through metal detectors. Then finally, the elevator ride to the floor where Scott would be waiting for me, shackled and locked in a room, waiting behind a glass window.

Scott always had that warm wonderful smile. He tried so hard to reassure me that I had nothing to feel guilty about; that this was about him. As many times as he has given me this lecture, I still don't believe it. I still feel overwhelming guilt.

The visits are always too short. It takes more time to drive up to the prison than the actual visit itself. What I wouldn't give to be able to hug my child again.

"Mom, we need to talk." During most of our visits, Scott was always smiling, happy just catching up on what was going on in the outside world. Today, he had a very stern look on his face. Something was definitely on his mind.

"What, honey?"

"Mom, you can't keep going like this. I know you better than anyone. I want you to listen to me. You are not the reason I am in here." My head dropped. The tears were streaming down my face.

"Mom, listen to me. This is not about you…it's about me. I got on the wrong track, not you. You didn't do anything." I looked in his eyes. It was killing him seeing me this way. I tried so hard not to cry in front of him, but I was never successful.

"Scott, I should have done something."

"What? What could you have done?"

"I don't know, something more…something more."

"Mom, I've been here a long time now…I've done a lot of thinking. You've got to go on with your life. This isn't helping anyone."

"I don't know how to, Scott…I just don't know how to. Why didn't God protect all of us? Why? If there were a God none of this would be happening!"

"Mom, listen to me. God had nothing to do with this. Remember, He gives us all free will." Why was Scott defending God?

"Mom, you have to get right with God again. You can't keep going on like this."

The guards interrupted our conversation to say our visit was over. I stood up and looked at Scott. I felt paralyzed. He smiles.

"Mom, it's going to be OK."

The guard again says the visit is over. As I approached the elevator, I glanced back at Scott. He smiled and waved; I waved back. What can I do to help him? What can I do?

Nine Years Later

All that's left is a world of heartbreak. Our marriage still has its ups and downs with much confusion, but we continue trying to piece our lives back together. The problems with Steve's family eventually became so severe and hateful that, now, there is no communication of any kind or any type of relationship with the exception of his one sister. The life that is left is so very painful; so empty at times.

Some of the hardest times are when Dave drives up to see his brother. After their visit, the call comes. Dave is sobbing. The pain of seeing his brother behind a glass wall in shackles is too much for him. "I need my brother, Mom," he cries.

The nights are sleepless for the most part. Tears flow through prayers to God to help our family. I pray for forgiveness for the things I have realized that I should have done differently; for all the mistakes that I have made, but the emptiness remains.

Through much love and persistence from my children and my sister and brother-in-law, I keep reaching for my faith in God. Most of the anger is gone…all that's left is the search for answers to the questions that weren't a part of Scott's trial, and the quest for justice.

I can't give up. I've taken all my energy and I'm determined to find a way to get to the truth. To find Justice. If, by writing this book, I can keep just one teenager from crossing the line, keep one person from making judgmental decisions, stop one person from saying a cruel word or committing a cruel act, get a single person to not let the system bulldoze his or her rights … if writing this book can do any of those things, then I have found a purpose, a reason to go on.

All I can do is pray that, one day, there will be someone out there that will help our family; that one day, Scott's case will be reopened and he will receive a fair trial and the truth will be known.

People of our world please understand the pain that the families of children of crime go through. Please understand that the cruelty and judgmental ways leave scars that never heal. We, too, have suffered a loss that never heals, added to the overwhelming, ever-present guilt.

Society may feel that justice has been served, but I can assure you that this family has paid a high price for this so-called justice.

The Injustice of Justice.

Where are they now?

Scott remains in the State Penitentiary serving his two life sentences. He has been subjected to solitary confinement for the past six years without any fresh air or sunlight.

Steve and Eve are still married, struggling to keep their marriage together in the hope that they will find their love for each other again.

Dave did finish his education and now runs a medical corporation. He is expecting his first child.

Alex Hunter did get reelected and is presently heading the JonBenet Ramsey case.

Judge Morris Sandstead is also presently involved with the JonBenet Ramsey case.

Judge not, and ye shall not be judged;
Condemn not, and ye shall not be condemned;
Forgive, and ye shall be forgiven.

Luke 6:37

Acknowledgements

To my children: I love you both more than you will ever know. Forgive me for the mistakes I have made and never forget that I will always be here for you.

To my husband: I am sorry for all the hurt and pain. You stood by me even when some thought you shouldn't.

Char, you've been like a mother to me. You'll never know how much your guidance and love has helped me through the years.

Special thanks and love to my sister Jan, my sister-in-law Norma and my brother-in-law Barry for not abandoning us. Thank you for your unconditional love to us all.

To my sister Sherry, who helped me with the perfect name for this book. We've shared the worst and best of times. I love you and wouldn't trade any of them.

To my brother Byron: Thank you for your love and always being there for me to help me find my way and keep my perspective.

Special thanks to my best friend Sandy. I treasure our friendship and I thank God for bringing you into my life.

I thank God every day for my family and all my wonderful friends who have supported me throughout this trying life that I lead. I love you all dearly.

With very special thanks to A. Olen Letourneau, Vice President of Editing Services, Leesa Gabel, Senior Editor and especially Ken Garner, Copy Editor. I had a story to tell and the three of you believed in me and helped me with my journey. You will always remain in my heart and always have my gratitude for your tireless efforts. You are all very special people. I can't thank you enough for your support and guidance through one of my most difficult endeavors I have taken on…writing this book.

About the Author

Eve was born in Morristown, New Jersey. Growing tired of life on the East Coast, she moved herself and two sons to Colorado in search of a simpler life. There she met her husband on New Year's Eve 1990. Not only was it a promising new year, but also a promising life ahead for Eve and her family. Until that dark night when her world came crashing in. Her oldest son was accused of murder, tried and convicted. Trying to regain control over her life, Eve began an organization called Parents of Prisoners. Unfortunately, this group did not flourish. Instead of giving up, Eve continued on her quest to help the troubled youth of Colorado. She began Dream Angel Charities. This nonprofit organization, with the help of local grants, will provide guidance for youths on the verge of a life of crime. Through local Christian high schools, these youths will get the guidance and education they need to turn their lives around and reach their dreams. She has dedicated her life to helping our youth turn their lives around so they do not end up in prison, or worse, dead.